Intellectual Disability, Trauma
and Psychotherapy

People with intellectual disabilities have emotional and mental health needs just like anyone else. Until recently however there has been little research of effective psychological treatment or direct, accessible psychotherapy provision for this client group.

Intellectual Disability, Trauma and Psychotherapy focuses on the delivery of psychotherapy services for those with intellectual disabilities. Leading professionals in this specialist field are brought together to describe the history, theory and practice of their work in twelve focused chapters that draw on the work of psychotherapists including Bion, Winnicott, Sinason and Alvarez. Topics covered include:

- therapeutic responses to cultural and religious diversity
- support for parents with intellectual disabilities
- developing healthy and secure attachments within the family
- dealing with intense feelings of shame
- helping clients to cope with traumatic sexual experiences.

Drawing on over a decade of pioneering practitioner experience at Respond – a government-funded psychotherapy service for people with learning disabilities based in central London – this book explores the practical issues in providing therapy to this client group, whether individually, in families, in groups, or by the use of telephone counselling. It closes with a chapter exploring the way forward for those who wish to develop services of this kind.

Tamsin Cottis has been a practitioner in the field of learning disability for over 20 years, as a teacher, trainer and therapist. She is also co-founder of Respond, one of the UK's leading providers of psychotherapy to people with intellectual disabilities.

Intellectual Disability, Trauma and Psychotherapy

Edited by Tamsin Cottis

Foreword by Anne Alvarez

Routledge
Taylor & Francis Group

LONDON AND NEW YORK

01264658

First published 2009 by Routledge
27 Church Road, Hove, East Sussex BN3 2FA

Simultaneously published in the USA and Canada
by Routledge
270 Madison Avenue, New York NY 10016

*Routledge is an imprint of the Taylor & Francis Group,
an Informa business*

© 2009 selection and editorial matter, Tamsin Cottis;
individual chapters, the contributors

Typeset in Times by RefineCatch Limited, Bungay, Suffolk
Printed and bound in Great Britain by TJ International Ltd, Padstow,
Cornwall
Paperback cover design by Design Deluxe, Bath, UK
Paperback cover image by Amy Jeans

This publication has been produced with paper manufactured to strict
environmental standards and with pulp derived from sustainable
forests.

British Library Cataloguing in Publication Data
A catalogue record for this book is available from the British Library

Library of Congress Cataloging-in-Publication Data
Intellectual disability, trauma, and psychotherapy / edited by Tamsin
Cottis.
    p. ; cm.
    Includes bibliographical references and index.
    ISBN 978–0–415–42166–9 (hbk) – ISBN 978–0–415–42167–6 (pbk)
1. Mental Retardation. 2. Psychotherapy. I. Cottis, Tamsin.
[DNLM: 1. Mental Retardation—therapy. 2. Mentally Ill Persons—
psychology. 3. Psychotherapy—methods. 4. Stress, Psychological—
therapy. WM 300 I599 2008]
    RC570.I662 2008
    616.89—dc22   2008005155

ISBN: 978–0–415–42166–9 (hbk)
ISBN: 978–0–415–42167–6 (pbk)

– 2 MAR 2010

This book is dedicated to the memory of Eibhlin Breathnach – a much-loved colleague and gifted psychotherapist.

Contents

Contributors

Anne Alvarez is Clinical Supervisor at Respond, Honorary Consultant Child and Adolescent Psychotherapist (retired Co-Convener of the Autism Service), Tavistock Clinic, London, and Visiting Professor, San Francisco Psychoanalytic Society 2005. She is the author of *Live Company: Psychotherapy with Autistic, Borderline, Deprived and Abused Children* (Routledge, 1992) and joint editor of *Autism and Personality: Findings from the Tavistock Autism Workshop. Being Alive: Building on the Work of Anne Alvarez* (ed. J. Edwards, Brunner-Routledge) was published in 2003.

Debbee Arthur is a psychotherapist who had a first career as an actor. She has worked in a number of long-stay psychiatric hospitals, devising interactive reminiscence theatre for psychogeriatric patients and people with intellectual disabilities. As a student psychotherapist she was involved in training volunteers in counselling skills for Victim Support. She has worked with people with intellectual disabilities for the past ten years in a number of settings – residential homes, supported living, self-advocacy and is the former Manager of the Respond Helpline.

Noelle Blackman is a dramatherapist, and Assistant Director at Respond. She is the founder of the roc Loss and Bereavement Service for people with intellectual disabilities, and deputy co-ordinator of the National Network for the Palliative Care of People with Intellectual Disabilities. She co-facilitates a user involvement group of older people with intellectual disabilities. Her published work includes *Living with Loss* (Pavilion), *Loss and Learning Disability* (Worth), *When Somebody Dies* (Books Beyond Words) and *Caring for People with Intellectual Disabilities Who Are Dying* (Worth).

Alan Corbett is a psychoanalytic psychotherapist with further training in forensic and child psychotherapy. He was Director of Respond from 1997 until 2003 and Clinical Director of the CARI Foundation until 2006. His publications include co-authorship of *Witnessing, Nurturing, Protesting: Therapeutic Responses to Sexual Abuse of People with Learning Disabilities* (David Fulton, 1996). He works in Ireland as a psychotherapist and is completing a doctorate in psychotherapy research at the University of Kent.

Tamsin Cottis is a co-founder and former Assistant Director of Respond. Formerly a teacher, she now works as a psychotherapist, consultant and trainer, providing assessment and treatment for intellectually disabled victims and perpetrators of sexual abuse and their carers. Tamsin is a founder member and former Trustee of the Institute of Psychotherapy and Disability. She has written widely about her work for professional journals and is co-author of *Witnessing, Nurturing, Protesting: Therapeutic Responses to Sexual Abuse of People with Learning Disabilities* (David Fulton, 1996). She has an MA in creative writing from Birkbeck College.

Richard Curen is Director of Respond. He has a diploma in forensic psychotherapeutic studies from the Portman Clinic and is Treasurer of the Institute of Psychotherapy and Disability, Chair of The Survivors Trust, and a specialist adviser to the Metropolitan Police 'Project Sapphire'. He is a visiting lecturer for the Tavistock and Portman NHS Trust, an editor of the learning disability magazine *Community Living* and a regular reviewer of books in *Community Care* magazine.

Judith Edwards is a consultant child and adolescent psychotherapist teaching and supervising on various courses at the Tavistock Clinic, where she is also course tutor for the MA in psychoanalytic studies. Apart from publishing papers in academic journals internationally, she has contributed to many books and conceived and edited *Being Alive* (Routledge, 2001) on the work of Anne Alvarez. She was joint editor of the *Journal of Child Psychotherapy* from 1996 to 2000, and has edited numerous books on psychoanalytic subjects, including *Live Company* (Alvarez, 1992, Routledge), *Arctic Spring: Potential for Growth in Adults with Psychosis and Autism* (Tremelloni, 2005, Karnac) and *Psychotherapy with Young People in Care: Lost and Found* (Hunter, 2001, Brunner-Routledge).

Shahnawaz Haque is a BPC-registered psychoanalytic psychotherapist working at Respond in psychotherapy and risk assessment, and a consultant psychotherapist at the Clinic for Dissociative Studies. He is also a Friday Imam and has a private practice as an Islamic therapist and counsellor.

Elizabeth Lloyd works at Respond as a sessional psychoanalytic psychotherapist. Between 1997 and 2000 she facilitated a group for women with intellectual disabilities who had experienced sexual abuse. In addition she is a therapist for the Clinic of Dissociative Studies and in private practice. She is a member of the Guild of Psychotherapists and has published papers about her work in a range of professional journals.

Winnie McNeil is a former Counsellor and Information Worker on the Respond Helpline. She has twenty years' experience of work with children and families, in both statutory and voluntary sectors, and for three years worked in a local authority adult learning disability team. She has a private counselling practice, specializing in areas of disability, trauma and bereavement. Winnie is a member of the General Social Services Council and of the Foundation for Psychotherapy and Counselling.

Chris Neill works as a sessional psychotherapist at Respond, undertaking assessment and treatment for victims and perpetrators of sexual abuse. He also works in private practice as a psychotherapist and as a trainer, group worker and supervisor. His professional background is in work with children and families in both community and residential settings. He is accredited and registered with the BACP and the UKCP.

David O'Driscoll is an Assistant Director of Respond and also works as a psychotherapist for people with intellectual disabilities for Hertfordshire Partnership NHS Trust. He is a UKCP-registered psychotherapist, a professional member of the Centre for Attachment-Based Psychoanalytic Psychotherapy (CAPP) and a founder member and Trustee of the Institute of Psychotherapy and Disability (IPD). David was News Editor of the *Psychotherapy Review* from August 1999 till 2001. He is a contributor to *Helping People with Intellectual Disabilities Cope with Bereavement* (1999, ed. Blackman, Pavilion).

Samantha Russell Small is a trainee psychotherapist with an advanced diploma in counselling and psychotherapy. She has experience as a workshop facilitator in creative arts with disabled children and adults, and has worked as a carer in a long-stay psychiatric hospital. She is currently a counsellor and outreach worker for Respond's telephone helpline.

Jason Upton is Manager of the Young People's Project at Respond. He has worked with people with intellectual disabilities for over ten years in a variety of roles and settings from statutory to voluntary services, and has worked as a dance movement therapist with children with special needs in a primary school setting. He is a UKCP-registered psychotherapist and has an MA in psychotherapy and counselling and an advanced diploma in existential psychotherapy from Regent's College. Jason is a professional member of the Association of Dance Movement Therapy UK and a member of the Society for Existential Analysis.

Foreword by Anne Alvarez

This is a brave book, well documented and researched, about the treatment of people with intellectual disabilities and the shocking level of bereavement, trauma, abuse and neglect to which many of them are subjected. Given the resulting level of emotional and cognitive damage, the treatment itself often seems to have arrived impossibly late. Yet the book contains remarkable examples of how some sense of personal dignity can be rebuilt and the capacity to use one's mind restored. It also describes how both victims and offenders gradually become less preoccupied with violence and begin to discover more ordinary ways of experiencing excitement.

Many people with intellectual disabilities may seem lacking in a capacity to communicate. Yet close examination of their relationship with the therapist, or family, or other carers often reveals faint, indirect signals – a flicker of light in a sometimes dull eye, a tiny change in facial features – which may at first need amplifying by others, but later can be sent more confidently and clearly by the individual himself or herself. Attention of this kind also reveals more than one source for the sometimes apparent mindlessness: the first may be a genuine genetic or other brain deficit; a second, the self-protective 'secondary handicap' identified by Sinason (1992) where the person behaves as if more disabled than he or she actually is; a third may arise from the habitual dissociation that follows from chronic or severe trauma (Perry *et al.*, 1995); a fourth may be the blunting that can occur following early and profound emotional neglect (Schore, 2003; Music, 2007) The original deficit or disorder may set a ceiling, but so too may the psychological damage, particularly where it exists from infancy, when the brain's growth is use-dependent – that is, dependent for its growth on emotional reciprocal interactions within the attachment relationship (Schore,

2003; Perry *et al.*, 1995). Eventually the ceiling may turn out to be more elastic than previously thought. Meanwhile, the therapist may have to function as a thinking and feeling self for the client, or patient, for a period of months or even years, while always looking for opportunities to facilitate the patient's own capacity to think and feel for himself or herself. There are no quick fixes for this level of damage to the personality and intellect.

Clearly, not all people with intellectual disabilities are either traumatized or abused. Even fewer are abusers, and not all are disturbed. This book is about a sub-group within a sub-group of the general population, but it raises fundamental issues for the care of all people with intellectual disabilities. All of them are vulnerable, and the proportion of victims and perpetrators of abuse (the latter have usually been victims) is higher among them than in the able population. Why? What is it about people with intellectual disabilities that often provokes such cruelty and contempt, or, at best, indifference and denial? What happens to our humanity towards their humanity? Is our own shame about our own inadequacy, or gracelessness, or physical or intellectual limitations so deeply buried that we prefer to avoid it or attack it? Even in the most devoted of families, the sense of disappointment (and in the saddest of cases, of distaste) may have been hard to acknowledge. But whether expressed cruelly or denied, where such feelings have not been processed, they may combine with the child's own sense of shame and thereby contribute to serious impairment in the sense of self-worth of both child and family. These issues raise philosophical, psychological, social and policy questions, all of which are addressed in considerable depth in the chapters that follow.

The contributors to this book have originally trained with more able and less emotionally damaged patients, but at Respond I think it is clear that they have gone on to become specialists not only in the development of delicate and respectful therapeutic techniques within the consulting room, but also in their careful practice of close liaison with, and support for, the families, carers and agencies involved with their clients. For example, fine distinctions have to be made between possible reasons for a woman's repetitive preoccupation with a rape that took place long ago: is she still preoccupied because the trauma has not been adequately heard and processed, or is she ruminating in order to keep herself interesting to herself and others, perhaps out of a quite unconscious fear that ordinariness and safety may lead back to dullness? Or both? This way of working alongside other carers and agencies may, incidentally, be helpful in other adult mental health settings. Respond does not only offer individual and group psychotherapy. The complex nature of the clients and their life situations has led the staff there to diversify into a range of additional services: telephone counselling, therapy for older people, for sexual offenders, for learning disabled parents, for ethnic minorities, and for the severely disabled. All of this work makes use of the psychoanalytic study of feelings within the relationships between the client and others; but it is also developmentally, psychopathologically and socially/culturally/ethnically informed.

The seriousness with which the staff approach their work is evident in the regularity of their peer group discussions, supervisions and also group consultations with an expert in the study of the effect of trauma on organizations. The clients' life experiences are disturbing enough, but sometimes they have gone on to experience or develop sexual perversions that may evoke deep feelings of horror and disgust in the therapist; and this in turn has to be worked on personally and talked about in supervision and in the group. In other cases, certain perpetrators may have a chillingly predatory and psychopathic lack of empathy that can be highly disturbing and indeed frightening. The tendency of groups to split – to side with either the actual victim or the hidden victim inside the perpetrator – is well documented (Hopper, 2003). Balance and humanity don't come cheaply in these situations. They have to be earned. The Respond group has made gargantuan efforts to treat traumatized people with intellectual disabilities with sympathy and honesty, to recognize their emotional and cognitive limitations and also, occasionally, their dangerousness, without patronizing them. It has written this book to alert us to the scale and complexity of the problem, not to shock us.

References

Hopper, E. (2003) *Traumatic Experience in the Unconscious Life of Groups: The Fourth Basic Assumption: Incohesion: Aggregation/Massification or (ba) I:A/M.* London: Jessica Kingsley.

Music, G. (2007) *Neglecting neglect: Some thoughts about children who have suffered neglect and deprivation and are 'undrawn' and 'unenjoyed'.* Personal communication.

Perry, B. D., Pollard, R. A., Blakley, T. L., Baker, W. L. and Vigilante, D.

(1995) Childhood trauma, the neurobiology of adaptation, and 'use-dependent' development of the brain: How states become traits. *Infant Mental Health Journal 16*, 271–291.

Schore, A. N. (2003) *Affect Regulation and Disorders of the Self*. London: Norton.

Sinason, V. (1992) *Mental Handicap and the Human Condition: New Approaches from the Tavistock*. London: Free Association Books.

Acknowledgements

Many people have contributed to this book, directly and indirectly, and helped to make its publication possible.

Firstly, all the named contributors to this book acknowledge their gratitude to Respond's clients, their carers and supporters. Thanks are also due to the funders whose generosity has made the work of Respond possible over the years.

My thanks are due to Judith Edwards, for sharing with me her skill, expertise and wisdom – as both an editor and a clinician. Her ideas, insight and support have been invaluable from the book's beginning to its eventual completion.

Many thanks to Joanne Forshaw, Jane Harris, Kate Moysen, and Sarah Gibson at Routledge for their consideration, support and efficiency.

Thanks also to: Julia Bell, Dorothy Bowers, Mark Brookes, Sylvia Brookstein, Malcolm Brown, Peter Burridge, Tamanna Choudhury, Isabel Clare, William Donovan, Andrew Gayle, Nadine Grieve, Nicola Harney, Claire Harris, Angela Hennessey, Sheila Hollins, Amy Jeans, Ayesha Janjua, Brett Kahr, Anup Karia, Anne Koch, Richard Kramer, Caroline Keely, Sean Kelly, Basil Lawrence, Mark Linington, Deborah Lyttelton, Gillian Miles, Mary Sue Moore, June Patterson, David Potter, Angela Powell, Leon Redler, Catia Serrano, Jake Spencer, Jo Sumner, Gloria Ugoh, Robin Van den Hende, Kiriakos Xenitidis.

Special thanks to Amanda Maffett and the Helpline Team for crucial support at times of extra stress!

And huge thanks from me, of course, to all the contributors – for their time, their work and their colleagueship. Anne Alvarez, Alan Corbett, Richard Curen, Elizabeth Lloyd, and David O'Driscoll went several extra miles to help bring this book to life. I'd like also to say a special thank you to Earl Hopper and Valerie Sinason for their inspiration and encouragement over many years.

Finally, my love as always to Nic, Rebecca, Georgia, and Rosie Newman.

Tamsin Cottis

Introduction

Tamsin Cottis

This book is an exploration of psychotherapy provision for people with intellectual disabilities,[1] with the consulting rooms at Respond as the fixed points on the journey.

Respond is a voluntary sector organization, based in Central London, managed by a Board of Trustees and part-funded by the UK Department of Health. It was established in 1991 and now provides a range of psychotherapeutic services to children and adults who have intellectual disabilities, most of whom have experienced abuse and trauma, often of a sexual nature, and some of whom have gone on to abuse others. The organization has interfaces with many other professional worlds including both mainstream and intellectual disability services, primary healthcare, schools, forensic services, and child protection teams. It also has a track record of campaigning for changes in law and policy to minimize the vulnerability of people with intellectual disabilities to sexual abuse. Since its inception it has grown from a staff of two to employ 20 people in both clinical and non-clinical capacities. Respond therapists treat up to 60 patients per week, and take an average of 200 calls per month on the telephone helpline.

It is the psychotherapy clients themselves that are at the heart of this book. In common with other practitioners who want to share

1 Terminology in this field is complex and contentious. Throughout this book, the term 'people [or clients or patients] with intellectual disabilities' is used to refer to the client group. While the terms 'people with learning difficulties' and 'people with learning disabilities' are widely used in the UK, 'intellectual disability' is currently the favoured international term. For a more lengthy, psychoanalytically informed exploration of the ways in which the evolution of terms reflects changes in the attitudes, values and feelings that inform our work, see Chapter 2 of this book, and also Sinason (1992).

their work with a wider audience, the contributors have had to address issues of confidentiality in order to produce a work that illuminates the clinical process but does not violate the privacy of the consulting room. Such issues are highly complex in relation to psychotherapeutic work with any group of vulnerable adults or young people. At no stage, for example, do Respond clients have the same degree of confidentiality as the non-intellectually disabled adult patient who is treated by a private practitioner. Organizational constraints, as well as the vulnerability of people with intellectual disabilities, mean that some information must always be shared within the clinical team. In addition, because of the limited means of communication available to some of our clients, we are usually working alongside referrers and other carers and are often in dialogue with them, especially regarding issues of risk and safety. At Respond, of course, organizational policies regarding confidentiality are in place, and the national legal and policy framework that surrounds the work done with people with intellectual disabilities who have been abused, or are vulnerable to abuse, has strengthened immensely over the past 10 years.[2] Notwithstanding these welcome reforms, it remains our experience at Respond that: confidentiality policies are regularly tested by events; high levels of vulnerability to abuse persist and should be recognized in the way our service is organized; and the field is complex and unpredictable. Confidentiality in the context of psychotherapy for people with intellectual disabilities is an organic and evolving process. Thus, seeking permission from clients who have intellectual disabilities to share material from their psychotherapy treatment is not straightforward. It can be difficult to be sure that someone has understood the implications of saying 'yes' to a request from a therapist to share the work with others. Also, many people with intellectual disabilities have spent their lives in a disempowered position and this means that a 'yes' can sometimes be no more than the product of a learned (and understandable) tendency to appease more powerful carers. However, wherever it has been possible to do so, we have sought that permission and tried to ensure that it is meaningful. Where this has not been possible we have disguised identities in ways that are aimed to prevent the possibility of

2   Policy guidelines such as the Department of Health's 'No Secrets' (2000; currently under review), as well as the Sex Offences Act (2003) and the Youth Justice and Criminal Evidence Act (1999), have sought to address the vulnerability to abuse experienced by people with intellectual disabilities, and their difficulties in giving evidence in court.

identification, while maintaining the educational value of the clinical material that has been shared. We are, of course, indebted to all our clients, as well as the carers and referrers who support them in their treatment.

Inspired, encouraged and educated by all our past and present clinical supervisors, and especially Anne Alvarez, Earl Hopper and Valerie Sinason, we have had the opportunity at Respond to apply innovative ideas to a diverse range of clinical services. The challenges of therapeutic work on the telephone (Chapter 10), with older people (Chapter 9), with those from ethnic minorities (Chapter 8), with sexual offenders (Chapter 6), with intellectually disabled parents (Chapter 7) and with those who have severe intellectual disabilities (Chapter 4) are all addressed here.

Most of the work described is psychoanalytic psychotherapy, and readers will find, for example, that terms such as 'transference', 'countertransference', 'attachment', 'containment' and 'the unconscious' are used in this context. A glossary clarifies these terms. However, the practice of our clinical work has required us to adapt our theoretical approach in ways that are sensitive to individual and particular need. All our treatment must begin with a profound respect for the humanity of the individual client, or patient. In this regard, we anticipate that all those who are seeking to provide thoughtful, person-centred services will find both recognition and ideas in this book. Our professional therapeutic challenge has been to be eclectic in approach without diluting the quality of the treatment or service on offer. The clinical work described in this book demonstrates that, as therapists, we have the responsibility to be flexible and adaptable practitioners, in order that our interventions are available, accessible and effective.

The development of psychotherapy for people with intellectual disabilities to date is seen here in its social, political and cultural context. As well as diverse therapeutic approaches, readers will find that we do not divorce our clinical work from the cultural and political circumstances of our intellectual disabled clients. Dick Sobsey's ecological model of abuse (1994) describes a dynamic process that operates in the individual, environmental and cultural spheres to heighten a disabled person's vulnerability to abuse. In Chapter 5, and in several other chapters, we see how this process can impact on families, who are operating in a culture that devalues disabled people and consequently provides inadequate support services for them and their families. Attachment relationships are in turn adversely affected as family members and disabled people themselves struggle to overcome emotional and practical difficulties.

There are also links between this ecological approach and a view that the therapy matrix in this context cannot be concerned only with the 'here and now' of a conventionally understood psychoanalytic relationship. When working with people with intellectual disabilities we have found that their lived experiences – culturally and historically as well as emotionally – cannot be divorced from their present experience. This is underscored most vividly by Hollins and Sinason's (2004) adaptation of Money-Kyrle's (1971) idea of the three Facts of Life. These are also explained by Steiner (1993). Hollins and Sinason describe these as the 'Three Secrets' of sex, dependency and death – which can be seen to exert a powerful effect on all aspects (individual, environmental and cultural) of Sobsey's ecological model and have been found to be highly relevant in our psychotherapeutic work. We have also been able to make links between an ecological view and that of group analytic thinking, where trauma in society can be seen to be reflected in the individuals of that society. Earl Hopper's work has had an especial resonance for us in this respect and is highlighted in Chapter 11.

Trauma and sexual abuse are also key themes. The majority of our clients have had deeply troubled lives and come to us with very painful histories. We recognize and witness this and have become very interested in and aware of the disabling effects of this trauma. When assessing the benefits of psychotherapy for this client group (this is an issue explored in Chapter 12) we have come to recognize that development and growth of a cognitive as well as an emotional kind can occur when patients are in long-term treatment.

Clinical examples described across all the chapters have encouraged us to make tentative links between an understanding of Kleinian paranoid schizoid functioning (as described by Hodges, 2003), of Main et al.'s Attachment Category 'D': disorganized attachment (1985), and of forensic psychotherapist Mervyn Glasser's (1996) theories (explained by Richard Curen in Chapter 6) regarding deeply held fears of annihilation and of a 'core complex' in the forensic patient.

All of these concepts (as well as the neuroscientific findings of Schore and others) would see that a child's attempts to defend against trauma inflicted by primary carers will cause deep and enduring damage both to their psychological well-being and to their cognitive and social development. We hope, as our work develops over the coming years, to focus even more intently on this issue, and to produce quantitative as well as qualitative data to demonstrate that the attempt, through psychotherapy, to recognize and repair some of this early deprivation can reduce a client's level of intellectual disability as well as their emotional distress. Teaching and supervision from Anne Alvarez and Mary Sue Moore have been especially helpful in our understanding of this subject to date.

At the beginning of the book, David O'Driscoll takes a historical view of psychotherapy with people who are intellectually disabled, describing 'episodes of interest' that have not taken a hold on service provision until very recently. In the past, the pressure was on the intellectually disabled patient to change to fit a prescriptive idea of a psychotherapy patient or be denied access to treatment.

In Chapter 2, Jason Upton describes the ways in which creative approaches, which seek to understand and employ alternative forms of communication, especially play, can be significant in work with those with cognitive or verbal difficulties. He provides a clear exposition of the theory that underpins his work with young people who have intellectual disabilities, and shows, through case material, how an approach that emphasizes creativity, flexibility and play provides an opportunity for the expression of previously suppressed experiences of trauma and distress.

Upton's approach is complemented by the psychoanalytic work of Alan Corbett, described in Chapter 3, which provides a detailed and clinically based exploration of long-term work with a severely disabled man. In this chapter, Corbett builds on the inspirational work of Valerie Sinason – and especially her theory of a 'secondary handicap' (1992), which is used as a defence against trauma by the intellectually disabled person – to raise the idea of a 'disability transference', where the disabled parts of the patient can disable the therapist in their thinking and understanding, in a way which can be felt to be almost literal. Anyone engaged in this psychotherapeutic work will identify with the sometimes slow pace of progress described here. By facing the consequences of this on us as practitioners we may be enabled to address the core difficulties and persist in work that can provide a unique and healing opportunity for hard to reach patients.

Like Corbett and Upton, Elizabeth Lloyd highlights (in Chapter 4) the appalling and visceral trauma experienced by many of her clients, and shines a particular light on how it is communicated through the body. She explains how therapy has offered her physically and psychically wounded clients the opportunity to develop a containing 'psychic skin'. The significance of somatic communications can be appreciated by all those who work with people with intellectual disabilities who have experienced trauma and perhaps struggle to put their experience into spoken words.

The effect of intellectual disability on the family can be profound, especially when unresolved grief is compounded by a later experience of trauma. In Chapter 5, Tamsin Cottis describes work with one family who were helped, through therapy, to rebuild family relationships that had fractured in the wake of their intellectually disabled son's experience of sexual abuse. We know from the work of, for example, Fonagy and Target (1997) that the attachment experiences of parents have a direct and profound effect on their own parenting. This idea is also explored in Chapter 5 in relation to our work with parents who are themselves intellectually disabled, and by Chris Neill and Tamsin Cottis in Chapter 7. The needs of parents who have intellectual disabilities and their children can be highly acute, complex and painful. Cottis and Neill stress the importance of a psychotherapeutic approach in this work which, while remaining at all times mindful of the needs of the child, can also respond to the emotional circumstances of the parents – who may be experiencing profound feelings of grief, shame, humiliation and confusion.

Almost from its inception, Respond has provided psychotherapy and assessment to people with intellectual disabilities whose experiences of abuse have led them to abuse others, or to act out sexually. The organization has a significant interface with forensic psychotherapy services, and the place of psychotherapy as a treatment option for sexual offending behaviour is explored in depth by Richard Curen in Chapter 6.

In Chapter 8, Shahnawaz Haque draws on his personal and professional experience to explore issues of ethnic, religious and cultural diversity in his work. Focusing on the experience of the Respond-based Equal Access Project, and using clinical examples, he reflects on the clinical and organizational implications of being proactive in addressing issues of diversity.

Respond works with intellectually disabled people of all ages and in Chapter 9, Noelle Blackman draws attention to the often overlooked needs of older people, or people who know they are nearing the end of their lives. She raises our awareness of an issue many would rather ignore, and describes the psychotherapeutic and supportive work of the Respond Elders Project.

Most Respond clients come to our offices in Euston and receive weekly or bi-weekly treatment there. However, another crucial part of our service is the telephone Helpline. Readers may already be familiar with the immediate and short-term advice and support that a telephone service can provide to people in need of help. In Chapter 10, Helpline counsellors Debbee Arthur, Winnie McNeil and Samantha Russell Small describe such practice and also explore the many challenges they face in their ongoing, longer term work with intellectually disabled clients who have experienced appalling levels of abuse and may be trapped in highly dangerous situations. For these Helpline clients, the telephone contact is often their only source of intensive therapeutic support.

In Chapter 11, Tamsin Cottis and David O'Driscoll explore the organizational impact of working with a highly traumatized and vulnerable group of clients. Reflecting on experiences from within Respond, as well as from their work in supporting external organizations, the pressures of the work are explored and linked to group dynamic theory and the idea of a social unconscious (Hopper, 2003), which suggests that trauma in the culture surrounding a patient can reverberate and resonate throughout the structural layers of an organization, including the consulting room.

Finally, in Chapter 12, Tamsin Cottis asks what the benefits of therapy might be for this client group, and makes a case for an expansion of provision as well as the need for vigilant attention to the quality of that provision. Developments such as the Royal College of Psychiatrists' Report (2004), which recommends the expansion of psychotherapy services for people with intellectual disabilities, are highlighted, and case examples are used to illustrate how individual therapy treatments may conclude and what the benefits of them may have been. We are excited at the prospect of future research that will provide more qualitative data regarding the benefits of this work.[3]

It is our aim that this book will add to the growing body of work that explains and promotes psychotherapy with people with intellectual disabilities. We have tried to be honest about the stresses, difficulties and limitations of the work. We know from experience and from our extensive work as teachers and consultants that fine ideals and theory can crumble to dust in, for example, the face of a client who appears closed down and lacking in affect, or the offender

---

3 Personal communication with Richard Curen (2007) regarding possible future research using the CORE Attachment Assessment tool.

whose lack of empathy makes it difficult to bear to stay in the room with him/her. Aided by the insights of our supervisors we are hopeful and positive in our practice, but wary of inauthentic optimism and vigilant about the possible consequences of this challenging work on ourselves as individuals, on teams and organizations.

We hope that all those who are developing their work as psychotherapists with people with intellectual disabilities, or who support people who are in therapy, or who have an interest in the emotional world of intellectual disabled people, will be able to find things in this book that relate to their lived experience and that they can translate into their own practice.

References

Fonagy, P. and Target, M. (1997) Attachment and reflective function: The role in self-organization. *Development and Psychopathology* 9(4), 679–700.

Glasser, M. (1996) Aggression and sadism in the perversions. In I. Rosen (ed.), *Sexual Deviation*, 3rd edition. Oxford: Oxford University Press.

Hodges, S. (2003) *Counselling Adults with Intellectual Disabilities*. London. Palgrave.

Hollins, S. and Sinason, V. (2000) Psychotherapy, learning disabilities and trauma: New perspectives. *British Journal of Psychiatry 176*(1), 32–36.

Hopper, E. (2003) *Traumatic Experience in the Unconscious Life of Groups: The Fourth Basic Assumption: Incohesion: Aggregation/Massification or (ba) I:A/M*. London: Jessica Kingsley.

Main, M., Kaplan, K. and Cassidy, J. (1985) Security in infancy, childhood and adulthood. A move to the level of representation. In I. Bretherton and E. Waters (eds), 'Growing points of attachment theory and research'. *Monographs of the Society for Research in Child Development 50*, 66–104.

Money-Kyrle, R. (1971) The aim of psychoanalysis. *International Journal of Psycho-Analysis 52*, 103–106; reprinted in *The Collected Papers of Roger Money-Kyrle* (1978). Strath Tay, UK: Clunie Press.

Royal College of Psychiatrists Council (2004) *Psychotherapy and learning disability*, Report CR116. London: Royal College of Psychiatrists.

Sinason, V. (1992) *Mental Handicap and the Human Condition: New Approaches from the Tavistock*. London: Free Association Books.

Sobsey, D. (1994) *Violence and Abuse in the Lives of People with Disabilities: The End of Silent Acceptance?* Baltimore: Paul H. Brookes Publishing Co.

Steiner, J. (1993) *Psychic Retreats: Pathological Organisations in Psychotic, Neurotic and Borderline Patients*. London: Routledge.

Chapter I

Psychotherapy and intellectual disability

A historical view

David O'Driscoll

On 2 June 1933, the distinguished psychiatrist and psychoanalyst Leon Pierce Clark (1870–1933), one of the founders of American psychoanalysis, left his comfortable consulting room on East 65th Street, on the Upper East Side of New York. He made the journey across the East River to the ramshackle Randall Island School for Mental Defectives in order to address (for the third year running) a meeting of the American Association for the Feeble-Minded. On this occasion, Clark presented his paper (1933a), 'The Need for a Better Understanding of the Emotional Life of the Feebleminded'. He used it to introduce the work of Freudian depth psychology, and told the society about his work with these ideas over the preceding decade. He gave the meeting examples from his case studies, showing the practical application of Freud's theories in an institutional setting. Clark finished the paper confidently: 'It is our endeavour to recommend these methods so that they may be carried out on a much larger scale in institutions for this class, and to be more patient to the fact that the potentialities for development in the "ament" [an early term for people with an intellectual disability] are not so hopeless as we have heretofore been led to expect' (Clark, 1933a p. 354).

This was historically important material for two reasons. First, Clark suggested that each mentally defective patient had an active emotional life, which in itself was worth exploring. He also believed that if they received help they could be kept out of the institution. This was a rather shocking statement at a time when most psychiatrists regarded mental defectives as unreachable and lacking in feeling (Trent, 1994). Secondly, Clark's initiative was the first attempt by a psychoanalyst to create a dialogue with specialists in this area and as such can be seen as a forerunner of today's multidisciplinary practice (see Chapter 11 for more on this). This paper was very soon followed by a book, *The Nature and Treatment of Amentia: Psychoanalysis and Mental Arrest in Relation to the Science of Intelligence* (Clark, 1933b) in which Clark was 'concerned to promote and exchange new ideas in the study and treatment of the 'feeblem-inded' (p. 354) as an alternative to the ideas of that era. In many ways Clark can be seen as a pioneer in expounding ideas and explaining practice that continue to inform psychodynamic and psychoanalytic treatments in the field of intellectual disability today. In this chapter I will outline the development of psychodynamic psychotherapy for people with intellectual disabilities, drawing on new research that describes Clark's work (O'Driscoll, 2000). A context to this historical view will identify key changes in the medical and government polices that informed care for people with intellectual disabilities. This includes the opening and closure of long-stay hospitals, the influence of the eugenics movement, and the principles of normalization and their culmination in the Government White Paper of 2001, *Valuing People* (Department of Health, 2001).

Several contemporary commentators have noted the historical reluctance of mental health specialists to provide psychotherapy treatment for people with intellectual disabilities (Bender, 1993; Beail, 1998), often referring first to Sigmund Freud's (1904) paper, 'On Psychotherapy' and to his comment that, 'Those patients who do not possess a reasonable degree of education and reliable character should be refused' (p. 254) and the view of Tyson and Sandler (1971) that, 'mental deficiency is generally regarded as a contra-indication for psychoanalysis'. Beginning with an examination of why Clark's early work did not take root, I will show how, in spite of the long-standing doubts about the efficacy of psychotherapy work with people with intellectual disabilities, and a tendency to favour cognitive and behavioural interventions, numerous modern practitioners including Sinason (1992) and Beail (1998; Beail *et al.*, 2005) have demonstrated that these patients can be treated successfully by psychodynamic psychotherapy.

An understanding of past experience, especially early life experience, and its part in a patient's current psychological state is considered central to successful psychoanalytic treatment. Even if the patient cannot form a coherent narrative of their life history (see Chapter 2), it is vital that the therapist has some sense of it. However, it is often the case that people with intellectual disabilities, especially older people who may have spent time in long-stay institutions, have little knowledge of their own life stories. The hospital's patient records concerning their background are often lost forever (O'Driscoll, 2007). It may also be difficult for staff to hold a person's past in their mind, particularly if it contains many painful experiences of abuse and trauma. But by failing to take account of personal histories, professional carers may be limiting the value of their therapeutic input as well as helping to ensure that people with intellectual disabilities are, in the words of Joanna Ryan (1991), 'still as hidden from history as they are from the rest of life. What history they do have is not so much theirs as the history of others acting either on their behalf, or against them' (p. 85).

The first significant work regarding disability was Jean Marc Gaspard Itard's French study of an abandoned and defective boy, *The Wild Boy of Aveyron* (1801). In this book, Itard showed that the education of an individual with intellectual disabilities was possible. Itard encouraged one of his pupils, Edouard Séguin (1812–1880), to follow in his path with further experiments in a similar vein. Séguin first published in 1846 an account of his attempts to teach an 'idiot' boy, after which he developed a system, in part based on moral treatment, which was an attempt to operate psychologically and was guided by a philosophical belief in the capacity of all persons to be 'made good'. Put simply, it was thought that if people were given suitable attention and training, they would improve. The tenets of this were to be kind, never abusive and to use physical restraint only in order to prevent harm. Recent enquiries into the abusive institutional treatment of people with intellectual disabilities in Cornwall and in Surrey (Health Care Commission, 2006, 2007), however, show that more than 150 years after Séguin's work, his apparently simple and uncontroversial approach can be difficult to put into practice. Séguin's philosophy was grounded in the relationships between workers and inmates. Clark's (1933a) view was that this reflected the relational basis of principles of psychodynamic psychotherapy – that is, the relationship between patient and therapist is seen as the primary therapeutic tool. Séguin believed that 'defectives' had use of their intellectual faculties but lacked the power to apply them because of poor resistance to competing stimuli. Séguin moved to America and was involved in the setting up of the first residential homes in the later part of the nineteenth century.

In England, the experience for many people prior to the 'asylum era' is not so well recorded. There was a classification of 'lunatic' meaning that the 'defect' was acquired and the patient's life was punctuated by particular times of madness. The term 'idiot' indicated that the defect was present from birth and constant (see Wright and Digby, 1996, for more information on this period). There are accounts of 'idiots' ending up in the workhouse system where the best they could hope for was benign neglect. (Interestingly, many of the workhouses were then turned into the first asylums for people with intellectual disabilities.)

The first group of asylums was opened in the 1870s and their population grew, especially as a result of the 1913 Mental Deficiency Act, the first piece of legislation to be applied only to this group. This continued to operate until 1959 and was the first attempt to distinguish people with intellectual disabilities from those with mental illness. When these institutions were first opened they were developed with the notion of being a short-term facility with the aim of training people for life in the community. In fact as late as 1929 the Wood Committee, which was established to explore the purpose of hospitals, concluded that the object of the early hospitals was 'not simply to confine [the patients] for life' and that the hospitals 'should not be a stagnant pool, but a flowing lake'. For the majority of patients, though, life in the hospitals was indeed 'a stagnant pool'. These hospitals were located in isolated positions, outside towns and with poor transport links. Post-war services saw no real change in the dominance of institutions despite a change of management from council care to the National Health Service. The majority of accounts by people who lived in the institutions spoke of mistreatment and cruelty (Cooper and Atkinson, 1997). These institutions seemed also to have pernicious effects on how staff behaved towards the patients, with reports of harsh and abusive treatment (Goffman, 1961). On leaving the institutions the least disabled, i.e. the majority of people living there, often struggled to develop 'ordinary life skills' (Felce, 2000). It also seems that these patients found themselves in a 'Catch-22' situation, as a visiting superintendent from Denmark remarked, 'The criterion for discharge (ability to support oneself in the community) indicated that these individuals should probably not have been in the institution in the first place' (Thomson, 1998, p. 145). It could be argued that while early attempts to provide psychotherapy for people with intellectual disabilities took place in a hospital setting, these settings were, institutionally, profoundly anti-therapeutic.

If the figure of Leon Pierce Clark is remembered today, it is for his work with people with epilepsy. His 1932 papers espoused controversial ideas on the 'epileptic's personality' that are now discredited

(Dwyer, 2004). Much less known is his pioneering work as the first psychotherapist with people with intellectual disabilities. Clark was born in 1870 and, after gaining his medical degree, spent most of his working life in various institutions around the state of New York, specializing in epilepsy. After going to Europe to study this condition further he developed an interest in psychoanalysis, visiting Sigmund Freud in Vienna and meeting the early analysts, which radically changed his approach. Using these new-found theories in his posting at the Letchworth Village for the Feeble Minded in the UK, he set about developing what he termed a 'psycholaborate institution for the feeble-minded' (1933a, p. 19). As this was the period when eugenics thinking was starting to be discredited, he was able to develop his innovative work here. He also started a short-lived psychoanalytic journal, *Archives of Psychoanalysis*, and translated the first version of Sigmund Freud's paper on anxiety (1926). He developed his work with intellectually disabled patients and went on to write his book (1933b). Clark's aims, as set out in the book, were modest: 'Psychoanalysis as a therapy would not claim to remove the fundamental causes of amentia. It would attempt, rather, to reduce the amount and depth of fixation so that the excessiveness of retardation may be avoided, even though the innate defect is not curable' (p. 15). He explained that this would be obtained through the radical application of Freudian theory: 'We believe that mental arrest should be presented in terms of the libido theory of Freud's, thus giving a broader, more vital conception of the whole process of feeblemindedness and increasing our knowledge of the proper training-treatment for this condition' (p. 15). Today, although Freud's influence remains, especially his developing a theory of the mind that includes the unconscious, most therapists in this field would work from a relational perspective. Clark acknowledged the importance of a modified approach to this group of patients, concluding that practitioners should be actively encouraged to extend their therapeutic repertoire. As Jason Upton argues in Chapter 2, it is beholden upon therapists in this field to have a solid theoretical basis to their work but to ensure, primarily, that it is flexible enough to respond to the particular communication needs of their patients who have intellectual disabilities. However, quantitative research of the theoretical trainings and therapeutic practices of therapists in this field has yet to be conducted.

Clark's book was supported by key members of the psychoanalytic community, and included a foreword by the President of the British

Society of Psycho-Analysis, Dr Ernest Jones: 'One can only admire Dr Pierce Clark's assiduity in the immense labours he has devoted to this field, usually considered so unpromising. It must be a source of gratification to him to observe that these hopes are beginning to meet with a degree of success' (Clark, 1993b, p. xi). Clark, in his acknowledgements, thanks a number of people, including the famous Hungarian psychoanalyst Sandor Ferenczi, who had visited Clark at his sanatorium. Today it is difficult to evaluate his work properly as he does not give much information on his 'therapeutic methods'. The analytic sessions reported seem to focus on the urging of ventilation of feelings and tolerating the effects produced – the 'cathartic method' – rather than interpreting the specific anxiety of the moment. Clark used the Freudian concept of 'narcissism' to explain states of mind in which emotional investment in anybody or anything outside the self appeared to have been withdrawn. Freud's early formulation was of an early developmental stage that followed autoerotism but was before anaclitic object choice. This became know as primary narcissism and is theoretically followed by secondary narcissism, a state of non-object relatedness, being fixated in a form of aloofness and an illusion of self-sufficiency. For Clark (1933b, p. 318) the key clinical point was for the 'client' to enter into a relationship with the support staff, to gain identification with them. Clark wrote about how the child takes in (introjects) the good objects (staff) and how this strengthens their ego. As more and more good objects are introjected, the child feels better about himself and discovers that others respond to his love. Clark felt that these experiences contribute to a stable personality. In this way, 'the narcissistic shell must be broken through in order to expose the real weaknesses, the fears and dependent needs which lie behind'. Clark believed the therapist should replace the narcissistic requirements of the patient's dependency on their mother: 'We hold that the primary narcissism is too rigidly attached to the ego in the severer forms of amentia (idiocy): and that only in the milder grades of feeblemindedness, where there is some degree of secondary narcissism can we hope to advance the ament toward a more adult ego and a greater object-cathexis.' (1933b, p. 50). This view would today be challenged by those practitioners (including several in this book), who find that improvement can be seen in the emotional well-being of even the most severely disabled people. Clark also believed that the therapist's task was to make the 'ament superego' less domineering (1933b, p. 51). It seems that here, Clark has identified one of the challenges that continue to face therapists in this field, who may struggle to understand what drives a patient's impulsive and challenging behaviour. It may often not be clear what behaviour is connected to the organic handicap or to subsequent trauma. The work of Sinason (1992) explores this in depth. She has shown that therapy which aims to alleviate emotional pain in the aftermath of trauma can provide relief from distress and so lead to a reduction in disturbed behaviour. Through his work in hospitals, Clark was able to develop Séguin's belief that people with intellectual disabilities have emotional lives. This was undoubtedly a very radical view for the time and for some time afterwards. In 1983 the historian of intellectual disability, Scheerenberger, wrote, 'The emotional and mental health life of intellectually limited persons had little interest and little impact, with few medical schools offering any training about this, a circumstance that had been not rectified by 1983' (1983, p. 90). Clark thought that his early Freudian view could be modified and changed to help this group of patients, believing that an understanding of the inner conflicts would help not only them but, crucially, their support staff, 'Handling of these behaviour problems can be advanced by a better understanding of the impulses and the emotional needs which are behind them' (1933b, p. 45). This is still a key point today, which is why therapy organizations working with people who have intellectual disabilities often offer support and training to support staff, in conjunction with the provision of psychotherapy to clients (see Chapter 11).

Clark's other main contribution was his view that the feeble-minded, as a group, are more fixated at a stage of primary narcissism than the average individual, and that this stops development. This is an interesting idea and resonates in work today, where a therapist may find that the patient with intellectual disabilities often has difficulty in conceptualizing the notion of 'the other' and in, almost literally, being able to put themselves in another's shoes. This can make the development of ordinary and rewarding relationships more than usually difficult, and may also impair the capacity for empathy in those who have gone on to offend against others (see Chapter 6 for a further exploration of offending behaviour). Clark also hypothesized that the excessive sleeping and foetal postures of handicapped patients represented a return to the foetal stage to avoid the damage of handicap to come.

Clark died in 1933. The economic depression of this time limited the potential to develop his work, as the state institutions started to look elsewhere for ideas. It seems that a very pessimistic outlook took hold of professionals working in the institutions (Trent, 1994) at that time.

In England in the post-war period, the advent of the National Health Service did not, unfortunately, increase funding for intellectual disability hospitals. The wider medical world looked down on colleagues who entered this area of work (Thomson, 1998). It was considered low-status work in the medical world and viewed as an unfashionable and neglected backwater for professionals. This, in part, led psychiatrists in particular to turn inwards to seek status. Here they concentrated on efficient economic management in their hospitals. They were not interested in developing new ideas about treatment, but rather adopted commonly held ideas about the value of fresh air, physical activity, work and discipline. Trent (1994) records how psychiatrists working in mental retardation did little more then administer medicine.

Despite this, there were some attempts at psychotherapy work. In 1949, Dr Simon Lindsay assumed a post in psychiatry at St Lawrence's Hospital for Mental Defectives in Caterham, Surrey, UK. At this time Dr Lindsay had completed a good proportion of his psychoanalytical training at the Institute of Psycho-Analysis in London, and as a trainee psychoanalyst he naturally began to wonder whether one might be able to apply psychodynamic ideas to this group of patients. Uncertain of the viability of psychoanalytical treatment for the disabled, Lindsay discussed this matter with his clinical supervisor, Dr Clifford Scott. Already well known in psychoanalytical circles for his pioneering work on psychotherapy for manic-depressive illness, Scott (1946, 1947) encouraged Lindsay. Indeed, Scott even gave the young psychiatrist a copy of the only full-length study on psychoanalysis and intellectual disability published at that time, namely Clark's (1933b) book. Lindsay worked with a patient, 'Betty', for four years, including a three-year period seeing her three times a week. Lindsay never published any of his work in his lifetime, though he wrote his qualifying paper for the Institute of Psychoanalysis on his experiences at St Lawrence's. Lindsay gave a copy to Scott, who later used it as a basis for a paper he wrote in 1962 for the Canadian psychoanalytic society. Each year Lindsay tested 'Betty's' IQ and found that it increased, which encouraged him to develop his work at the Tavistock Clinic, where he carried on treating a few 'mental deficiency' patients. He worked with John Bowlby and Donald Winnicott but never developed this work or wrote about it in journals, moving on to other professional interests. It was, it seems, another opportunity lost. Lindsay was not alone in attempting some psychoanalytically informed psychological work in such institutions, although again we see a situation in which a clinician gives a positive report yet it is not developed into an available treatment option. In England, Linda Mundy (1957) wrote a positive account of her work with children in an institution, while at the Foundation Hospital, London, Sara Neham (1957), a clinical psychologist, wrote a review of the psychotherapy literature concerning people with intellectual disabilities to date, noting that, 'It is sometimes assumed that psychotherapy with the mentally retarded is inadvisable because of their insight and poor verbal development' (p. 3). Neham concluded, 'the weight of evidence presented indicates that for psychotherapy to be effective . . . there may be improvement but only within the limitations of their mental deficiency' (p. 7). This was a recurring conclusion with the majority of clinicians, including Clark (1933b) and Lindsay (1952). A number of papers were published in *The American Journal of Mental Deficiency*, which, for a period, started to explore psychological approaches, and in particular group approaches (e.g. Mundy, 1957; Vail, 1955). Neham wrote, 'Psychotherapy or treatment for the most part, was administered to reduce tension and distress and was not usually considered to be a method of changing the cognitive status of the retardate.' (1957, p. 3).

Another clinical psychologist, Sarason, co-wrote *Psychological Problems in Mental Deficiency* (Sarason and Gladwin, 1949), which explored the complications of psychotherapy with this group. Developing a critical attitude about the hospitalization of people with intellectual disabilities, he wrote about his experience working in such an institution: 'For a year after its opening, Southbury existed for its residents: after that, the residents existed for the organisation' (1988, p. 168). He also noted that, 'I call them residents, but in those days we referred to them as children, regardless of their age. I knew about the self-fulfilling prophecy long before it became a subject of psychological study' (p. 154). Trent (1994, p. 266) has written of the start of the infantilization of 'retarded' people in this period, moving from the idea of them being a 'menace'. Similar processes were developing in the United Kingdom. While participating in the Tavistock Mental Handicap Workshop in the 1990s, psychotherapist Brett Kahr (unpublished work) coined the term 'infanticidal introject' to describe the way that, because the majority of people in society – from parents to support staff – treat people with intellectual disability as children, they in turn introject this and come to feel it about themselves. Sarason (1988) wrote that the majority of his patients did not have organic brain damage but were from impoverished economic backgrounds, or had had brushes with the law. Sinason (1992) wrote that intellectual disabilities are often the result of social and psychological distress in early life. Sarason (1988) gives an example of how a person's IQ became all-consuming: 'If an individual got an I.Q. score of 70 or above, the legal question would be asked: Have we grounds for keeping the person in the institution? There was no question about the differences between 69 and 71' (p. 170). While at Southbury, Sarason (1988) decided to attempt a series of 'studies' in psychotherapy with this neglected group of patients: 'In those studies, I accorded them the status of persons and personhood, emphasizing our similarities as thinking and feeling people and trying to counter the dominant view that they are incomplete, damaged, semi-empty vessels who are obviously human but equally obviously devoid of the "inner life" we know so well.' Sarason concluded: 'The number for whom that approach was applicable was probably not overwhelming; the psychotherapeutic endeavor is one of repair and not of prevention: and as endeavor of repair, its results are far from perfect' (pp. 157–158).

Unpublished research from Respond (Clarke, 1997) likewise show-ed that, following psychotherapeutic treatment, there was slow yet incremental improvement in the psychological state of clients.

Sarason (1988) decided that psychotherapy would be the best way to help patients at Southbury. If it led to a greater self-understanding on the part of patients, or to an increase in their IQ, it might help to keep intellectually disabled people out of the institutions. But first, Sarason had to have his own psychotherapy and then obtain a supervisor for this work. Sarason found a New York psychoanalyst. 'The analysis was of enormous help to me at Southbury. For one thing, I came to understand the residents in relation to me (and vice versa) in a more complex way, both in my therapeutic work and in diagnostic work' (p. 173). The benefits for a therapist in this field to have been in personal therapy are great and, in line with full therapy training, this is something to be advocated in respect of professionals wishing to specialize in this work. There is often a lack of under-standing about why people want to work with this client group. Sarason approached various psychoanalysts, all of whom refused him, and was turned down for a clinical training by the New York Psycho-Analytic Institute.

The American psychiatrist Frank Menolascino (cited in Russell, 1997) wrote on the psychological impact of life in an institution and, drawing on the work of John Bowlby, suggested that behavioural problems in hospital patients may be the result of attachment and relationship difficulties, rather than the disability itself. Such an understanding has been an essential tenet of contemporary psycho-therapeutic practice with people with intellectual disabilities (Hollins and Sinason, 2000). Menolascino also highlighted the importance of 'dual diagnosis', i.e. the recognition that a person could have intel-lectual disability *and* a mental health problem. This is now firmly established in professional practice.

Two notable psychiatrists, both trained in psychoanalysis, spent their professional careers working in a major hospital, Harperbury, near Radlett in Hertfordshire, UK. Professor Lionel Penrose quali-fied in medicine at Cambridge and later pursued an interest in psychology, psychiatry and psychoanalysis, going to Vienna to work with Freud and the Viennese group for a while. He trained as a psychoanalyst but after qualification decided not to practice, focus-ing instead on research and writing a number of seminal publica-tions (Penrose, 1905). His colleague at Harperbury, Alex Shapiro, also trained as a psychoanalyst and worked at the hospital from 1939 until his retirement in 1976. Shapiro did not discount psychoanalysis on the basis of the patient's low intelligence. He developed a modi-fied group analysis approach and a version of a therapeutic com-munity in one part of the hospital, but unfortunately never wrote fully about this. Today he is remembered more for his opposition to long-stay hospital closure, having campaigned very strongly against the closure of the hospitals.

In 1992, a collection of psychotherapy papers was also published (Waitman and Conboy-Hill, 1992) outlining different therapeutic approaches. Since then, however, only two of these approaches, psy-chodynamic and cognitive behavioural therapy (CBT), have been developed further. CBT grew out of behavioural therapy, which was widely used in the hospitals. Behavioural methods were developed in the 1930s and became very popular in the 1960s, particularly as a treatment option for people with intellectual disabilities. Essentially, the method reinforces good behaviour by rewarding it, while bad behaviour is ignored.

While behaviour therapists are encouraged to study and record the antecedents to incidents of challenging behaviour, they are not encouraged to seek explanations for it in the client's past or in his/her emotional world. It is popular because outcomes can be measured and treatment time is generally 6 to 12 sessions, therefore it is a much shorter term treatment than psychoanalytic psychotherapy. Today it is widely used in anger management, enabling the client to express emotions appropriately. There is much ongoing discussion on CBT techniques, for example on the reliability of self-reporting of the client, which is a key factor in the development of new skills for dealing with negative behaviour. It seems that, in the future, practitioners of CBT may be more likely to use the psychodynamic concept of transference in their work and thus will develop a bridge between the two therapeutic approaches. For a full account of these developments, see Kroese *et al.* (1997).

Maud Mannoni, a French Lacanian psychoanalyst who practised as a child psychologist in Paris, wrote 'A Challenge to Mental Retardation' (1965). Mannoni examined the ways in which intellectually disabled people experienced significant difficulties in building and maintaining relationships (an issue also researched in the UK by Richardson and Ritchie, 1989). While making it clear that she did not deny the existence of organic damage, Mannoni felt that its psychological aspects were not fully understood. In 1972 Penguin published a special education edition on her work with children with intellectual disabilities: *The Backward Child and Her Mother*. It appears to have generated little interest in the UK.

The key breakthrough regarding psychoanalytic psychotherapy for people with intellectual disabilities came with the work of Neville Symington in the 1980s. His work coincided with the widespread development of services for people with intellectual disabilities according to principles of normalization (Wolfensberger, 1974), which in turn led to the development of the self-advocacy movement in the UK (see Chapter 10 for more information about self-advocacy). Long-stay hospitals were closing and people with intellectual disabilities were moving into the community. Wolfensberger was influenced by psychoanalytic ideas and wrote of the role of the unconscious is the ways in which services were set up and delivered. His work on 'deathmaking' cultures is also significant in relation to therapeutic work, and is referred to in several other chapters in this book.

Psychotherapist Neville Symington was encouraged to offer treatment to a man with intellectual disabilities after reading Clark's book (1933b). In Symington's now classic paper (1981) which describes his work, it is clear that the patient, 'Harry', made progress in his therapy. It is also notable that many of the challenges in the treatment, which Symington identifies, remain live issues in the provision of psychotherapy to people with learning disabilities. In particular, Symington describes his efforts to work alongside Harry's other carers, and to enlist their support for the treatment. He says, 'The staff were very willing to help. But to communicate what I had learned in a therapeutic encounter, through rational explanations, was only minimally successful' (p. 192). Symington also made attempts to engage Harry's parents in a form of family therapy, as he identified that Harry's family relationships were key to his emotional distress. However, he was met with resistance. Harry was also unsure of his mental capacities and this caused him great confusion and sadness. Part of Symington's work was to witness Harry's pain at his identity as a disabled man. Symington concluded that despair was a central problem for professionals working with this group. He wrote, 'There is a strong tendency for people to despair as soon as the word organic is mentioned . . . Neurological growth can be stimulated and is not static. What remains static are people's expectations that change can occur' (p. 199). Symington started the Tavistock Mental Handicap Workshop, which Valerie Sinason joined; she started to develop her own pioneering ideas, especially that of a 'secondary handicap', which is explored in subsequent chapters.

Since the early 1990s the field of psychotherapy and intellectual disability has been enriched by the work of Nigel Beail (1998, 2004; Beail *et al.*, 2005), also referenced in Chapters 3 and 12, who has conducted significant research into the effectiveness of psychodynamic psychotherapy with people with intellectual disabilities.

To conclude this historical review, it could be argued that each new therapist that writes about their work with people who have intellectual disabilities has to begin again to make the case for the value of the work. American psychiatrist Dr Howard Potter (1965) reflected on his long career in the field of intellectual disability. He had been active in New York in the period when L. P. Clark was developing his therapeutic work, frequently chairing many of the meetings in which Clark presented his work. Potter writes, 'some psychoanalytic studies have been reported . . . showing that intensive psychotherapy in some cases of mental retardation results in striking improvement of intellectual functioning. There are dozens of reports on the technique and stabilising value of group psychotherapy with mental retardates.' He concluded by asking (rather pessimistically), regarding his fellow professionals, 'Could it be that the nature of mental retardation is such that the modern psychiatrist is not so well prepared to be of service to the mentally retarded as was his nineteenth-century counterpart?' (pp. 541–543). Trent (1994) wrote that many psychoanalysts view this client group as 'boring'. Karl Menninger wrote an early paper with a colleague (Chidester and Menninger, 1936) in which he reported some successful therapeutic work; despite going on to establish the world-famous Menninger psychoanalytic clinic in America, he never developed the work further. While I was doing my psychotherapy training there seemed relatively little interest in this work compared with, for example, the work undertaken with psychotic patients. In my view, as Symington suggested, despair can be a key element in this work, along with a sense that the therapist's narcissism is under attack as they feel unable to cure the individual in the therapy process.

The history of the treatment of people with intellectual disabilities can, at best, be described as benign neglect. 'Mental defectives' were construed as a social problem at the end of the nineteenth century. They were seen as an abhorrence to civilized society and as a genetic danger. While today these attitudes may seem abhorrent, we know that services reflect the wider attitudes and policies of the time. For example, eugenics programmes represent the darkest expressions of the dehumanizing view of people with intellectual disabilities, and have their apotheosis in the Nazi T4 programme (Burleigh, 1994). It could be argued that here, in the twenty-first century, we have been more successful in correcting the horrors of state institutions than in developing humane alternatives in the community. In order to cope with society's collective intolerance, it has historically 'split off' and controlled people defined as dangerous, sick, incompetent or unpredictable by placing them in institutions where they are out of sight and out of mind. In splitting off these people, we do not have to come into contact with the handicapped or mad parts of ourselves.

Nevertheless, the place of people with intellectual disabilities in society has changed for the better in a number of ways. Advances in legislation pertaining to human rights and the implementation of the Disability Discrimination Act (2005) stand as powerful reminders of the ethical and societal obligation to treat people with disabilities with respect, and of ensuring a greater sense of equality and integration. Why then, have advances in psychotherapeutic provision lagged so far behind other societal advances (notwithstanding very recent improvements such as the foundation of The Institute for Psychotherapy and

Disability in 2000 and the Royal College of Psychiatrists' Report, 2004, into psychotherapy and intellectual disabilities, as well as the fact that specialist trainings are currently being developed in at least two British universities)? Why has the progress of the pioneers described in this chapter taken such a long time to filter down to mainstream therapeutic practice? Why are contemporary practitioners, such as Sinason, Hollins and therapists at Respond, still described as pioneers rather than as mainstream clinicians? It may be helpful to view the failure of psychotherapeutic practice to embrace fully the needs of people with intellectual disability through the lens of the disability transference (see Chapter 3). A subtle overidentification with intellectual disability may have led some of the early twentieth-century pioneers to hide their work from public view, in much the same way as families have often sought to hide their disabled child from the glare of the community. A complex mix of shame, guilt, rage and hatred may have served to overshadow the attendant feelings of pride, joy and love that are often also present in the disability transference. A slowness, or failure, to process our transferential feelings of hatred (and love) of our patients may be seen to have been enacted in the psychotherapy community's larger disavowal of patients with intellectual disabilities. The reluctance of the majority of psychotherapy training institutes to allow their members to train with patients with intellectual disabilities points not only to an abandonment of respect and equal opportunity, but also to a primitive wish to abort people with intellectual disabilities from our minds.

The past 15 years has seen much, if not enough, change. To write or talk about one's clinical experiences of patients with intellectual disabilities does not have quite the same charge of public shame that it once did. Most clinicians working with clients with intellectual disabilities over the past two decades are familiar with countertransferential feelings that are stirred up through engaging in professional clinical networks. Although it happens less frequently as the sheer weight of clinical evidence from the consulting room grows, we still remember all too well fighting to speak about disability at mainstream conferences and in mainstream journals. To describe ourselves to colleagues as working therapeutically with people with intellectual disabilities could, in the past, cause us to be treated and responded to as if we ourselves had some form of disability. In addition to, for example, specialists such as the Tavistock Learning Disabilities Service, organizations such as the International Association of Forensic Psychotherapy, the Guild of Psychotherapists and the Centre for Attachment Based Psychoanalytic Psychotherapy have an increasing awareness of the needs of patients who have intellectual disabilities at their core, most vividly demonstrated by an increasing number of clinical papers and keynote presentations at their conferences being concerned with the possibility of psychoanalytic work with people with intellectual disabilities. These are small but significant steps, and mirror not only the patient's slow, painful and gradual shift from the paranoid/schizoid to a more depressive position (a journey that, for some, may take decades), but also the psychotherapist's long struggle to process his or her painful responses to dealing with clinical issues of trauma, damage and difference. Thus the answer to the question of why psychotherapy has been so slow to begin thinking in a non-defensive and non-rejecting way about the emotional needs of patients with intellectual disabilities may lie in the very centre of the psychotherapeutic endeavour – the transference and the countertransference. As we become more adept at describing our work in ways that illuminate the depth of clinical exchanges happening around the UK, so we are reminding our colleagues of how the similarities outweigh the differences. As most chapters in this book seek to demonstrate, the differences are profound – as are the similarities. Living with intellectual disabilities is different from living without them. But it is also the same. The core struggles of life – who we are, how we express our sexuality, and how we deal with the unavoidable fact that one day we will die – are felt and communicated by all human beings, regardless of ability. Being a psychotherapist working with people with intellectual disabilities is different too. Nevertheless, concepts of the unconscious, of splitting, projective identification, the transference and the countertransference are as deeply embedded in this work as they are in work with neurotic patients and people with borderline personality disorder, psychosis and dissociative identity disorders. Perhaps the biggest lesson we can learn from the history of psychotherapy with people with intellectual disabilities is that the history is as dictated by the unconscious as we are, patients and therapist alike.

References

Atkinson, D., Jackson, M. and Walmsley, J. (1997) *Forgotten Lives: Exploring the History of Intellectual Disability*. Kidderminster, UK: BILD Publications.

Beail, N. (1998) Outcome of psychoanalysis, psychoanalytic and psycho-dynamic psychotherapy with people with intellectual disabilities: A review. *Changes 13*, 186–191.

Beail, N. (2004) Method, design and evaluation in psychotherapy research with people with intellectual disabilities. In E. Emerson, C. Hatton, T. Parmenter and T. Thompson (eds), *International Handbook of Methods for Research and Evaluation in Intellectual Disabilities*. New York: Wiley.

Beail, N., Warden, S., Morsley, K. and Newman, D. W. (2005) Naturalistic evaluation of the effectiveness of psychodynamic psychotherapy for people with intellectual disabilities. *Journal of Applied Research in Intellectual Disabilities 18*, 245–251.

Bender, M. (1993) The unoffered chair: The history of therapeutic disdain towards people with intellectual disabilities: A review. *Clinical Psychology Forum 54*, 7–12.

Burleigh, M. (1994) *Death and Deliverance: Euthanasia in Germany, 1900–1954*. Cambridge, UK: Cambridge University Press.

Chidester, L. and Menninger, K. (1936) The application of psychoanalytic methods to the study of mental retardation. *American Journal of Orthopsychiatry 6*, 616–625.

Clark, L. P. (1932a) What is the psychology of organic epilepsy? *Psychoanalytic Review 20*, 79–85.

Clark, L. P. (1932b) The psychology of idiocy. *Psychoanalytic Review 19*, 257–269.

Clark, L. P. (1933a) *The Need for a Better Understanding of the Emotional Life of the Feebleminded*. Proceeding address of the American Association on Mental Deficiency. Minutes of meeting, vol. 38, 348–357.

Clark, L. P. (1933b) *The Nature and Treatment of Amentia: Psychoanalysis and Mental Arrest in Relation to the Science of Intelligence*. London: Bailliere, Tindall and Cox.

Clarke, A. W. (1997) *An Initial Analysis of Respond's Psychotherapy Services* (unpublished research).

Cooper, M. and Atkinson, D. (1997) My life story. In D. Atkinson, M. Jackson and J. Walmsley (eds), *Forgotten Lives: Exploring the History of Learning Disability*. Kidderminster, UK: BILD Publications.

Department of Health (2001) *Valuing People: A New Strategy for Learning Disability for the 21st Century*. London: The Stationery Office.

The Disability Discrimination Act (2005) (Commencement No. 2 (C113)). London: HMSO.

Dwyer, E. (2004) The state and the multiply disadvantaged: The case of epilepsy. In S. Noll and J. W. Trent (eds), *Mental Retardation in America: A Historical Reader (The History of Disability)*. New York: New York University Press.

Felce, D. (2000) *Quality of Life for People with Learning Disabilities in*

Supported Housing in the Community: A Review of the Research. Exeter, UK: Centre for Evidence-based Social Services, University of Exeter.

Freud, S. (1904) Freud's psychoanalytic procedure. Reprinted (1953–1974) in the *Standard Edition of the Complete Psychological Works of Sigmund Freud* (trans. and ed. J. Strachey), vol. 7. London: Hogarth Press.

Freud, S. (1926) *Inhibitions, symptom and anxiety.* Standard Edition, vol. 20. London: Hogarth Press.

Grafton, G. (2005) *Interview with Valerie Sinason* (personal communication).

Goffman, E. (1961) *Asylums: Essays in the Social Situation in the Mental Patients and Other Inmates.* New York: Doubleday.

Health Care Commission (2006) *Investigation into Services for People with Learning Disabilities at Cornwall Partnership NHS Trust.* London: HCC.

Health Care Commission (2007) *Investigation into Services for People with Learning Disabilities at Sutton & Merton Primary Care Trust.* London: HCC.

Hollins, S. and Sinason, V. (2000) Psychotherapy, learning disabilities and trauma: New perspectives. *British Journal of Psychiatry 176,* 32–36.

Kroese, B. S., Dagnan, D. and Loumidis, K. (1997) *Cognitive-Behaviour Therapy for People with Learning Disabilities.* London: Routledge.

Lindsay, S. (1952) *A Psychoanalytic Approach to Mental Deficiency.* Presented to the Psychotherapy and Social Psychiatry Group of the Royal Medical Psychological Society (unpublished paper).

Mannoni, M. (1965) A challenge to mental retardation. Reprinted in M. Mannoni (1972) *The Backward Child and her Mother.* London: Penguin.

Mannoni, M. (1972) *The Backward Child and her Mother.* London: Penguin.

Mundy, L. (1957) Therapy with physically and mentally handicapped children in a mental deficiency hospital. *British Journal of Clinical Psychology 13,* 59–64.

Neham, S. (1957) Psychotherapy in relation to mental deficiency. *American Journal of Mental Deficiency 55,* 557–572.

Noll, S. and Trent, J. W. (2004) *Mental Retardation in America: A Historical Reader (The History of Disability).* New York: New York University Press.

O'Driscoll, D. (2000) *The Need for a Better Understanding of the Emotional Life of the Feebleminded: Two Pioneers of Psychoanalytic Psychotherapy with People with Learning Disabilities.* Unpublished MA dissertation, Regent's College/City University, London.

O'Driscoll, D. (2007) The Hertfordshire History Project. *Down's Syndrome Association Magazine,* spring.

Penrose, L. S. (1905) *Biology of Mental Defect.* Cambridge, UK: Cambridge University Press.

Potter, H. (1965) Mental Retardation: The Cinderella of Psychiatry. *Psychiatric Quarterly 39*, 537–549.

Report of the Mental Deficiency Committee (The Wood Report) (1929) London: HMSO.

Richardson, A. and Ritchie, J. (1989) *Developing Friendships: Enabling People with Learning Difficulties to Make and Keep Friends.* London: Policy Studies Institute.

Royal College of Psychiatrists Council (2004) *Psychotherapy and learning disability*, Report CR116. London: Royal College of Psychiatrists.

Russell, O. (1997) *Seminars in the Psychiatry of Learning Disabilities*, Royal College of Psychiatrists. Glasgow: Gaskell.

Ryan, J. with Thomas, F. (1991) *The Politics of Mental Handicap* (revised ed.). London: Free Association Press.

Sarason, S. B. (1988) *The Making of an American Psychologist: An Autobiography.* San Francisco: Jossey Bass.

Sarason, S. B. and Gladwin, T. (1949) *Psychological Problems in Mental Deficiency* (3rd ed.). New York: Harper and Brothers.

Scheerenberger, R. C. (1983) *A History of Mental Retardation.* Baltimore: Paul H. Brooks.

Scott, W. C. M. (1934) Book Review of L. P. Clark's *The Nature and Treatment of Amentia. International Journal of Psychoanalysis 15*, 93.

Scott, W. C. M. (1946) A note of psychopathology of convulsive phenomena in manic depressive states. *International Journal of Psychoanalysis 27*, 152–155.

Scott, W. C. M. (1947) On the Intensive Affects Encountered in Treating a Severe Manic Depressive. *International Journal of Psychoanalysis 27*, 152–155.

Séguin, E. (1846) *Traitement moral hygiene et education des idiots et des autres enfants arrieres ou etardeés dans leur development.* Paris: Bailliere Tindall.

Sinason, V. (1992) *Mental Handicap and the Human Condition: New Approaches from the Tavistock.* London: Free Association Books.

Symington, N. (1981) The psychotherapy of a subnormal patient. *British Journal of Medical Psychology 44*, 211–228.

Thomson, M. (1998) *The Problem of Mental Deficiency: Eugenics, Democracy, and Social Policy in Britain 1879–1959.* Oxford, UK: Oxford University Press.

Trent, J. (1994) *Inventing the Feeble Mind: A History of Mental Retardation in America.* Berkeley, CA: University of California Press.

Tyson, R. L. and Sandler, J. (1971) Problems in the selection of patients for psychoanalysis: Comments on the application of 'indications', 'suitability' and 'analysability'. *British Journal of Medical Psychology 44*, 211–228.

Vail, D. J. (1955) An unsuccessful experiment in group therapy. *American Journal of Mental Deficiency 60*(1), 144–151.

Waitman, A. and Conboy-Hill, S. (1992) *Psychotherapy and Mental Handicap*. London: Sage.

Wolfensberger, W. (1974) *The Origin and Nature of Our Institutional Models*. Syracuse, NY: Syracuse University Press.

Wright, D. and Digby, A. (eds) (1996) *From Idiocy to Mental Deficiency: Historical Perspectives on People with Learning Disabilities*. London: Routledge.

Chapter 2

When words are not enough

Creative therapeutic approaches

Jason Upton

As Chapter 1 has described, for many years it was believed that people with intellectual disabilities could not make use of psychotherapy. If a client was not able to communicate their experiences well enough using words, and to *think about* their thoughts, feelings and behaviour, then they were considered unable to benefit from therapy. Even today, it is our experience at Respond that many mental health services still refuse access to therapy for people with intellectual disabilities. And while belief that this group should have access to effective emotional and psychological therapies has perhaps changed over recent times, what has perhaps not changed sufficiently is the therapists' abilities to make the therapy itself appropriate and accessible.

Can creative approaches help to make psychotherapy meaningful for people with intellectual disabilities, enabling them to find not only means for self-expression but also opportunities to process and work through emotional and psychological issues? In particular, I want to draw attention to different levels of creative expression, from embodiment to representational and symbolic levels. These levels can enable clients with intellectual disabilities to find expression that corresponds to their particular level of development. I will also explore how an important characteristic of many creative techniques, such as an awareness of indirect communication, can play an invaluable role in overcoming some of the key factors that typically are thought to prevent the intellectually disabled client from making use of therapy.

Self-expression and therapy

Self-expression is a universal given for all human beings. Essentially, it is the way in which I reveal myself to myself, to others and to the world. This expression includes all aspects of lived experience from past, present and future; and contains emotional experiences such as anxieties, hopes and fears; as well as perceptions and understandings of the self and others. In many ways, all this is being expressed constantly through every act, decision, gesture, spoken word, vocal utterance, etc. From the moment we are born, we are constantly expressing our experience of being alive, and as we develop we normally acquire more sophisticated cognitive and emotional capacities to enhance and enrich the subtleties of this expression. A young infant may suddenly burst into tears at the departure of his mother, while a ten-year-old girl is able to express to her father that she feels sad because she is unable to live with him.

This capacity for self-expression, in whatever form it may take, is very much at the heart of all human relationships. We express ourselves to one another and are keenly attentive to how others are affected by this, and respond to us. In his pioneering studies into the infant–parent relationship, Daniel Stern (1985, 2004) has shown how each moment of the relationship reveals an intersubjective matrix where both implicit and explicit (unconscious and conscious) felt experiences are expressed and then shared by the infant and parent. He demonstrates how the expression of subjective experience is inseparable from this co-created intersubjective matrix. Thus, one's self-expression is deeply embedded in one's relationships to other people.

Psychotherapy is grounded in such notions of self-expression, and similarly believes that this expression unfolds within the context of a relationship – the therapeutic relationship. Therapy is typically about people telling the story of their life – either past or present – to a therapist. This is usually because there is something troubling them in their life that they cannot understand or change. Often they may not even know what exactly is troubling them. They may be unable to express their difficulties verbally, but these difficulties are being both experienced and expressed through how they live their lives. The therapist will encourage the client's self-expression until these troubles reveal themselves and can be understood. Thus, the dialogue and the relationship to the therapist nurture the client's self-expression, and in turn self-reflection.

Narratives, therapy and people with intellectual disabilities

Following on from this, we can see how therapy has become deeply reliant on narratives as a means to explore the client's experience. Systemic therapists Vetere and Dowling (2005) observe that a central tenet of their therapeutic work is an interest in the client's stories, accounts, narratives and biography. Of course, psychoanalytic psychotherapy emphasizes the significance of the unconscious, and uses free associations and dreams as well as narrative and conversation, but the analyst makes use of sometimes rather complicated explanations of why the patient needs his symptoms, and such a 'talking cure' may be felt to be beyond the limits of some clients who have intellectual disabilities. It remains the case that the client's capacity for narrative-based self-reporting is a significant part of many psychotherapeutic approaches and the client's ability to convey accounts of their past or present experience may be regarded, by therapist as well as referrers and clients, as crucial for psychotherapy to be effective. Typically, in a therapeutic process, this narrative-based self reporting relies on:

- verbal communication
- direct communication
- factuality – i.e. being grounded in some kind of reality.

Verbal communication refers to the means of expression through which clients convey their experience. Narratives may involve the use of images, metaphors and analogies, or refer to real-life events, fantasy or imagination – but nearly always these narratives are conveyed through words. Direct communication refers to the client's ability to communicate their story directly to the therapist. Clients recall their life experiences and report them using the range of language available to them. And finally, all these client narratives are usually grounded in and made referent to the client's actual life history or experience.

These key features of narrative-based self-reporting, which usually enable clients to make good use of therapy, can help us to understand just why many clients with intellectual disabilities may struggle to do so. For many people with intellectual disabilities, narrative-based self-reporting is difficult. This can be due to such factors as:

- poor memory
- struggles in making cognitive connections between feelings and behaviours, as well as understanding the cause-and-effect nature of relationships
- poor language and communication skills – especially the inability to name their emotional and subjective states.

Each of these difficulties means that providing a direct and verbal narrative account of their life experiences is going to be either limited or simply not possible. When we add to this the emotional defences that often inhibit any client (with or without an intellectual disability) in therapy, and the emotional issues that are too painful to acknowledge, then we begin to arrive at a position that asks whether or not people with intellectual disabilities can indeed benefit from psychotherapy. Many professionals still struggle with clients who have intellectual disabilities, believing that such narrative-based self-reporting coupled with a high-enough level of reflective functioning is a precondition for any psychotherapy or psychological intervention. However, I would like to argue that this is most certainly not the case. The therapeutic limitation comes not because intellectually disabled clients struggle to express their life narrative, but because the therapist requires that it be presented and worked with in a particular fashion. It is precisely at this point that, I believe, psychotherapists need to be open and sensitive to the vast array of expressive means that these clients *already* have at their disposal, and be willing to enter into an encounter where that expression can be nurtured, and heard as meaningful articulations of their lived experience.

Creative expression and projective techniques

The development of the art therapies over the past 30 years has opened up the therapeutic world to the possibilities of using creative approaches for the purpose of facilitating therapeutic change. While it is not my intention to give an overview of these approaches here, I do wish to explore how creative approaches can assist clients who have intellectual disabilities to make use of therapy.

In the therapeutic context, creative expression can be divided into the following two categories:

1   *Embodied expression*

- Whole-person movement
- Dancing and music
- Acting, characterization, masks and role-play
- Embodied games

2   *Projected expression*

- The whole mind is used and drama is projected onto objects outside the client
- Art – painting and drawing
- Sand tray, puppets
- Written stories, poetry

Within this categorization of creative expression, the key difference comes in defining where the creative narratives take place. Either the creative expression involves the whole person (embodied expression) or it is projected onto something outside of, or other than, the person (projected expression). In the former, clients engage in expression that involves their whole body/mind, from dancing to embodied games. These embodied activities convey directly their experience and can be developed to the level of dramatic expression that contains characterization and acting out actual narratives. In the latter, the client's experience is projected onto external creative activities such as through painting or using sand-tray figures. While undoubtedly this expression is still completely from the client, what occurs here is that she or he retains a level of distance from the creative product.

There is a tremendous benefit in these embodied and projected forms of expression for a client who has intellectual disabilities. Making reference to the key features of narrative-based self-reporting, these benefits include the following.

- They are not dependent on verbal communication.
- They allow for indirect communication.
- They work with both imagined and factual narratives.

All these forms of communication can allow for a self-expression that matches the client's level of emotional or cognitive development and, thus, still enable the client to express the narrative of their lived experience. In other words, despite any challenges of poor memory, poor verbal and communication skills, or poor capacity for cognitive linking, clients can still express their life experiences, their perceptions and understanding, and their emotional and behavioural response to life. These are the fundamental prerequisites for the therapeutic process to take place.

Developmental view of expression

An important aspect of creativity that can enable clients who have intellectual disabilities to express their experiences comes via the correlation of different types of cognitive and emotional expression. Several creative arts therapists have written about continua of play and self-expression that correlate to human development. Courtney (1980) provides a detailed account of creative play that can be seen at differing stages of an infant/child's development. And Jennings (1990) offers a simpler model that suggests a progression through embodied play to projective play to role-play. Most of these developmental approaches are based around theories of developmental psychology such as Jean Piaget's line of cognitive development. The following is a brief overview of a development approach that I have personally found helpful.

Concrete/embodied expression

Here, expression is embodied and is largely a physical experience. An object, such as a ball, is merely an object and is related to purely through a physical/sensory relationship. It is important to highlight that while this expression remains mostly embodied or physical/sensory, it is still rich with emotional qualities and endowed with significance and meaning. For instance, a client who repeatedly and aggressively discards objects may be expressing himself at this concrete level, but is simultaneously revealing a strong emotional and relational experience – for instance, anger and abandonment. At this level, the therapist must pay close attention to how the client's expression affects him/her in what is called the countertransference.

Representational expression

At this level, expression moves away from the merely embodied to contain images or depictions of representations. Thus, an object is no longer just an object but can *represent* something else. For instance, a figure of a tiger is not just a piece of plastic but represents an actual tiger. Similarly, my body can represent an animal, a tree, a building, etc. At this point, simple narratives become possible due to the ability to designate definable characters and images with specified qualities or traits. Clients can also develop relationships between such representations. For instance, a client may draw a picture showing a person being scared of a snarling tiger. While this narrative remains simple, it nevertheless reveals a vivid depiction of both emotional and relational significance. In this respect, it has strong affinities with children's play and drawings.

Symbolic expression

Finally, in this simple developmental presentation, the client moves beyond the merely representational towards the symbolic. Here, not only can an object *represent* something that it is made to look like, but it can now become a symbol for something else. For example, the painting of the tiger now moves beyond merely being a depiction of an actual tiger, and instead symbolically expresses a bully at school, a threatening adult, or strength and courage. Again, symbolic expressions convey a rich account of a client's emotional, relational and cognitive experience. Invariably they tend to enable a more sophisticated level of self-expression, as symbols allow the client to capture more complicated and abstract experiences in one image. In a later vignette about a client called Steve, we will see how a client can move developmentally along these stages of self-expression, employing levels of expression that best capture the experience in that moment.

Indirect communication and defence mechanisms

One of the benefits of creative approaches is that they can allow the client to engage in indirect communication. This permits the client to retain some psychological distance from the emotional expression that takes place once removed. This means that issues that are too psychologically painful can be expressed without the client feeling overwhelmed from a more personal encounter with his/her feelings. For some clients, it is easier to refer to the feelings of a character than to their own feelings. While direct communication about the client's own feelings is ultimately preferable, this approach can help prevent the client from closing down in the face of strong emotions. It also helps to relax emotional defence mechanisms, as the self feels less vulnerable or threatened when engaged in indirect expression. From a therapeutic perspective, when emotional defences or usual coping strategies are suspended, clients often convey rich narratives of their inner world – revealing their internal representations of how they understand and experience themselves, others and the world. Even while such narratives more typically represent the client's inner world, rather than outer world/reality, they nevertheless shed significant light on the issues they are struggling with and provide valuable clues to their everyday experience. The therapeutic benefit for the clients is that they are able to give expression to their issues in a way that is not too confrontational.

Case study: Jack

Jack, who has mild intellectual disabilities, came to us for therapy after a recommendation was made with regard to a concern that his cousin had been sexually abusing him. He was 12 years old and had been living in a foster home for the past five years. Both his parents had mental health problems, and he was taken into care on grounds of neglect and suspected abuse. The neglect of Jack was so bad that he was found desperately malnourished and sleeping on a cardboard box, practically naked and completely uncared for. His foster carers were struggling with his defiant behaviour, which they couldn't understand, and at the time Jack was refusing to go to school because he feared being bullied.

From the outset, it was clear that his emotional defences were very strong. Any attempt by me to encourage dialogue about his difficulties resulted in him yelling over the top of me, simply ignoring me or walking out of the room. Directly addressing his difficulties proved to be too much for Jack. Fortunately, he relished using creative expression. Over time, he created a wealth of characters and storylines that conveyed events too difficult for him to confront or bring into full consciousness. While others around Jack found his aggressive and challenging behaviour hard to understand, it become clear that such behaviour was a defence against a deep-seated fear of abandonment, betrayal and being hurt. His defiance was actually a call for affection and attention. And as his foster carers felt they offered him as much as they could, his behaviour was simply hard to comprehend.

Themes that emerged in his stories expressed his experience vividly. He played characters who fell off cliffs and broke all the bones in their bodies, and he frequently regressed to being a one-year-old baby, completely vulnerable and in need of attention. In particular, he often portrayed a character who had blades stabbed into different parts of his body. This character needed endless operations, which usually failed to extract all the knives. Often the blades would break off during the operation and just end up going deeper. Having been placed, by Jack, in the role of the surgeon – he was ensuring that I experienced the failure and powerlessness of somebody unable to help him – I not only felt helpless, but also questioned whether or not, just as the blade went deeper, I was making things worse. Was I helping Jack or hurting him? This countertransference response told me a great deal about how Jack experiences others – not as helpers but as hurters; and how he experiences himself – helpless and hopeless. It also gave me a good insight into the feelings of his foster carers as they struggled to provide good care for him. From his perspective, all this care and attention could not uproot this pain. Such scenes were re-enacted over and over, week after week. It made me wonder at times whether his profound experience of trauma and his endless need for attention/affection could ever be worked through.

Throughout this time, Jack still found direct communication about his behaviour and experiences too overwhelming, igniting his defences. Eventually, within some of his stories there emerged a shift and some capacity to reflect. One story saw a baby covered in blades. Again, all attempts at operation were unsuccessful. At the end of the story, however, Jack commented that the baby had died because the mum had not shown him any love or respect. I asked what he would do. He said show him some love and take all the knives out. In the coming weeks, the same story continued with striking developments. The main character began to be awake during operations, and even assisted the surgeon. Operations slowly began to be successful, with the injured patient commencing periods of recovery. This was coupled with an emerging theme that the character could take responsibility for 'helping himself'. All these shifts occurred through indirect narratives of dramatic role-play with very little formal reflection. These were little steps, but indicated a significant transition from total vulnerability, which was helpless and hopeless, to being able to receive help, and helping himself.

After 18 months of therapy I learnt that Jack's sister, who had been placed in a therapeutic community, was experiencing a total psychotic breakdown with paranoia attacks and auditory and visual hallucinations. Hearing this news, I felt as if I understood some of the importance of Jack's defensive patterns. It could have been that they were to avoid such a psychological deterioration on his own part. While this remains merely conjecture, it does perhaps point to the significance of how strongly he defended himself against direct communication and bringing issues into full conscious awareness. Bearing this in mind, we can begin to see the importance of indirect communication, through either projective techniques or such embodied expressions as Jack's characterized narratives. It can allow for issues to be expressed in a manner that does not overwhelm the client, helping to bypass emotional defences, if you like, without destroying their important purpose. However, even more pertinently than this, it can allow for clients to reflect both indirectly and pre-reflectively on their issues, enabling them to explore and employ new psychological positions.

Indirect communication: demonstrating is easier

Another advantage of indirect communication for clients who have intellectual disabilities is the fact that it is more demonstrative. A client may not have the words to describe an experience of abuse, but she or he may be able to draw it, or animate figures to demonstrate it. Clearly, this is much easier for many people with intellectual disabilities as it does not require a high level of language, or indeed any verbal skills. What it does allow is the expression of pre-reflective and pre-verbal memories and experience. A good example of this can be seen in the following vignette of Steve.

Case study: Steve

Steve was 19 years old on referral. He has moderate to severe intellectual disabilities with limited verbal communication. He was referred over concerns about his aggressive behaviour towards others, and the beginnings of sexually inappropriate behaviour. Steve was adopted when he was seven years old, having been taken into care on suspicions that he had been repeatedly sexually abused by several male members of his family.

At the commencement of therapy, Steve's relationship to both the resources and myself was one of objectification and functionality. Throughout the early stages, Steve made use of many animal figures, in particular the dinosaurs. Steve would relate to these figures not as animals but as objects. He would hit them together or against the table, or they would be thrown around the room. The predominant themes were of aggression and functionality. Steve would use each animal to convey an experience of aggression and then they would be discarded immediately. At other times, he would investigate the figures as if they were objects of scientific examination, dead and lifeless. There was little sense of 'otherness' in his expression, rather an outpouring of chaotic aggression that objectified and deadened. This was also reflected in our relationship. While Steve was never physically aggressive towards me, his relation to me was primarily functional. I provided him with access to the resources and materials, and at other times it was as if I didn't even exist. Most of my attempts to engage Steve directly through words or gesture were either ignored or 'killed off' by his insistence on keeping me out of his creative expression. My countertransference response oscillated between feeling cut off and desperately isolated, to feeling as if I was an intruder and a violator of his play whenever I attempted to establish contact. These responses gave me important insights into Steve's experience. If others are potentially so threatening or intrusive, then perhaps 'killing them off' or turning them into objects is the only way to manage the distress and fear they would otherwise cause.

After a few months in therapy, Steve began to develop this play – moving from a concrete level of expression to a more representational and symbolic level. Initially, Steve began animating the figures as if they were living animals: they would meet and fight, with one viciously attacking and killing the other. Over time, Steve developed this simple narrative to more complex and sophisticated levels. He began clearly to identify different characters, with different motivational intent and responses to one another. It is important to emphasize here that the emergence of such a story would normally have been considered most unlikely for someone with his level of intellectual disability; certainly he would not have been able to communicate this verbally.

Steve's narratives depicted characters who had clear predatorial intent, and who planned and manipulated a situation in order to disable and overcome their victim. A strong theme was that of a group of predators attacking others. They would often use their numbers to chase and corner their victim. Within all of this was an overwhelming sense of helplessness and hopelessness on the part of the victims. They were nearly always totally overcome, viciously attacked, and killed. Steve would reinforce their death by calling out 'dead, dead' on many occasions, adamant that they were now lifeless and could not be moved by either himself or me. While this indirect communication does not tell us anything about the historical details of Steve's life, what it painted was a picture of the world as Steve experiences it, full of vicious and violent predators, and hopeless victims.

Processing and working through on a pre-reflective level

Clients like Steve, who have very little verbal language, will usually lack the cognitive capacity for reflection. In other words, Steve would struggle to conceptualize the importance of his narratives and see the significances for his everyday life experience. But does that mean that he cannot process or work through his emotional issues? I do not believe so. Instead, the processing takes place pre-reflectively.

In simple terms, working through a difficult issue means moving from one emotional/psychological position to another. This can happen via differing means such as a new-found acceptance or resolution, or an alteration of how one perceives or understands oneself, others or one's experience. This changing perspective not only influences how we interpret our experience, but then affects what we place value upon, how we relate to others and how we behave. While this may be the specific and conscious intent of psychotherapy, it is also, by extension, a natural and normal part of human development. Winnicott (1964, 2002) demonstrated beautifully how children's experiences of play help to facilitate their development. The creative process itself facilitates an exploration of *new and possible* ways of understanding, viewing, and relating to one's experience. In this way, many emotional issues, for children, are worked through without (or indeed even prior to acquiring) a high level of reflective functioning. Thus, creativity can help a person to open up possibilities that can be taken up on a *pre-reflective* level.

Initially Steve's play contained little expression of 'otherness'. In other words, other people, animals or characters were merely objects to be manipulated and upon which were vented furious emotions. For many months, Steve's play involving the dinosaurs exhibited them as predators, and the victims were still very much object-like. Slowly, this objectified way of relating to others began to change and with it the acknowledgement of feelings in the other, and for the other. The victims started to display fear and helplessness at their continual besiegement. And some of the characters began to show a response to death and loss. When one of the animals from the predatorial group was killed and knocked across the room, another from the same group appeared to go looking for it. This was the first emergence of a sense of loss, as well as concern for another – both of which had remained otherwise absent from his play. Essentially, Steve's symbolic expression was allowing for internal *possibility* – new ways of relating, perceiving and feeling.

Another example of an issue being worked through came with the first signs of protection and defence. After a few more months, one of the human characters managed to protect himself from the vicious attacks, by stabbing and killing the animals, and by being able to hide and outwit the dinosaurs so that they could not find him. This emergence of protection/defence indicated a significant transition from a mere helpless position on the part of the victim. The victim was no longer completely at the mercy of the power of the aggressors, but now had some internal resources to draw upon that could protect him. The psychological significance of this for Steve was huge – the world was no longer *merely* a place where helpless victims are hideously violated. It was now a place in which victims (and, by interpretation we could say, he himself) felt able to survive and protect themselves. This new psychological and emotional position meant that Steve now had the capacity not always to experience other people in his everyday life as violently threatening (whether they actually were or not). The consequence of seeing others as less threatening and himself as more secure *could* mean that he experienced less need to fear other people, in his everyday life, and to be aggressive towards them. Reports from his home and college environment told us that Steve's levels of aggression had noticeably reduced. Now, of course, that might have been as a result of a multitude of factors, but it is probably safe to assume that his therapy played an important role.

Creatively assisting the client's capacity for reflection

After the creation of a narrative, a psychoanalytic approach encourages, where possible, the client to reflect upon and make sense of the significance of the narrative for his/her life. This therapeutic attitude is possibly one of the defining differences between psychotherapy that employs creative approaches and many art therapies, which tend to emphasize the role of creativity as being the central healing agent. Given the limitations that many people with intellectual disabilities have with cognitive reflection, often they are referred to a creative arts therapist where issues can be expressed and processed pre-reflectively, as with Steve. However, I believe that for many intellectually disabled clients the two approaches can be integrated, so that they can develop from a pre-reflective to a reflective level of emotional processing, facilitated by creative means. For example, at Piaget's (1999) *pre-operational stage* a client is not yet able to conceptualize abstractly and still needs concrete physical situations for both expression and understanding. As the client moves to the *concrete operational stage*, he or she develops the ability to separate thought from action and slowly learns to think or reflect *about* something – he or she is now able to step back and develop a view about an experience, a feeling, oneself or another. This developmental transition is often a challenge for people with mild to moderate levels of intellectual disabilities. Action and thought are often tied together, and developing the capacity to reflect upon one's actions, behaviours or feelings can be difficult. A therapeutic approach that encourages reflection is also helping to facilitate development.

Being aware of the struggles of this developmental transition, it is possible for the therapist to help the client build bridges from one stage to the next. For instance, once a projected or enacted narrative has been created, it can often be challenging for the intellectually disabled client to make a transition from self-expression to self-reflection. To assist this transition, I have found it very helpful to concretize the reflective process. This can be by creating physical depictions of the story and characters using drawing, images and words. Once this has occurred, the narrative is concretized and is physically located in space. If a client forgets part of the narrative, the images hold it for him/her. Holding two drawings in your hand can assist with holding two ideas or feelings in your mind. As Pattis Zoja (2004, p. 14) comments on her use of sandplay in therapy, 'psychic substance is materialised with the help of the hands'. For instance, an ambivalent client who struggles to reconcile loving and aggressive feelings towards a parent may create narratives where characters switch from good to bad, from being loving to angry. If this narrative is concretized on paper, the client can physically hold the two emotions *at the same time*, and thus literally learn to hold this ambivalence in his/her mind. In this process, it can be far easier to identify key interpersonal issues and circumstances that give rise to each feeling, they can be compared and cognitive links can be made. In essence, the physical or concrete distance between the client and the depicted narrative can support a similar psychic space to emerge or open up. This is a development from a pre-reflective to reflective capacity.

Conclusion

People with intellectual disabilities, like all human beings, have the same desire for self-expression and the need to process or make sense of their life experiences. Because they may struggle with language, and their cognitive capacities for conceptualization and reflection may be limited, this does not mean that they cannot find meaningful ways to express themselves. The above vignettes have shown how creative expression can play a vital role in facilitating both self-expression and a working through of emotional issues. It can allow a client to find an expression that fits with his/her level of development and creates an encounter between himself/herself and the therapist where issues can be addressed pre-reflectively. Even further to this, we have seen how creative approaches can assist a client's development from a pre-reflective to a reflective stage.

A significant feature of creative expression which I have highlighted in this chapter is that of indirect communication and how this benefits the client who has intellectual disabilities. With Jack, it offered him the opportunity both to express and to work through incredibly painful emotional issues pre-reflectively without having to uproot and confront his necessary defence mechanisms. And with Steve, we saw how it enabled him to communicate his internal experience despite his limited language and communication skills. For all this to take place, it was first vital that I, as the therapist, was open to allowing my clients to express themselves in these ways. Being open to creative approaches challenges the psychotherapist to engage with the client in a manner whereby the client's self-expression can flourish. The therapist not only needs to develop sensitivity to the meaningfulness of such creative expressions but also must be willing *to respond* accordingly while paying keen attention to their countertransference responses. As previously noted by Stern (2004), self-expression only ever arises, and has any meaning, within the context of relationship. The extent to which the therapist is capable of entering into such a creative exchange has an enormous impact on the client and his/her ability to take advantage of its benefits. Bearing this in mind, I hope I have communicated directly, and perhaps indirectly, just how much psychotherapy and creative approaches can assist people with intellectual disabilities. The challenge is not so much in their ability to make use of therapy but rather in our ability, as therapists, to provide the opportunities for both self-expression and working through to take place.

References

Courtney, R. (1980) *The Dramatic Curriculum*. New York: Drama Books Specialists.

Jennings, S. (1990) *Dramatherapy with Families, Groups and Individuals*. London: Jessica Kingsley.

McMahon, L. (1992) *The Handbook of Play Therapy*. London: Routledge.

Pattis Zoja, E. (2004) *Sandplay Therapy – The Treatment of Psychopathology*. Einsiedeln, Switzerland: Daimon Verlag.

Piaget, J. (1999) *The Growth of Logical Thinking from Childhood to Adolescence: An Essay on the Construction of Formal Operational Structures* (new edition). London: Routledge.

Stern, D. (1985) *The Interpersonal World of the Infant*. London: Karnac.

Stern, D. (2004) *The Present Moment, in Psychotherapy and Everyday Life*. New York: Norton.

Vetere, A. and Dowling, E. (2005) *Narrative Therapies with Children and Their Families*. London: Routledge.

Winnicott, D. (1964) *The Child, The Family and The Outside World*. Bungay, UK: Chaucer Press.

Winnicott, D. (2002) *Playing and Reality* (new edition). London: Routledge.

Chapter 3

Words as a second language

The psychotherapeutic challenge of severe intellectual disability

Alan Corbett

Freud (1904) declared that 'a certain measure of natural intelligence' was required of patients entering psychoanalysis. This misconception went largely unchallenged throughout much of the twentieth century. It began to crumble in the 1980s, challenged by the pioneering work of clinicians such as Valerie Sinason and Anne Alvarez in the UK and authors such as Johan De Groef and Evelyn Heinemann (1999) in wider Europe. As already acknowledged in this book, Valerie Sinason (1992) is, arguably, the foremost theoretician and practitioner in this field, gifting us with invaluable concepts such as those of primary and secondary handicap, disability as a defence against trauma, and the handicapped smile. All of these concepts have a particular relevance to the work I wish to discuss in this chapter, namely psychoanalytic psychotherapy with people with severe intellectual disabilities. I will explore the growth of such work and examine ideas of psychological mindedness and intellectual capacity as indicators of readiness to engage in an analytic process. The emerging notion of mentalization will be considered, with particular references to a man with severe intellectual disabilities and Down's syndrome, and I will introduce here the concept of the disability transference. I will also touch on some issues relating to the psychoanalytic frame in which this work is conducted.

There is now a growing number of theoreticians and practitioners working in this field. As clinical experience develops, work with patients with intellectual disabilities can be examined and explained in ways that make this work relevant and useful for a wider range of psychotherapists. Nevertheless, people with severe intellectual disabilities may still find themselves as a minority within a minority. Current research tools are not equipped for the challenge of analysing the changes made through therapy with those whose verbal and receptive communication skills are severely impaired. The benefits of the therapeutic process are felt significantly by the patient but may be extremely difficult for a researcher – or, I suggest, an analyst – to discern. Having said this, recent years have seen a growth in the number of outcome studies into psychotherapy with people who have intellectual disabilities (Beail *et al.*, 2005; Beail, 2003; Newman and Beail, 2002) which, combined with the groundbreaking study by the Royal College of Psychiatrists (2004) into psychotherapeutic approaches with people with intellectual disabilities, should help provide more of an evidence base for the development of work described in this chapter.

This chapter is as much about 'otherness' as about severe intellectual disability. The otherness I refer to here is not just the otherness of living with a severe cognitive deficit and of having difficulties in conceptualizing time and space and forming a narrative. It is the further disabling of those processes through a later sexual attack, whether it be in infancy, childhood or, indeed, as an adult. This is where Sinason's (1992) concept of secondary handicap is helpful in delineating the primary severe organic disability that exists in most cases from birth and in some cases is acquired through brain injury, and the secondary handicap that develops as a defence against trauma.

An important place at which to start is language. In writing and co-authoring various papers about psychoanalysis and disability (Corbett, 1996, 1999, 2000, 2004a, 2004b; Corbett *et al.*, 1996), I have been struck by how the bibliography tends to act as a potted history of the changing language with which we describe cognitive otherness and lack. As Sinason (1992, pp. 39–40) writes, 'No human group has been forced to change its name so frequently. The sick and the poor are always with us, in physical presence and in verbal terms, but not the handicapped. What we are looking at is a process of euphemism. Euphemisms, linguistically, are words brought in to replace the verbal bed linen when a particular word feels too raw, too near a disturbing experience.'

Thus, perhaps every decade or so, people with intellectual disabilities find themselves facing another name change. Working backwards historically, we come across 'intellectual disability' to the now unacceptable 'mental handicap' to 'mental retardation' to 'feeblemindedness' and then even further back to terms like 'spastic', 'imbecile' and 'cretin', all of which were perfectly acceptable, socially sanctioned phrases of their time. Sinason underscores the relationship between these terms and the word 'stupid', which itself is derived from 'stupefied', meaning, 'numb with grief'. It is my view that unless, as clinicians working with severe disability, we are making some attempt to work with that numbness we may be missing one of the core components of someone's persona.

As psychoanalytic psychotherapists beginning to open the consulting room door to patients with severe intellectual disabilities, what should we expect? Our preconceptions about patients who are severely intellectually disabled (alongside the service demands of those involved in referring such patients for psychotherapy) are likely to make it very difficult to attain the state that Bion (1967) posited as the optimum for engaging in psychoanalytic work – 'to be without memory or desire is the mental state which prepares the analyst best for the forthcoming clinical session'.

It is difficult to be the memoriless, desireless analyst when the analytic encounter tends not to be solely between analyst and patient, especially because my patients do not come to me alone. They have paid carers and drivers. One man lives seemingly on the cusp of such catastrophic epileptic seizures that, in addition to the crash helmet he wears to his sessions, he is accompanied by two carers. These are worried, anxious, shadowy parental figures who have had to fight their desire to come into the consulting room with him, so disbelieving are they that I could cope if the patient were to have a seizure. At a barely unconscious level, they fear that for him to come into a room alone may actually kill my patient. With these figures tending to people the borders of the analytic space, I am never truly by myself with an intellectually disabled patient.

Thus, the clinical work I am describing occupies a unique place in the matrix of psychoanalytic theory and practice. I am thinking not just about the otherness embodied by those whose cognitions differ from the norm, or who have also experienced sexual abuse. Our patients carry a strong sense of otherness – and the analytic frame can often feel cluttered by the considerations of referrers, and members of the patient's support network. In tailoring our psychoanalytic approaches to this particular group of patients it is not enough to consider the symbolic notion of the other – the others are also there.

This evokes important questions about how possible it is, within the constraints of this particularly crowded therapeutic endeavour, to work to the spirit of Anny Cordié's (1993) words, 'The analyst asks neither that the subject gets better nor that he become normal;

the analyst requires nothing, imposes nothing. He is there so that the subject may gain access to the truth of his desire, his own desire, and not so that he may respond to the other's demand' (p. 299).

It may be useful here to consider the links between psychotherapy with people with intellectual disabilities and child psychotherapy. I would argue that both endeavours require the analyst to keep alive some memory, if not desire, on behalf of the patient who, for cognitive and/or developmental reasons, does not keep it alive himself or herself. It is also a means of creating a parallel analytic process by which the surrogate parental figures are provided with their own space in which to think and reflect. Martha Harris (1989) writes with insight on the importance of the psychotherapeutic space for the parents as well as facilitating the main analytic work with the child or infant, and as a secondarily important space for the parents themselves.

Thus, in considering psychoanalytic work with patients with severe intellectual disabilities, our assessment cannot focus solely on the patient himself or herself. As therapists we are required also to assess the psychological capacity of the carers to support the analytic project. This should not be limited to the practicalities, important as they are. Questions have, of course, to be asked about who will help bring the patient to their sessions, who will let us know (if the patient cannot) of any breaks coming up and, importantly, who will pay for the sessions. The impact of our patients living in a financial subclass is enormous, and one I will not address in this chapter.

However, individual clinicians also have to decide how much information they will seek to get from the patient's carers, and how much they trust will emerge from the patient himself or herself. For example, I have sometimes asked for speech and language assessment reports, knowing that intellectual disability is a world that inhabits many different professional territories. I have learned, for example, that simply because someone can form words cogently, it does not mean they can understand words that have more than two syllables.

This is particularly important when working with patients with severe intellectual disabilities where the receptive language is key. I recall working with a group of men, all of whom had experienced sexual trauma, and all of whom had gone on to act out that trauma against others. Within that group were men with mild, moderate and severe intellectual disabilities. Much time was spent throughout the life of the group seeking to clarify issues of who could understand what, who needed particular help with following the discourse of the group and how we would know when such help was required. One man, whom I will call 'Keith', delighted in hiding his deficits. His presentation in the group was often of a man with mild disability, with good verbal skills and a seeming ability to comprehend much that was lost on the more disabled members of the group. It was some time before the group came to grasp what I had already seen in my original assessment of this man – that what he said and how he said it masked large and significant problems with processing information. Words of more than one syllable were like words of a foreign language to him, and sentences – even simple ones – were likes mazes in which he would get lost, growing simultaneously more frightened and more triumphant that his shameful secret, that he was more disabled than he appeared, remained hidden from the world.

The need to consider one's tone of voice and rhythm of delivery is of particular but not exclusive importance when working with people with severe intellectual disabilities. It is my view that such consideration should be given to patients at all stages of the disability spectrum. We construct our consulting rooms with great attention to the detail of fabrics, colours and therapeutic tools made available. Such importance should be given to the way we speak our words, too. It is not just the content of our interpretations that holds the key to a truly therapeutic process for our patients; it is the way in which such interpretations are delivered. Developmental psychology points to the importance of infant-directed speech between carer and infant. In this process one's intonations, register and sentence length are adapted (consciously and unconsciously) to meet the developmental and educative needs of the infant but also, I suggest, to provide an aural sense of holding and containment. Later in the chapter I will describe how a mutually understood language – of words, of body language and of unconscious communication – developed between myself and one severely disabled patient.

I have been interested by the emergence of the terms 'mentalization' and 'mentalizing' and their relevance to work with patients with cognitive deficits. Holmes (2005) provides a useful outline of the four interrelated aspects of mentalization as follows.

1   Mentalization is a 'meta-cognitive' phenomenon, in the sense that it refers to the capacity for *interpretation* of thoughts and actions – to think about thinking or, to use Meins *et al.*'s (1998) phrase, to be 'mind-minded'.

2   It is concerned with the meanings we attribute to our own and others' actions – that is, to the implicit or explicit hypotheses we use to understand why we, or another, might have thought or done such and such a thing.

3   This links with a third aspect, which picks up on mentalizing as a key attribute of *persons*, as opposed to the inanimate world. Implicit in this is the capacity to have projects, desires and wishes.

4   Finally, mentalizing is not a fixed property of mind, but a *process*, a capacity or skill that may be present or absent to a greater or lesser degree.

Case study: Barry

To explore the link between mentalization and patients with severe intellectual disabilities, I would like to talk about a patient I will call Barry, who was referred to me for psychotherapy following a sexual assault at his day centre. The sexual assault was not reported to the police, and might never have been discovered were it not for the tenacity of Barry's social worker and the work of a researcher who, while undertaking some work with a group of men with intellectual disabilities on the area of sex education, uncovered Barry's history of trauma.

Barry had Down's syndrome and a severe intellectual disability. At the time of initial referral he was in his thirties. He did not use many words and found it difficult to form any kind of a narrative. His body was broken down. He was very arthritic and moved through the world, I felt, carrying with him a sense of immense fragility and fear. It was hard to be with him without thinking about his terrible susceptibility to harm and injury, and the way in which his body seemed to communicate an almost primal sense of vulnerability.

He wore hearing aids although, as our work progressed, it became clear that he did not actually need them in order to hear me. He would shake his head about, causing the hearing aids to hang down like strange plastic earrings. Sometimes he would leave them on the chair as he exited the session, as if leaving behind a useless and unwanted part of himself. He did not maintain eye contact and his first entry into the clinic in which I worked conveyed a deep sense of desolation and despair. I recall the receptionist commenting on the sadness he carried with him as he made his way to the waiting area (a countertransference response that, despite lying outside or on the edge of the psychoanalytic frame, was important to consider).

How much to engage with patients' support teams is an important point in relation not just to assessment but to the maintenance of psychotherapy with people with severe disabilities. It is further explored in Chapter 11. I have worked with support teams where the lack of containment of their own anxieties regarding the severely intellectually disabled patient, as well as the psychotherapeutic process itself, has been such that they have contributed consciously and unconsciously to a sabotaging of the therapeutic work. This may happen, for example, through ensuring the patient is late for sessions, or that they don't arrive at all, and that other, apparently more important, activities are scheduled at the same time as therapy. If key supporters are themselves sceptical about the likely efficacy of therapy I have found that these negative expectations can affect the transferences in the work. In some cases these expectations may have almost paralysed the thinking of the team, so over-identified are they with the severe disability and the sense of damage, emotional impoverishment and trauma it symbolizes.

It may even be that there is some envy of the severely disabled patient as they receive an expensive treatment for hard-to-understand difficulties. Thus, it can be useful to establish a space in which to voice, for example, feelings of anger that time and money are being spent on the patient who may be perceived by their carers as being unable to use something as specialized and seemingly word-based as psychotherapy.

Barry was referred by his social worker, who had worked with him for some years and clearly developed a close bond to him. She had worked hard to attain a high level of services for him and through the first year of therapy acted as a valuable bridge between the therapy and the rest of Barry's life. After meeting with her, I arranged to meet with Barry's team, and was struck by a very different set of feelings being carried by them. I would characterize this as benign indifference. They were not guilty of failing Barry in any way. In fact, they were exemplary in their wish to ensure that the structure of his days was good, he had enough activities to keep him stimulated and his physiological care was exemplary. In contrast to the social worker, however, they had little interest in his psychological world. In sitting with them I was aware of a high level of passive aggression in the room. They articulated their scepticism about the role of psychotherapy in Barry's life, and stated their desire that he be allowed to simply get on with his life without attention being drawn to any difficult feelings he may have buried. I experienced a strong reaction to this, soon feeling impatient with them, feeling scrutinized and denigrated by their strongly anti-therapy stance and regretting having agreed to meet them in the first place. It is important that such reactions are monitored and noted as they form an instructive part of the referral matrix. I came away from them with an understanding of how easy it was to forget that Barry had a brain that was capable of thinking, and emotions that could be felt. I was reminded of the need not to retaliate against them by shutting them out of the therapy completely. Their scepticism about psychotherapy would need to be heard rather than defended against. There is sometimes a risk when faced with such scepticism of retreating into defensive mode, of seeking to sell the benefits of psychotherapy in an unrealistic way. I had to fight the desire to tell them that Barry would certainly benefit from therapy, that he would learn how to process the trauma he had experienced, he would develop great insight and find better ways of relating healthily to others. These were, of course, my hopes, but they had to be tempered with the Cordié (1993) stance quoted earlier – a stance that is useful in processing one's own need to fight scepticism with certainty.

This touches on the area of expectations and outcome in psychoanalytic work with people with intellectual disabilities, and the need to pay careful attention to the desires, realistic or otherwise, of the matrix of others supporting the patient. There are times when there is simply not a sense of shared expectation about the psychotherapeutic process. The number of different thoughts about what therapy is for is probably as large as the number of people involved in the enterprise – psychotherapist, social worker, residential team, family members and the patient himself or herself. Thus the pre-therapy process is not simply about gathering information; it is also about embarking on a shared therapeutic process with a group or team, a process in which difference will have to be talked about.

We would not necessarily think of convening this sort of pre-therapy engagement in cases where an intellectual disability is absent, and there is always inevitable discomfort for the analytic practitioner in so much information-gathering taking place before they have encountered the patient. Here again it is useful to consider connections with the world of child psychotherapy, and the attention it pays to the child's family circumstances and history before meeting the child himself or herself. Having said that, the pre-therapy work with Barry did not necessarily prepare me for the moment when I finally met him.

My first session with him was a baffling one. The team in his home had worked hard to tell him about where he was coming to and who I was. He sat down, placing a cup of hot chocolate beside him. It lay untouched for the whole of the session, as it did for most of the sessions we had together. He suddenly smiled at me, revealing a mouth of missing teeth, and the smile vanished as suddenly as it had appeared. He seemed interested in me and I found myself being interested in him. He made a series of grunts and groans, all of which seemed different from each other. I could make out one word – 'People'. This was a word he was very attached to, one that he would repeat at intervals throughout our work together.

Beyond that there was confusion, and I ended the session with the sense that he had wanted to come, but without as clear a sense as I would have liked to have had that he actually knew what he was coming for. This was a patient for whom one session was clearly not going to be enough to answer the question I had in my mind, namely: 'Was he consenting to enter therapy?' That is, did he have an understanding of what therapy is, in particular that it is not an ordinary social exchange; the kind of conversation he could have with anyone in the rest of his life? I wondered if Barry had been able to understand, or even to experience in that first session, the way in which psychotherapy is something highly unusual; that it is a psychological process that will involve an exploration of his emotional world. It is also worth wondering how many patients without intellectual disabilities come away from their first session with a clear sense of the process that is about to unfold.

It took much longer than one session for me to find my answer. Looking back, I would say that the first year was an *ongoing* assessment process, involving the two of us gradually constructing an understanding of each other. This 'extended assessment' also had to involve members of his support team. They formed the other part of this triangulated therapeutic process, and had become extremely important, particularly in those early days when I would frequently ask a colleague to phone them to double-check that Barry still wanted to come, and that it was more to him than just a nice day out, a good opportunity to have a Big Mac after the session – reassurance that, in those early sessions, I could not find out from Barry himself. The team assured my colleague that the sessions seemed to be the high point of Barry's week, and that, in his coming to his psychotherapy, his demeanour and mood were different from when he was engaging in his more socially based activities. They described this as a qualitative change – the rather manic, feverish excitement about some activities was missing, replaced by a more measured, thoughtful approach to the journey to therapy. This was extremely useful information to have, mirroring as it did the change I had begun to observe within the consulting room. All this supplementary information should be worked with as part of the overall assessment process, a process that can be as much about the patient's external landscape as about their internal world.

Psychoanalytic psychotherapy is about language. It can provide us with a language with which to describe, understand and process our histories. Sometimes, however, that language is not made up of words. There are times when words are not enough. Barry became more adept at teaching me which words were useful to him and which were not. I developed a way of commenting on his entrances into the room, whether he seemed to be entering with happiness, fear, joy, energy or foreboding. In one session he seemed to bring with him a tremendous sense of sadness. He slumped into the chair, staring down at the floor, not moving for some time. I commented on how different he seemed today and what feelings he might be experiencing. He was usually interested when I talked about feelings, and over the preceding months I had begun to think that he was beginning to form a deeper understanding of emotions and feelings. I tentatively suggested that he might be feeling sad today, as he was so unlike his usual self, which had been, in the sessions leading up to this one, brighter, more focused on the sessions and generally lighter in affect.

Barry reacted with shock to my use of the word 'sad', and brought his hands up over his face, shaking his head ferociously. I said that the word seemed to have a real power and, indeed, seemed to be a word he did not like. He managed to say, 'No, not sad. Not sad.' As he said this, he slapped his hands down on his legs, underlining the words with each slap. Some weeks later he appeared to be extremely low once more, and slumped down in front of me as if bereft. This time I said little, and we sat together for some time. He looked over at me hungrily. I commented again on how he seemed today, taking care to say that I know the last time I wondered if he was sad he really hadn't liked it, so maybe I needed to use another phrase, like 'Fed up'. Barry put up his thumb at this and nodded. He repeated the words to me, although it took several attempts until they began to resemble the words I had used. We had stumbled upon a phrase that would be extremely useful to us both throughout our work.

Barry enjoyed trying to form the words in his mouth, and seemed increasingly in tune with them as a barometer of his emotional state.

There were many times in the sessions when words became a secondary means of communication between us. Barry would come in and place down his cups of hot chocolate carefully beside him. After the first year he began making two cups each session, although they both remained untouched. I found myself thinking of this as more evidence of his ability to conceptualize the 'you and I' aspect of the work. There were two of us, communicating, feeling and thinking about each other. With this came a deeper sense of his thinking of me as an other who could be helpful. He would then sigh deeply. Sometimes he would say, 'People, people', laughing as he did this. We stumbled upon the word, 'body' together. It was a word he could say more clearly than others, and he enjoyed the sound of it. He would point at himself and then at me, saying, 'Body, body'. I wondered aloud about our two bodies, mine and his, and what he might be feeling about the differences between them. He would sometimes hold up his fist, as if to show me his stiffly curled fingers that had been gripped by arthritis and could do very little. I would comment on these fingers, the difference between their rigidity and the flexibility of my own, and how fed up he may be about not having fingers or a body that could do all sorts of fantastic things.

It was at moments like these that I came to think we were in the presence of a trauma far deeper than the sexual trauma he had experienced. The abuse he suffered featured in our work. He had learnt the word 'abuse' from his team, and had formed a link between that and the experience of someone touching and entering his body when he had not wanted it to be touched or entered. At times, he would seem very enervated by explorations of his experiences of abuse, although there remained much confusion for me as to what sense he was actually making of remembering the terrible things that had been done to him. I look back now at those sessions as encapsulated moments in which he managed to think about his experiences of sexual trauma without feeling all the attendant feelings of shame, guilt, pain and depression that had previously gripped him.

In my view, what preoccupied him more than his experience of abuse, however, was his sense of who he was and, through this, his relationship with his disability. In working with intellectual disability we are of course not just working with notions of IQ, cognition and memory. We are working with lack, absence, and the birth of the baby who is both longed for and not longed for. It was through

Barry's use of dolls that we both found ourselves thinking about the nature of his earliest relationships and his notions of himself as a baby. In around the third year of our work together Barry began to really pay attention to the dolls in the consulting room, and picked them up, discarding most but selecting two in particular to work with – a mother and a baby doll. His use of them seemed extraordinarily intuitive and smooth. For some weeks he cradled the baby in his arms, singing to it and soothing it with an air of gentleness that was new to me. I commented on how maybe he was showing me all sorts of things – his ability to nurture and to love as well as his desire to be nurtured and to be loved. Perhaps, I ventured gently, he was also showing me something about himself as a baby too. He then moved on to the female doll. The gentleness vanished then, with an abruptness that took me aback, and I watched as he began to pick at the doll with a cold viciousness. He poked his fingers into the doll, pulling at its hair and eventually throwing it across the room. There was a powerful silence in the room, broken only by my noting how much anger he had shown, and my sense that the anger might be to do with the baby doll as him and the adult doll as his mother.

The interpretation I did not make at this point was about me and him and his hatred of me for putting into words so many painful feelings and experiences. These interpretations came later on in our work.

Barry never wanted his sessions to end. When the 50 minutes was up, he would simply sit in his chair while I explained that it was time to go. He would stare back at me as I repeated myself, gently inviting him to go out to his member of staff out in the waiting area. I tried many different strategies for dealing with this. I drew a picture of blocks of time remaining until we finished. I would remind him at five-minute intervals that we were approaching the end. These methods felt extremely punitive, as if rubbing salt into a wound. They were, however, all ignored by Barry. In the end a compromise was reached whereby I was the one who left, while his worker came into the room. This was always a dreadful way to end the session, although Barry himself appeared perfectly content. I think he was conducting a powerful enactment around separation and loss but from a safe position, ensuring that others (not just me but also his workers) were caught up in something that felt potentially abusive but within which he could attain a certain level of power and agency. This was no small achievement for a man who occupied one of the lowest rungs of society's ladder.

As the treatment progressed I came to believe that Barry's relationship with his disability was a tremendously painful one. He felt himself to be an alien, belonging to a race that acted, felt and looked different. It is difficult to be specific about why I believe this, beyond considering my countertransference response to him – in itself, of course, an important research tool. When working with disability it is important to monitor one's own countertransference responses, as a way of considering the various manifestations of projective identification that weave their way through the fabric of analytic work. In many sessions I was aware of holding heavy, dreadful feelings of hopelessness, dread, deadness and fear. These can be usefully thought about as forming part of the 'disability transference', in which the patient projects into the therapist the disavowed feelings that are simply too unbearable to hold. The disability transference is, I suggest, more intense the more severe the disability is. With Barry I felt intense projections of difference, otherness and shame that I struggled to hold in mind, let alone put into words (this is where the value of effective clinical supervision is paramount, as it can provide a space in which the projections can be analysed and made sense of, and provide the therapist with a sense of understanding as well as relief).

The issue of embodiment was a core one for Barry. He had a very broken-down, distorted body that often seemed fused with his broken-down mind and distorted thoughts. For him, the mind and body difference was an agonizing one, as it was suffused with loss and undoubtedly added to the weight and intensity of the Disability Transference. This links back to Freud's (1923) notion that 'the ego is first and foremost a bodily ego' (p. 364). I had to work hard to facilitate a process of mourning in Barry for the self he could never be, to enable him to really think about that loss rather than, as had been the case beforehand, to shut down, or to act out as a defence against thinking and feeling. Susie Orbach (2003) has paraphrased Winnicott's (1960) 'There is no such thing as a baby. There is only a mother and a baby' to 'There is no such thing as a body, there is only a body in relationship with another body'. Her insight is a powerful reminder of the particular intensity of working with those whose damage is not just cognitive, or internal, but also physical and external.

My sense of my own embodiment was intensified through working with Barry. I thought more than usual about the fragility of bodies, my own as well as others. I began to notice people's injuries much more, at one point seeming to see arms in slings everywhere. I unconsciously scheduled my sessions with Barry for the middle of the day, and invariably found myself leaving the office for a brisk walk, as if needing to remind myself of the aliveness of my own body as opposed to the deadness of Barry's.

In one session, while we were exploring his feelings about his birthday, Barry wet himself. For weeks he had been repeating key birthday words – 'Coke', 'cake' and 'party' – to the point where I felt I could no longer bear to stay in the room with him while he repeated them again. It was useful to remind myself of Anne Alvarez's (1992) courageous flagging of her own sense of boredom sometimes when working with autistic children, a boredom that can feel murderous, or as if it is impossible to remain fully alive in the face of severe deprivation, abuse or mindlessness. A shift occurred, however, when I talked about birthdays also being 'fed up' times for some people, where you are expected to be happy but sometimes you don't feel like it. They can be a reminder of being born different, being something other. A look of grief crossed Barry's face and I suddenly became aware of the wetness around him. We ended the session as best we could, and worked with the sense of such mess being present in the room, alongside a sense of his regression when faced with thoughts of loss. There was also, I think something parental he needed to play out with me as I dashed for a towel to mop up the mess, and helped make sure he was dried off properly.

Barry died before our work was completed. His heart condition worsened and his already weakened body gave up. I won't focus on his death now, as that is a discussion that deserves a separate space. I would like to consider the very alive use Barry made of our work, and to consider his capacity to mentalize. I consider Barry to be someone who engaged in a meta-cognitive process, someone who, despite his lacks and deficits, was able, to use Meins et al.'s (1998) phrase, to be 'mind-minded'.

Holmes (2005) argues that countertransference in its modern garb is but a specific example of mentalizing – the therapist must always be asking himself/herself 'Why am I thinking and feeling in this particular way at this specific moment?' Alvarez's (1992) work with autistic children alerts us to the primacy of the countertransference, and it is a primacy that extends to working with children and adults with severe intellectual disabilities. She also points us to the work of Spillius (1988) and the modern use of the transference and countertransference making the analyst less attuned to whether he or she has given the 'right' interpretation, and more to whether he has communicated his understanding to the patient in a way that is receivable.

A complex process of projection and projective identification ebbed and flowed throughout the work with Barry. Over the course of the five years I found myself often unable to think and unable to process thought while I was in the room with him. There were also times when it seemed hard for me to speak with any fluency: as if, returning to my thoughts on the role of the disability transference, I was the disability, the attack on thinking, one of the holes in his mind. I was also the disavowed murderous rage, hating him and hating his disability. I recall sessions where it seemed as if we were both on the edge of death. I was sometimes gripped by intense boredom, hating the mindlessness of our work, yearning for a patient who could talk, who could form connections between thoughts, someone whose mind was truly alive. I would become the murderous mother, appalled at and ashamed of this poorly functioning child I had given birth to (it may be useful at this point to recall the words of the father of a baby with Down's syndrome, Hannam, 1975): 'Having a handicapped child evoked in me a great sense of failure . . . I thought of killing my child.'

Alongside my feelings of curiosity and nurturing for Barry, I was sometimes acutely aware of wishing to abort him from this analytic project that I periodically lost faith in.

In working with severe disability we can ourselves feel like the other. It is work that tends not to be talked about in psychoanalytic trainings and, when it is, it is usually on the margins, bracketed away. This is wrong on so many levels: politically, socially and, I argue, psychoanalytically. I have found it useful to draw on the work not just of pioneers in the field of disability, but also of clinicians such as Searles (1965), who writes with such insight about the challenges and successes of working with schizophrenic and psychotic patients. I found his thoughts on integration and differentiation in working with the 'non-integrated patient' particularly useful, as are his constant reminders of the importance of careful monitoring of the countertransference in working with patients who bring with them agonizing history of damage, fragmentation and loss.

It strikes me that Searles (1965) could, in much of his work, be writing about the disability transference, and the sometimes overwhelming tide of primitive emotions this work can evoke in us. This sums up much of the transferential tone of the work not just with Barry, but with other patients with severe intellectual disabilities. Bewilderment and pain coexist with curiosity and wonder. It is an exciting time for psychotherapy with this client group, although a great deal of work remains to be done. In seeking to capture some of the flavour of the work I have used analytic thinking as a way of understanding a process that can be difficult and frightening as well as, I would argue, hopeful. I have outlined some of the adaptations that need to be made to the analytic frame in order to accommodate the patient with intellectual disabilities. It is important to end with a reminder that the adaptations and the differences should not outweigh the similarities. The process is still a psychoanalytic one. I suggest it is a *particularly* psychoanalytic one, so central is the use of the transference and the countertransference and the disability transference, particularly when working with those for whom words are not the first language. Relatedness becomes more important than cognition, though research has shown that ego development is accompanied by cognitive growth. This is, of course, a by-product rather than an aim of the therapeutic process. In alerting clinicians to the possibilities of working analytically with patients with intellectual disabilities, the map we are creating is a map of the psyche of the other, and in order to navigate that map we also need to keep alive a sense of our own otherness. To paraphrase Freud (1904): to work with this client group, a certain measure of natural otherness on the part of the analyst is required.

References

Alvarez, A. (1992) *Live Company*. London: Routledge.

Beail, N. (2003) What works for people with mental retardation? Critical commentary on cognitive behavioural and psychodynamic psychotherapy research. *Mental Retardation 41*, 468–472.

Beail, N., Warden, S., Morsley, K. and Newman, D. W. (2005) Naturalistic evaluation of the effectiveness of psychodynamic psychotherapy for people with intellectual disabilities. *Journal of Applied Research in Intellectual Disabilities 18*, 245–251.

Bion, W. (1967) Notes on memory and desire. *Psychoanalytic Forum 2*, 271–280.

Corbett, A. (1999) *Psychotherapy and the learning disabled offender*. International Association of Forensic Psychotherapy Conference, Sheffield, UK.

Corbett, A. (2000) *Psychotherapy with Those Who Do Not Pay*. Confer

Clinical Enquiry Series: Money and Psychotherapy. London: Tavistock Clinic.

Corbett, A. (2004a) *Words are Not Enough: Psychotherapy with the Non Verbal*. Irish College of Psychiatrists Conference. Belfast, UK.

Corbett, A. (2004b) *No Man's Land: Forensic Psychotherapy and Disability*. International Association of Forensic Psychotherapy Conference ('After Trauma: within Families and between Strangers'). Dublin, Ireland.

Corbett, A., Cottis, T. and Morris, S. (1996) *Witnessing, Nurturing, Protesting: Therapeutic Responses to Sexual Abuse of People with Learning Disabilities*. London: David Fulton.

Corbett, A., Howlett, S., McKee, A., Pattison, S. and Peckham, N. (2007) The delivery of a survivors' group for intellectual disabled women with significant learning disabilities who have been sexually abused. *British Journal of Learning Disabilities* 35(4), 236–244.

Cordié, A. (1993) *Les cancres n'existent pas*. Paris: Seuill.

De Groef, J. and Heinemann, E. (1999) *Psychoanalysis and Mental Handicap*. London: Free Association Books.

Freud, S. (1904) Freud's psychoanalytic procedure. Reprinted (1953–1974) in the *Standard Edition of the Complete Psychological Works of Sigmund Freud* (trans. and ed. by J. Strachey), vol. 7. London: Hogarth Press.

Freud, S. (1923) The ego and the id. Reprinted (1984) in *On Metapsychology: The Theory of Psychoanalysis*. Freud Library, Vol. 2. London. Penguin

Hannam, C. (1975) Reprinted in N. Blackman (ed.) (1999), *Living with Loss: Helping People with Learning Disabilities Cope with Bereavement and Loss*. Brighton, UK: Pavilion.

Harris, M. (1989) The child psychotherapist and the patient's family. In *Collected Papers of Martha Harris and Esther Bick*. Strath Tay, UK: Clunie Press.

Holmes, J. (2005) Notes on mentalizing – Old hat or new wine? *British Journal of Psychotherapy* 22(2), 179–197.

Meins, E., Fernyhough, C., Russell, J. and Clark-Carter, D. (1998) Security of attachment as a predictor of symbolic and mentalizing abilities: A longitudinal study. *Social Development* 7, 1–14.

Newman, D. W. and Beail, N. (2002) Monitoring change in psychotherapy with people with intellectual disabilities: The application of the Assimilation of Problematic Experiences Scale. *Journal of Applied Research in Intellectual Disabilities* 15, 48–60.

Orbach, S. (2003) There is no such thing as a body. *British Journal of Psychotherapy* 20(1), 3–26.

Royal College of Psychiatrists Council (2004) *Psychotherapy and Learning Disability*, Report CR116. London: Royal College of Psychiatrists.

Searles, H. F. (1965) *Collected Papers on Schizophrenia and Related Subjects*. London: Karnac.

Sinason, V. (1992) *Mental Handicap and The Human Condition: New Approaches From The Tavistock*. London: Free Association Books.

Spillius, E. (ed.) (1988) *Melanie Klein Today, Vol. 2: Mainly Practice*. London: Routledge.

Winnicott, D. (1960) The theory of the parent-child relationship. *International Journal of Psychoanalysis 41*, 585–595.

Chapter 4

Speaking through the skin

The significance of shame

Elizabeth Lloyd

The young woman says nothing. She sits and looks at me and smiles a wide, vacant smile but her eyes are dead. Her wrists and the ends of her fingers are wrapped in plasters, grubby and fraying where she has chewed the fabric, unable to tear at her own skin. While still fixing me with her chillingly blank smile she raises her knuckle to her mouth and starts gnawing at it. She is in her early twenties but is dressed like a middle-aged woman. The smile is fixed and then suddenly shatters and she starts to cry, with uncontrollable sobs.

Susie has been referred to Respond for individual psychotherapy following a disclosure to her care workers that she had been raped as a child by her father – disclosures endlessly repeated in a flat, affectless monotone with the same fixed smile. As described in the previous chapter, Sinason (1992) first noted what she termed the 'handicapped smile': the outward sign of a psychic defence against the unbearability (for themselves and for the other) of the horror of handicap. An 'I'm not fooled and neither are you but let's pretend' smile.

Susie has been inscribing her experience of abuse on her body – not only in the re-enactments of the cutting and tearing of her skin but also in her assault on her own bodily boundaries, on the physical and psychic skin that separates her sense of me from her sense of not-me. That sense can never feel wholly safe and reliable for any of us – our bodies don't always do what we want them to and are prone to leaking and bleeding and to an overall messy unpredictability – but somehow, particularly through the use of language, we are able to carve out a sense of reality. And the carving does not have to be on our own body. For someone with an intellectual disability, where language is difficult and fraught with traps, this creation of self is so much harder. For someone with an intellectual disability who has been sexually abused it becomes a marathon task. As a psychotherapist at Respond I see people, mostly women, who are struggling and often failing with this task. I want to consider here some of these struggles and the issues raised for me as a therapist both clinically and theoretically in this work.

The sense of herself that Susie brought with her was suffused with an overwhelming sense of shame – shame at a bodily level of 'wrongness' and damage and shame at her own sense of worthlessness. Her actual experiences, of rejection and abuse (in reality), only served to underline the shame. For those people with an intellectual disability fortunate enough to have positive experiences of family and childhood, there is some hope of the shame being worked through and counteracted, though I would argue that there will always need to be a struggle to overcome the disappointment and shame at that initial loss of the non-handicapped child, however much the reality becomes something positive in time. This idea is explored further in Chapter 5.

Shame, horror and disgust are fundamental cultural constructs used to structure human emotion and social patterns. Anthropologists such as Mary Douglas (1966) have written about the need to create separate categories based on these constructs as a way of managing human experience. In her study *Purity and Danger*, she explores the significance of borders as a way of making sense of human experience – the universal human need to categorize through casting out as much as through keeping in. Psychoanalysts such as Julia Kristeva (1982) have developed this into the realm of the unconscious. In her earlier writings Kristeva had developed the idea of 'abjection' as integral to the human psyche – the regressive combination of fascination and horror with the limitations of the human body, the pull back towards the maternal body and the recoiling away from the traces of that dependence. She saw the quest for identity as the quest for the boundary that would separate the me from the not-me and how this is constantly sabotaged from within by the unreliability of those boundaries, constantly at risk of dissolution, slippery and unsafe. Without the aid of language it would become almost impossible to find a way to fix those boundaries – Kristeva draws a connection between *propre* being the French word both for 'clean' and for 'own'. For people with intellectual disabilities, their own words might be limited or non-existent and they would depend on the words of others to anchor them in their own bodies and their own place in society – in Lacanian (1978) terms, their place in the Symbolic Order. For Susie, her place in the world was a series of abusive fictions. She was abandoned by her birth mother and brought up by her aunt, whom she believed to be her mother. Her uncle, who she believed to be her father, abused her sexually and physically. She was reclaimed by her birth mother, who she had thought was her sister, and abused by her stepfather, who she had thought to be her brother-in-law: a nightmare tangle of lies and abuse. Eventually, when she told her mother of the sexual abuse by her stepfather she was disowned and thrown out, as her mother preferred to keep her allegiance to her abusing partner and not to her daughter.

When she began therapy she was in the habit of changing her name from week to week – both first and second names – so that neither she nor I would ever know who she would feel herself to be that day. After about a year she began to announce her arrival with 'Here I am again', adding the name she had chosen that week. The smile had long disappeared. She began to piece together – for herself as much as for me – the falsehoods and misrecognitions of her childhood and she was able to draw a connecting thread that linked her to me in the transference of the therapy, and linking this to the disparate parts of herself. She ceased the gnawing and tearing of the skin of her fingers and hands – the marking of her own bodily boundaries and extremities. Her recurrent sore throat and loss of voice, which had been extensively investigated, disappeared after she had, over many months and very haltingly, described how her stepfather would blow cigarette smoke into her mouth as he raped her. Eventually, with support from her residential workers she embarked on a journal mapping the secrets and lies of her upbringing and decided to fix her name by deed-poll to her middle forename, which her family had never used, and her mother's maiden name. She moved into her own flat. In parallel with the internal changes she had been making she had transformed the way she looked so that now she no longer appeared mismatched and misshapen – she was no longer wearing her sense of damage and difference as a protective skin around her. On first moving into her flat she described, very movingly, going to buy a 'teapot for one': she had for so long been in institutions where all of life was communal – even the teapot – that having something of her own was miraculous. Within that communality she had presented the world with the false jollity of her 'handicapped smile' while her desperate search for a coherent individuality led her to mark her own borders with her teeth.

This need to mark the boundaries of the self has been explored by writers such as Louise Kaplan (1991) in her concept of 'delicate self-cutting'. The need to make incisions in the skin is first and foremost a communication that something unbearable is being unconsciously re-enacted through the body upon its own surface, and that re-enactment takes on its own ritualized desperation.

Case study: Jean

'How can I tell you if I don't have the words?' – that was the anguished question of another young woman, Jean, who had come for psychotherapy. Her way of 'telling' had been to cut her arms and wrists repeatedly into an intricate pattern of interwoven scars in a desperate attempt to create a pattern of order and linkages out of the disorder and chaos of her own life. She was someone who actually did have the capacity to use language but her experiences had been so traumatic and so early in her life, before she had access to words, that translating them from body memories into words felt an impossible task. As we began work a symmetry began to emerge between the process of cutting and the experience of her own life. Like almost all the patients I see at Respond her life had been marked by abandonment and abuse – the phrase 'marked by' describing precisely what she was doing to herself – marking her skin with the scars that would stand as testimony to the abuse she had suffered, in a way words would never feel able to do.

Her earliest memory had been of her mother breaking a bottle of beer over her head and of being wiped down by her, soaked in a mixture of beer and blood, before being rushed to hospital to be stitched up. Maternal care and maternal fluid were toxic and damaging and yet desperately longed for, the merger with the maternal care-giver was both desired and feared, and the cutting of her skin, the stitching and scarring all served as a re-enactment of this maternal trope of intermingled love and hate. The cut was not only the index of abuse and damage from her mother but also a signifier of the possibility of a different care outside the maternal order which severed her from a terrifying dependency on a relationship that had been for her omnipotently damaging. This desperate need to escape the over-powerful object of both need and terror is symptomatic of so many people who have suffered severe sexual trauma from a care-giver – that which is most dreaded and feared becomes, unconsciously and despite themselves – that which is most longed for and most powerfully desired. This idea is also explored in Chapter 6 in relation to Glasser's (1996) 'core complex'. Hence, the recurrent theme of the individual who, as a form of self-harming behaviour, unconsciously places themselves at risk. It is also possible to think about this pattern in terms of attachment theory whereby the infant's earliest patterns of attachment become an unconscious template to be replayed. For someone with a chaotic pattern of attachment stemming from a violent and abusive parental figure this leads to a confusion as to where safety and danger lie, as both are contained in the same person. This in turn leads to what has been termed a disorganized attachment pattern (Category D) (Main *et al.*, 1985) where the feared and hated figure is also sought out as a source of love and security. Such a pattern sees people putting themselves at risk of further harm through seeking damaging or dangerous situations and relationships. In Jean's case, throughout her life she had continued to re-enact these unconscious and opposing desires. She would repeatedly find herself trapped in abusive relationships where she would long for the same pattern of violence and care, of abuse and reparation. She would seek to be ejaculated over and then wiped down, would cut herself so that the blood would be intermingled with semen. The cutting would sometimes be intricate and careful in patterns on her forearms, sometimes wildly, thrusting her hands through panes of glass. The bleeding, the wiping, the cutting, the stitching: these were all replayed in a grotesque distortion of maternal care. The experience was trapped in a re-enactment devoid of signifiers and driven by action, not words. The translation into words was a long and difficult process that eventually proved too terrifying to continue. Jean became increasingly distressed as memories became clearer to her and more available for thought and, after discussion with her care team, therapy was postponed until she was more able to bear the impact of the self-knowledge. This might take many years of gradually developing a secure enough base for her to bear the sadness of confronting the past and not re-enacting it.

For Jean, the unconscious phantasy of love had become too interwoven with the phantasy of damage for a therapeutic relationship to emerge at that point. Had she been able to feel safe enough to form a relationship with me it might have allowed these to be unravelled rather than replayed through her body.

This is, however, not always the case. Someone else, whom I saw in therapy for several years, was able to use the therapeutic space as somewhere she could disentangle desire and damage, love and shame.

Case study: Jenny

Jenny was referred for an assessment as to whether she had the capacity to consent to a sexual relationship for which she seemed to be expressing a wish – her verbal capability was severely limited. The boyfriend, another day-centre user, was thought to be putting her under some pressure to agree to this. Through the use of drawings, and of play with anatomical dolls, Jenny's capacity to understand the meaning of a sexual relationship could be assessed. However, what had not been expected was graphically detailed 'accounts' of sexual acts to which she had definitely not agreed and which she had, indeed, experienced as assaults. It emerged that her family had expressed concerns over several months about her levels of distress at attending the centre and about the many occasions when she would return with underwear soiled with blood and faeces. Jenny had been anally raped by at least three other day centre users over a long period – and her experience of these assaults had been horrifying for her but had been accepted as fitting in with her sense of herself as damaged – bleeding and soiled. Additionally, there was the perverse sense of excitement that existed alongside the horror and that could be triggered by the intimate self-care her level of disability required. She would be horrified yet excited by the need to have soiled sanitary towels changed, at one time wanting me to participate in the ritual of this. Her carers had to be aware of the level of phantasy aroused by bodily care that might lead to allegations of abuse – an abuse both dreaded and desired, as in her fantasy that her carer had, as Jenny said, 'dug into my stomach with her fingers and left her bright red nails there'. Her drawings would consist of sheet after sheet of a single egg-shaped object, the next paper seized upon before the last one had reached the floor where she had dropped it, rather as sheets of a wound dressing, or lavatory paper might be used.

The therapy took many years of regular weekly sessions – alongside work with her family and carers – but gradually her behaviour became more settled. Her body no longer regurgitated its contents in bulimia and soiling, she no longer revelled in the smell and sensation of her own waste products, and her menstruation became less of a focus of thrill and taboo. This took time. There was no possibility of a quick fix for Jenny to repair a sense of herself as one so immersed in her own abjection and so in thrall to her own bodily horror. Gradually, the story unfolded of a child who had been already locked into her own sense of a damaged self long before the actual abuse took place; a child who had soiled and smeared faeces until her early teens and whose desire had become caught up in the care – and disgust – her own body could arouse.

Any therapy needs to find a way to address this fundamental sense of something wrong before being able to move on to thinking about the actual experiences that have served to compound this sense of damage. Jenny felt herself to be a body managed by others – a source of revulsion kept in check by an exaggerated objectification. Although she had few words and little sense of language Jenny would, at the beginning of therapy, offer me lists: a list of what she had eaten for breakfast, a list of what she had subsequently vomited up, a list of the bath and shower lotions she was going to buy, a list of violent film heroes, a list of grotesque martial arts fighters. These lists seemed to encapsulate her confusion between inside and outside, danger and desire, cleanliness and dirt.

Over time, through her use of art materials, she was able to construct for herself a sense of her own body that was not a collection of objects – foods eaten or expelled, blood and faeces – but a body that she could inhabit and enjoy. My role, as therapist, was to provide a space for this to happen, not to be overwhelmed with disgust but neither to be overly excited. In the transference there had to be the possibility of something and someone different.

The therapist's position in the transference is very often the best clue to the patient's own experiences – for someone who has been abused, that position can oscillate between being experienced as abuser or abused. Many of the patients we see at Respond find being alone in a room with one other person a very confused mixture of fear of potential abuse and longing for the intimacy of a close relationship. If their earliest experiences of intimacy are coloured with shame and horror, as well as with actual abuse, then the longing and the fear can be unbearable. The therapist has to be very aware of their own bodily transference to try to gauge where on the continuum of desire and disgust they might be from moment to moment.

For example, a young woman whom I was seeing evoked in me immensely strong feelings of discomfort and unease. Ordinary therapeutic tasks such as sitting with her to reach into the dolls' house or to lay out the art materials seemed fraught with danger and sexual unease. Then, in one session she launched herself at me, digging her nails in my arm and, staring fixedly past me, roaring in a mixture of sexual frenzy and terror. Later in that same session she was able to reveal that she was being sexually abused by her mother – an activity she found horrific but at the same time gratifying. The confusion aroused in her (literally sexually aroused) was leading to her unmanageably self-harming and aggressive behaviour. For her care staff there was a terrible dilemma of dealing with her longing to see her mother while protecting her from her mother's abuse and this dilemma heightens the problems posed by client self-determination. This is never straightforward when someone has been abused, as it is so difficult and yet so vital to distinguish the conscious wish from the unconscious re-enactment. Someone with an intellectual disability is perhaps always going to have to manage a degree of dependence that most other people discard, and this can lead both to real practical difficulties and also to an unacknowledged internal shame at needing so much more. I am thinking here of another young woman, a member of a group I ran for four years for women with intellectual disabilities who had been sexually abused, who said she wanted a sexual relationship with her boyfriend. Her staff supported her in this although they were uneasy but could not specify why. Eventually it emerged that she was unconsciously replaying with him the nightly rapes carried out by her father when she was a child. The moment of realization came when she described how her boyfriend would bang her head against the head of the bed which she associated with that very same precise detail in the rapes. She was able then to make the connection with the sexual activity itself, a much more traumatic and hence deeply buried experience, and was able to say that what she wanted was not sex but the intimacy and closeness of a relationship – along with its status and specialness. Her sense of herself had been so bound up with an internal damaged core that to replay that damage seemed normal. It seemed to her that abuse was the price to be paid for attachment. She had described her birth as immensely painful (she meant physically but undoubtedly also emotionally) for her mother, and that she had been born, 'the wrong way round' (hers had been a breech birth). This sense of wrongness had come to be translated into a psychological wrongness, just as her mother's physical pain had been used as an explanation for her mother's abandonment of her to her abusing father.

We are all constantly creating and re-creating our sense of our own identity, positioning ourselves in relation to others – both the external others we encounter in our own experiences and the internal others we carry with us. Disability has a profoundly distorting effect on this process of self-creation. For someone with a physical disability there is still the possibility of making sense of the world and finding a place in it through language and relatedness to others. There is still a profound sense of difference and of loss, of shame at not meeting an internalized ideal, but there is the possibility of reparation through a capacity to think. When this capacity itself is damaged, as for someone with an intellectual disability, then reparation is more problematic.

It might be the case that for some patients this reparation is more possible in the therapeutic space of an analytic group than in individual psychotherapy. The group can come to be a re-enactment on a smaller and hopefully safer scale of the original trauma – a fractal image where the whole is refracted through a part. For this group of women, who had experienced their own bodies as being torn and shredded, their experience of the group was as something likewise torn and shredded that could never hold and contain them safely. In a group, the analyst would be interpreting not only the transference between therapist and patient but also those between the group members and between the group members and the group itself. This possibility of multiple transferences can be particularly helpful when a corporeal sense of shame is central. By its very nature a group throws up the question of the individual's relationship not only with herself but with the other – and here the disabling power of shame, over and above the disability itself, can be addressed.

In a group for women with intellectual disabilities who had been sexually abused the sense of bodily shame and self-disgust was overwhelming. Each woman had her own experience of disability and abuse that she had tried to absorb in her own way – perhaps through the practised compliance of the disabled smile or through a retreat into psychosis. In the group each one began to see herself reflected and refracted through the experience of others. The group itself came to be experienced like a bodily membrane. Initially, the group skin was one that was torn and leaking with no capacity to contain its members, but gradually the group boundary came to feel more complete, enabling them to stay in the room without feeling either trapped or leaking.

For each one of them their experience of themselves as disabled had been reinforced by their abuse and this had compounded the sense of shame colouring their very existence. Their sense of the shamefulness of their own being had in itself led to their vulnerability to abuse. Carol recounted the narrative she had constructed around her birth, perhaps based on some historical reality but, more importantly, encoding her own reality: 'When I was born I couldn't breathe so the doctor hit me on the back, and then my dad punched the doctor and he fell to the floor and dropped me. Then, that's when I started to breathe. So you see, I owe my life to my father and he had a right to do what he did.'

Carol's father had gone on to rape her from the age of three until he was convicted and imprisoned when she was a teenager, and he had continued to rape her when he was released from prison and she was a young adult. She felt she owed her life to him and had no choice but to accept what he saw as his due. For her to have a different sense of herself would take a long and difficult therapeutic struggle – and would entail a loss of the distorted 'specialness' she had felt she had in her eyes and his. This perverse mixture of shame and excitement is one of the hardest areas to loosen – particularly when this special excitement is the only colour, however horrific, in a colourless world.

One of the therapist's tasks becomes that of conveying the very different colour and aliveness of the ordinary. So often, the only experience that has come to signify being alive has been sexual and the therapist has to work hard to ignite an interest in the other-than-sexual; to help the client discover that, for example, there are other things the dolls in the dolls' house might want to do than have simulated sex, there are other ways of capturing the therapist's interest than exposing oneself or disclosing abuse. In an effective therapy, the client can discover other sparks to the imagination as the therapist becomes the voice of the everyday, and represents the ordinariness of a non-erotic attachment. In terms of Melanie Klein's (1923) theory, there has to be a giving up of what she called the paranoid-schizoid position and an acceptance of the ordinariness of the depressive position. This is most evident at points of highest anxiety in the therapy – particularly around breaks.

Case study: Mary

Mary, who had been referred because of her own dangerousness towards children, found breaks particularly hard. She had been abandoned at birth – literally left on a doorstep in a cardboard box. She had then been abused in her residential care home. She could not imagine – or allow herself to imagine and have – any attachment other than abusive. She had been sexually used by a group of men and had eventually been imprisoned for abducting and abusing a small child. Gradually, like Susie, she began to have some belief in the continuity of the thread connecting us. This took time to develop: after our first meeting her response to my 'I'll see you next week' had been to itemize all the catastrophes that could befall me, such as sudden and fatal illness or being run over by a bus. More than most she had a highly developed sense of the precariousness of life, and carried with her deep fears of annihilation (as identified in Chapters 5 and 6). There was a significant turning point in the treatment when she realized that we had a shared frame of reference of the predictability of the seasons. She would love to itemize the different weather that had linked our meetings and to concretize these changes in the different clothes she and I had worn. She developed a sense of the rhythm of predictability that both encompassed us and was out of our control – but not in the sense of a potentially personal disaster. Gradually she accepted that she would miss me during the time between sessions, but the longer time during holiday breaks was still too painful and she would translate her sadness into anger. She brought in the letter I had sent her with the holiday dates and tore it up and threw the fragments of paper away in my room. But she also said she had made a copy and kept it under her pillow. Then, one summer break when the sadness was no longer turned into anger, she thought to hold me in the only other way she knew and very slowly, fixing me with a hungrily intent stare, she bared her breast to me. This seemed to epitomize her confusion of maternal need, hunger and feeding with the eroticization and distortion of the maternal bond. I very gently asked her to put her top back and said how confused in her mind these things had become. She seemed immensely relieved and was able to accept an interruption in the therapy with the knowledge that we would be returning.

Eventually, she herself decided that she no longer would need to come to see me. She would, I think, always pose a potential risk to children in whom she could enviously attack the maternal bond she had never experienced, and her staff were very aware of that. But she had developed a life with other satisfactions in it and the potential for other relationships that did not have to fall into the old and familiar pattern of damaged and damaging.

This work may not always use the analytically familiar language of words, but it does use the analytically familiar language of the unconscious revealed through the body. It becomes a shared language between the therapist and the client – the bodily counter-transference experienced by the therapist having a very significant meaning in terms of the patient's unconscious communication of trauma: the client's own body communicates unbearable experiences not processed by the ordinary mechanisms of memory. Psycho-therapy in this field can then be seen as a different reading of a different text – a textual analysis of the body.

References

Douglas, M. (1966) *Purity and Danger: An Analysis of Concepts of Pollution and Taboo*. London: Routledge.

Glasser, M. (1996) Aggression and sadism in the perversions. In I. Rosen (ed.), *Sexual Deviation* (3rd ed.). Oxford, UK: Oxford University Press.

Kaplan, L. (1991) *Female Perversions*. London: Harper Collins.

Klein, M. (1923) Infant analysis. *International Journal of Psychoanalysis 9*, 167–180.

Kristeva, J. (1982) *Powers of Horror: An Essay in Abjection*. New York: Columbia University Press.

Lacan, J. (1978) *The Four Fundamental Concepts of Psychoanalysis*. New York: Norton.

Sinason, V. (1992) *Mental Handicap and the Human Condition: New Approaches from the Tavistock*. London: Free Association Books.

Chapter 5

Love hurts

The emotional impact of intellectual disability and sexual abuse on a family

Tamsin Cottis

This chapter describes work with a family that was in treatment for one year. It explores the psychological impact of disability on family functioning, with particular reference to circumstances when a person who has intellectual disabilities experiences sexual abuse perpetrated by a non-family member.

Mr and Mrs Lee sit in the therapy room. Their severely disabled son, John, has been sexually abused – anally raped by another resident of his respite care home – possibly over a period of many years. The family's outside battle is now with the management of the home, which does not accept John's version of events and refuses to acknowledge the damage done, far less accept responsibility for it. An apology may imply responsibility and lead to civil action and financial compensation.

Mrs Lee is physically frail, with chronic asthma, so her breath whistles as a constant reminder to her family and to me of her frailty. Today she also has a black eye because John hit her last night in what she describes as a random, unprovoked attack. Since he disclosed the abuse he's been prone to violence towards her. John's older sister, Melanie, is here in the therapy room too. I know from our sessions that she experienced depression as a teenager and briefly ran away from home.

John had a separate treatment, with a different therapist but within the same organization, which lasted for three years. Initially, it was just John that was to receive therapy, because of the sexual abuse he had suffered. However, it quickly became clear that this family were so traumatized that they too needed support. After the abuse, John's parents were finding it difficult to trust any professionals and would intrude on his sessions, as well as confronting the therapist and demanding that he tell them 'what John has said this week'.

The family was engaged in a tortuous battle with the authorities to have the abuse recognized at an official level. It is our experience that such legal battles can last several years, and are, literally, maddening for the families involved. The lack of evidence, the disability of the victims, the difficulties for (and sometimes reluctance of) the police in pursuing the case when both alleged victim and offender have intellectual disabilities, and the determination of authorities to keep a lid on accusations, militate against justice. When families have to bear witness alone to the fact their child is victim of a sexual crime, it can exacerbate feelings of isolation and injustice that may have been there since the disabled child was born.

In the Lee family, Mrs Lee saw her existence as being woven into John's. I came to understand that the brutal and violent abuse which John had experienced had been viscerally disturbing for Mrs Lee – it was almost as if it had been perpetrated against *her*. She had reacted with anger and grief. Somatic symptoms had flared and she spent many hours ruminating over what happened, tortured by feelings of guilt. These reactions were what I would have expected to see in an actual victim. Since disclosing the abuse, I heard that John had developed an obsessive interest in violent computer games, becoming very excited by their incidents of aggression and extreme violence. His family said that he played these games to the exclusion of almost any other activity. His therapist understood him to be somehow discharging his feelings of distress and confusion regarding the violent and physically coercive sexual abuse that he had endured. At home, we heard, he was unusually aggressive, uncooperative and usually highly distressed. He was full of rage directed especially at his mother. It was as if John was discharging his pain through his mother and she felt it on his behalf. Of course, a lot of mothers feel like this when their children are distressed, whether or not their children are disabled. Indeed it can be seen as an entirely appropriate communication of a secure attachment process (for a more detailed explanation of attachment theory, see the glossary). However, in the Lee family, this process had got stuck. There had been little or no individuation between John and his mother, and the consequence was an enmeshed attachment – unmediated by the normal development and evolving independence of the child. Tustin (1981) employs the term 'post-natal womb' to describe the way in which mothers of autistic children continue to offer a shield of protection to the child who may be slow to develop a sense of me/not-me. In her unpublished paper 'Lost and found', Amy Jeans (2003) suggests that this may act to create a feeling of merged existence for both, beyond a time where separation is possible: 'The sensory state of early development and maternal protection of the child from "not-self" [Tustin] awareness before they are ready may mean that experience and feelings are translated through a somatic, pre-verbal realm'. Lechavalier-Haim (2001, p. 93) writes of her work describing a mother 'almost in a relationship of complete fusion with her [autistic daughter], always anticipating what [she] might want and leaving her no opportunity to take initiatives'.

Such maternal behaviour can be seen perhaps as in some way compensatory – an attempt to make good the gap between the child and its relations with the outside world. This feeling can be expressed in more everyday terms thus: 'Speaking as Domenica's mother, it is hard to describe the love you have for a child who is handicapped. It is peculiarly intense. Your natural maternal protectiveness is much sharper . . . I am always conscious of her aching vulnerability' (Rosa Monckton, *Daily Mail*, 4th Nov 2005). Ms Monckton goes on to say, 'Yet [Domenica] is very much her own person. She is funny, witty, an excellent mimic. Fearless and brave.'

Jeans (2003) too, goes on to describe the way in which movement work and dramatherapy supported an autistic child and his mother to work through some of these issues and to begin to develop a sense of themselves as separate from one another.

It is my experience that not all parents are able to make the move forward emotionally, to experience their disabled child as 'their own person'. The capacity to do so may depend on many internal and external factors.

As Sinason (1993, p. 15) has described, the birth of a disabled child may itself be experienced initially as a shock, and as a loss, as the hoped-for perfect baby has not arrived. There may also be feelings of shame and of fear. These early feelings may then be compounded by practical lived experience where it seems that no one else has the needs of the disabled child as central to their lives. Many parents find that, in terms of accessing the right support for their child, they have to fight all the time.

The Lees seemed not to see John as a separate person, with his own rights and feelings. They were furious for him and were existing in this state of unprocessed, all-consuming, anger and distress. He, however, seemed at first in therapy to be unaffected and was calm and polite in his sessions as he recited lists and talked obsessively about computer games. His affect increased as his family began to receive their own therapeutic treatment.

The Lees, like almost every parent of a disabled child I have ever spoken to, were hugely preoccupied with fears for John's future once they had died. They spoke freely of the advantages if he were to die before they did as this would be preferable for him to a life without their care and love. These feelings are, of course, far from irrational. Services can be sometimes be so patchy, or even non-existent, as to make this feel like a reasonable response. I would argue that these rational feelings are fed and magnified by the traumatic effects of having a disabled child in the first place. An individual's relationship with issues of mortality and with the creative potential of life is profoundly altered by the experience of having an intellectually disabled child. Sheila Hollins's work regarding the 'three secrets of disability' (Hollins and Sinason, 2000) is highly pertinent here. Developing Money-Kyrle's ideas of the Facts of Life as set out by Steiner (1993), Hollins identifies sex, dependency and death as core issues underpinning any therapeutic work with people with intellectual disabilities. All three 'secrets' are influenced by the presence of an intellectual disability: sex is experienced (by parents and, unconsciously by the child) as potentially damaging, rather than creative and healing; dependency issues are paramount as the possibility of eternal childlike dependence permeates the mother–infant relationship; and death is experienced as a live trauma, running counter to ordinary parental experience, throwing up questions about whether the life should have occurred in the first place, or a belief that perhaps the child would be better off dead. In families, there may also be a profound wish that the disability will end with this child. Therefore, the desire to avoid a pregnancy can become very powerful and lead to a denial of the disabled person's sexuality. This can stand in stark contrast to the more usual wish for grandchildren and a desire to see one's progeny flourish and procreate.

I saw the Lee family struggling with all these issues, as well as trying to process the traumatic effects of sexual abuse, and this struggle affected their attachment behaviour. Many things in life may challenge the development of secure attachments – death; family breakdown; inconsistent, cruel or abusive parenting; poverty and attendant family stress. The presence of an intellectual disability in a child can also make the development of secure attachment a greater challenge. The disability itself may affect the communication between parent and child: an unresponsive child is hard work; hospitalization in infancy may interfere with bonding and thence attachment processes. The attachment experience of parents profoundly affects their attachments with their own children. Writing about his work supporting foster carers to look after children with severe attachment disorder, Daniel Hughes (2006, p. 4) says:

> For a child to develop well, she needs to have a positive impact on the key people in her life . . . the danger is that she will have a negative impact on them. Her anger, rejection, withdrawal, defiance, and indifference may activate within the parents doubts about their parenting abilities . . . they are not likely to feel safe with their child. Their worth, value and abilities are being questioned continuously . . . For this reason, each parent's own attachment history is an important factor . . . If the child's behaviour activates within [the parent] aspects of her own relationships with her parents that were unresolved and poorly integrated, she is likely to react with anger or anxiety in response to her child.

Mr and Mrs Lee were devastated to discover that John had severe intellectual disabilities. He had been floppy and unresponsive as a tiny baby, but also very distressed and difficult to console. The early years of his life had been characterized by exhaustion and a terrible sense of failure. It would have been very difficult for John to internalize a sense that he had, in Hughes's words, 'a positive impact on the key people in his life'. Melanie, aged three when John was born, had to cease being a baby overnight. She was catapulted into an early carer role, and soon learned that, at home at least, she needed to be a very good child who would not add to her parents' burden. Melanie learned quickly to suppress her own normal ambivalent feelings of envy, frustration and hate for her new sibling. As Peter Burke (2004, p. 45) has said, 'siblings also share the stress experienced by their parents at the birth of their disabled sibling or at the time when the realisation of disability sets in . . . The impact on siblings of having a brother or sister with disabilities will increase the sense of being "left out" which often goes unrecognised within the family.'

Melanie, like her parents, experienced great difficulty in saying out loud that she had any negative feelings towards John himself. The family had been terribly wounded by the fact of his birth but their wish to love him and protect him was fierce. It was also fragile. In my view they were defending against ambivalent feelings with their fierce protectiveness and had always done so. That John had been abused while *not* in their care added further fire to this dynamic. The family could not admit to the ambivalence because to do so would potentially leave him all alone in the world. Perhaps the fact that there would be more negativity – that he was not the able child they wished for and that the expected pattern of their lives as parents and as a sister had been overturned because he was intellectually disabled – meant that to admit any negative feelings at all would be to open a floodgate. A parent may start their parenting life of a disabled child with an emotional package of hurt, shock, sadness and a strong sense of feeling 'on the outside' and 'not like other people'. If these were feelings that were prevalent in the parents' life before they had children, they are likely to be magnified by the experience of disability. What happens next may ameliorate the situation or it may make it worse as the struggle for services sets the family apart, and means that it is experienced as troublesome. It takes a very robust family indeed to withstand these pressures, to avoid definition of themselves as problematic and excluded. Research from the charity Contact a Family (Shapiro, 2004) found that in families with a disabled child, relationships were helped by a number of factors, especially the availability of respite care, and 'the ability of the parents to communicate'. Evidently not all families collapse under the strain of a disabled child but Shapiro found that, while almost 25 per cent of those surveyed felt that having a disabled child had brought them closer together, a similar number felt that having the child had caused significant problems in their relationship (one in six disabled children is brought up by a single parent). Seventy-five per cent of the respondents had experienced stress, depression and/or tiredness or lack of sleep linked with disabled child. Almost 66 per cent of respondents had received counselling or said they would have liked to have had the opportunity to do so.

It became clear quite quickly that the Lees were not a robust family and the experience of having John had profoundly affected the whole family's attachment behaviour and relationships. The family members were feeling very tightly bound together, primarily as a defence against the outside world, which was experienced as hostile and rejecting of them because of John. Of course, in some ways this was true – the handicapping effects of John's disability had caused them many practical difficulties and militated against them functioning as members of 'mainstream' society. The social model of disability emphasizes this in its understanding of the consequences of disability for families and individuals. In my view, however, too complete an emphasis on it may be used to defend against the very real pain, at an emotional and psychic level, of disability. Parenthood involves ambivalence, as Rozsika Parker (2005) has written. This ambivalence can be very difficult for families, especially mothers, to acknowledge. And ambivalence here does not simply mean, 'mixed feelings' but rather, 'the concept developed by psychoanalysis according to which quite contradictory impulses and emotions towards the same person co-exist. The positive and negative components sit side by side and remain in opposition' (Parker, 2005, p. 7).

Parker makes a connection with Kleinian thinking, and the gradual progression to a position of integration where positive and negative can be managed so that love outweighs hate. Klein describes this as the 'depressive position'. Parker also cites Klein's view that sometimes extreme life experiences (for example, loss and mourning) may make the achievement of depressive-position functioning more difficult. Parker argues that motherhood itself is one of those experiences. I suggest that becoming a mother to a disabled child could be regarded as an even more 'extreme life experience'. Parker (2005, p. 8) takes Bion's idea that there is also a clash in the mind between knowledge and understanding, and suggests that it is the conflict between love and hate that drives a mother on to understand her child, and her relationship with the child. If the ambivalence, and therefore conflict, is denied, understanding cannot be advanced.

John, as a severely disabled boy, had his identity fixed in his family's mind as such. His disability was the defining thing about him. He was not as they would have wished him to be, but, now he was with them, they were paradoxically resistant to him being less disabled. The family's expectations of John were minimal and all members adopted the view that he was, to all intents and purposes, an infant with infant needs. His expressions of emotion were regarded by them and by other professionals as part of his disability. He could be very aggressive towards Melanie, for example, but this was perceived as a situation that it was Melanie's responsibility (as a non-disabled child) to address. As a result, John became quite monstrous in the demands he made on his family, and neither he nor they received any psychologically oriented support to help them manage this highly charged and stressful situation. Navigating separation and individuation can be difficult for any parent and child. As Parker (2005, p. 45) says, 'Mothers are expected to function as their small children's sole life-support system and then to drop them off unproblematically at school or the playgroup door.'

If a parent of a disabled child has no confidence that their child will be welcomed, appreciated or understood by those outside the family and, indeed, this has been a lived reality, as well as a profound emotional experience triggered by the birth of the disabled child, then surely it will be even harder for them to see their child as separate from them, and to let go and believe that anyone else will care for their child as they do.

Melanie, perhaps with the distance of sibling rather than parent, was more able to begin to talk about these things as therapy progressed. She talked to me alone at first, then tentatively to her parents, of the losses of her childhood – the pressure on her to be good, her lack of friendships outside the home, 'all because of John'. Hence, her expressed view that she would sacrifice her life for John if her parents could no longer cope. This family did not have any confidence in the idea of 'shared care', no sense that Melanie might love John and also want space away from him, or that Mr and Mrs Lee might both love him and care for him yet also hate him for the demands and pressures he placed on them.

As Hodges (2002) explains, Klein's understanding of paranoid-schizoid and depressive-position functioning is helpful here. Early infancy is characterized by extreme and extraordinary feelings. Until the baby learns that her all-consuming hunger or cold or fear will be assuaged by attuned parenting, the world is a terrifying place. She learns that she can be restored, comforted and loved, and she internalizes this process. She becomes able to calm herself until her needs are met, as she knows that they will indeed be met. Such experience, or, in Winnicott's (1962) phrase, 'holding' by the mother – or containment of the baby's emotional and physical needs – means that an individual learns to manage negative and fearful feelings and does not experience them as potentially catastrophic or annihilatory.

In our therapy sessions, I learned that Mrs Lee had already experienced a great deal of trauma in her childhood. She had lost her mother in late childhood and had spent her teenage years sacrificing her education and social life to care for her younger sister. She fled the family home to a secret marriage to Mr Lee, and all contact with her birth family was lost. She saw Mr Lee as her saviour and felt that she owed him everything. She could experience no 'middle way' with her family's demands on her and she felt such guilt at leaving her sister that in some ways she experienced the lifelong dependence of John as a punishment for her abandonment of her responsibilities to the sister. Mrs Lee's experience of dependence in parent–child relationships was thus already damaged before John was born, upsetting them further. Mrs Lee's childhood experiences of a lack of containment were also reactivated by the trauma of having a severely disabled son. She found it very difficult to feel any equanimity about her situation – it was inherently traumatic, and left her feeling uncontained and isolated. Trauma can generate a post-traumatic stress state where fear is expressed though acute anxiety. If early experiences have been extreme or traumatic, this can lead to a susceptibility to these feelings recurring.

Mrs Lee's losses had never been mourned, as to do so might have threatened the relationship with Mr Lee. It is likely that even if John had not been disabled, the Lees might have felt themselves to be a family under stress and without the moorings of mutually supportive extended family networks. John's disability, and their family experience of it, compounded these difficulties. John's individuality had become lost and Melanie, as she had grown up, experienced depression and eating disorders. It was only in sessions alone with me that she felt safe to name the terrible effect that John had had on her life and to express the anger and grief at what she had lost. She and her parents maintained for several months that all their problems and difficulties were perpetrated from outside the family. I came to realize that it was only because I believed that John had been abused, when others were reluctant to do so, that I was allowed 'in'.

Mrs Lee feared being told to put John in the care of others. From the point when she realized there was something wrong with him, her role in his life was characterized by the fear of annihilation that we encounter in Glasser's (1996) work on the psyche of the offender and Hopper's (2003) on the effects of trauma on the life of groups. The fear of annihilation can perhaps be linked to the Kleinian understanding of paranoid-schizoid functioning – a life of extremes in which balance and emotional equilibrium are very elusive. With her experience of the premature death of her mother, and then of caring for her sister, Mrs Lee already knew something of the unreliability of central relationships, the fragility of life. Although Mrs Lee was offered some support when John was a baby, she was frequently overwhelmed by the feeling that everything was down to her and that she was alone with John. She functioned in emotional extremes. As Parker (2005, p. 12) says:

> The individual mother is left to grapple with the fact that she is not only the source of life but also of potential death for her

child ... anxiety mobilised by motherhood can magnify the conflicts provoked by ambivalence ... Some may enjoy a new sense of potency and agency but others, besieged by images of loss and disaster determined by their own social circumstances, states of mind, or possibly their child's physical condition may be swamped by depressive guilt.

Mr and Mrs Lee's relationship was under strain from the outset. Mr Lee found it hard to express the feelings of fear, failure and vulnerability that had been triggered by John's birth and at times Mrs Lee experienced him as shut off from her. This exacerbated her feelings of neediness and the sense that she had been literally abandoned to cope with this lifelong trauma of John. After he was born, Mr and Mrs Lee became isolated from each other, with very few positive experiences to bind them. Their sex life suffered, as intimacy became bound up with the creation of something damaged and damaging. Mrs Lee had found John's adolescence very difficult, and the development of his secondary sexual characteristics was painful and also shocking for her. The onset of his adolescence connected her more acutely with the fears for his future and the recognition that he would never achieve the usual milestones of male adulthood. His behaviour was often embarrassing as he frequently masturbated in public. It was due to the intervention of a community nurse, who developed a relationship of trust over many years and who could see the terrible strain that care for John placed on the whole family, that Mrs Lee was eventually able to make use of respite care. Mrs Lee became used to projecting many of her feelings of hurt and abandonment into John, or at least into his disability. For as long as they had a disabled child there had been a place for the family to put sad feelings. Just as an intellectual disability may cloak mental distress in an individual, it can serve the same function in a family. John, with his acute needs, incessant demands and lifelong dependence, had become the reason that the Lees experienced themselves and were experienced by others as an unhappy family. As John could never be made well, or 'undisabled', so the family would never be happy. This may have actually exacerbated the extent of John's disability. Reading reports from the respite home that he attended, it seemed that he was able to do far more for himself that he was allowed to at home. Mrs Lee dressed and bathed him and even supervised him in the toilet. He was not allowed in the kitchen at home and never went out alone. It was clear from these reports, however, that John could manage some self-care and help out with simple kitchen tasks. Although he did not go out alone, he was able to enjoy excursions and supervised trips to the shop. The staff there were working according to their professional guidelines, to maximize his choice and independence. They spoke of their frustration at what they saw as the family's 'overprotectiveness' and commented that the family frequently denied permission for John to participate in certain activities. When John had begun to display sexualized behaviour they had seen this as in some ways appropriate to his age, and found the family's difficulty in accepting that John may develop sexual interest in females as part of their 'trying to keep him like a child'. As it turned out, neither party was right, although the family were closer to the truth. John began to strip off in public places and his masturbation increased. His attempts to grab women became more violent in intent. It is likely that this behaviour was, as the family perceived, a sign of disturbance, as it was John trying to communicate his abuse. When the family asked that an investigation take place, John was able to say that another resident had come into his bedroom, and he used signs to indicate the ways in which this man had abused him. The family then felt vindicated in their view that John needed to be protected at all costs, and were angry with the staff for failing to keep him safe. John was denied access to all services as trust broke down between the family and service providers. John lost contact with the friends he had begun to make, including a woman who he had told the staff was his 'girlfriend'. In therapy he said how much he missed her and his therapist began to feel that some of his difficult behaviour at home – including the violence – could have been due in part to his boredom and frustration at being permanently stuck inside. The family were unable to accept John's possible need for a mutually rewarding friendship, or even relationship with a woman. They had struggled to do so for Melanie, their non-disabled child, who had been discouraged from having boyfriends in her teenage years. Now that the small steps towards more independence of self that John had been allowed to take had ended, as the family saw it, in disaster, he had to revert to total dependence. It was a terrible situation, which would take time to ease. The therapeutic issues were complex. To some extent the sexual abuse, about which more information became available as the investigation progressed, seemed to be experienced by Mr and Mrs Lee as an abuse of them. Mrs Lee especially experienced post-traumatic distress, and memories of a teenage experience of sexual assault were evoked. Mr Lee felt impotent, emasculated, disgusted and furious.

Therapy allowed the gradual exposure of some of these very powerful feelings. Our work initially was concerned with the trauma of the sexual abuse, and there was a thread throughout the work of it providing a space for Mr and Mrs Lee to vent their rage and frustration at the obstructive behaviour of the local authority. We also began to peel back the layers of family attachment patterns. In sessions without Melanie, Mr and Mrs Lee began to talk about their relationship. John had been between them from the start. Sleep was constantly disrupted and Mrs Lee generally slept in the same room as her son, affording John an Oedipal victory. Mr Lee had been pleased when Mrs Lee finally agreed to make use of the respite care service, and at this stage he had begun to recover an intimacy with his wife. The abuse had shattered this and added to his distress and frustration at what had happened. He was able gradually to concede some resentment that his fragile plans for closer times with Mrs Lee were in pieces. Mrs Lee talked of her feeling that Mr Lee's desire for intimacy and time alone were like another demand on top of the excessive demands placed on her by John. I was reminded of parents of new babies where the father is temporarily displaced by the new baby – in the marital bed and in the mother's heart and mind. Mr Lee had a traditional view of his role as husband and father and anticipated that he would draw satisfaction from supporting and protecting his family. Yet, because of John, Mrs Lee felt that she could never be happy. Mr Lee's feelings of failure had been horribly exposed by the abuse – in his eyes he had failed to keep John safe, and now, with John at home 24 hours a day, he could not keep his wife safe from John's violent frustration. He also could not seek direct revenge on the attacker because he was also disabled and, therefore, 'the same as John'.

From the outside, it was clear that it was not tenable for the family to be alone with John 24 hours a day, seven days a week, rejecting all offers of help – apart from the therapy – as potentially too dangerous. They accepted therapy only because they experienced the organization as independent of the services in which the abuse had occurred. It seemed likely to me that Mrs Lee would soon break down completely. The key to the work was, I think, the slow development of trust, while all the time the Lees fought this. They were so fixed in their belief that no-one else could possibly understand them that there was a lot to lose in letting go of it. They let Melanie take a lead in some ways – she encouraged them to come to therapy and would often speak up in my defence in sessions, as though emboldened by the presence of another. When Melanie began to say that the family would need to plan realistically for John's future, they were able to listen because she was on the 'inside'. Both Mr and Mrs Lee experienced relief through the therapy and attended alone to talk with me about incidents from their childhood. This was an entirely new experience for them and they were very tentative. They struggled with the boundaries of my analytic approach and I had to be flexible to some extent to make it possible for them to engage at all. I also felt a strong need to recognize, rather than interpret, the horrors of their battle for legal recognition and justice.

In the later months, Mr and Mrs Lee found it much easier to let the other speak, and express negative feelings about what happened 'in' the family as well as 'out' of it. They loved each other and began to access these feelings underneath the legacy of long years of stress – what Hopper (2003, p. 54) has described as 'loss, abandonment and damage which may be understood in terms of the Chinese water torture *strains* of daily life, the *cumulative* build up of small incidents into an overpowering wave of oppressions and/or the *catastrophic* violation of the safety shield . . . Trauma is always a matter of failed dependency on other people and situations for containment, holding and nurturing in both personal and social domains' (emphasis in original).

Towards the end of the therapy, the treatment became quite task-focused. Mr and Mrs Lee identified an activity they might be able to do together – an afternoon walk by the river near their home followed by a drink in the pub, for example. The therapist's role was often to set the boundaries within the sessions and ensure that each person got a chance to speak. Mr Lee could be very domineering, while his wife would retreat into an angry silence which, I learned, would explode after the session. Whatever triggered this distancing and anger, it became clear to the Lees that their different feelings about John were often at the heart of it. Mrs Lee knew that Mr Lee would welcome a break from John and feared he would insist that John live away from the family.

My countertransference in my work with the Lees frequently mirrored the experience of enmeshed attachment. I found myself drawn into their long and lurid accounts of John's suffering, weighed down by their distress, and often struggled to get hold of their individual, separate selves in my thinking and my interpretations.

In conclusion, we can see how the outside and inside worlds collide in families who have a child with intellectual disabilities. There is, in the therapeutic matrix, the reality of their unsupported and battle-strewn lives – exerting stresses and strains that all but the most robust families will struggle to survive. It is important, in therapy, to recognize the reality of this. However, there can also be psychic wounds inflicted by the fact of having a disabled child. Sexuality, dependency and death – the three 'facts of life' – will all be impacted by it, requiring more than usual resilience. The human journey to depressive-position functioning is likely to be more rocky, as the impact of disability raises fears of annihilation and offers a life lived at emotional extremes. The child's own pain, distress and fear may be harder to contain by the parent, especially if their disability affects the way in which they relate to carers. Paranoid-schizoid functioning makes the admitting of ambivalent feelings very difficult, and the thinking and understanding that allows for constructive ambivalence may not take place.

Psychoanalytic psychotherapy, which can contain but also work assertively with the terrible reality of the family's life, as well as recognizing the significance of siblings' relationships, can slowly allow for space to develop between mother and child. She will gradually begin to experience her child as separate from her and attend better to her own needs and those of the other members of her family. As well, she can begin to hope for the maximum independence possible for her child.

The Lee family situation was fraught and complex, for John had indeed been inadequately protected by his non-family carers. This did not mean, however, that he must never ever be allowed independence. A non-disabled victim of a sexual crime may experience profound difficulties in relationships in the aftermath of the attack, but that is not same as wanting to be, essentially, denied one's liberty. Therapy played a crucial part in being a bridging service for the family. By the end of the therapy, Mr and Mrs Lee were communicating more effectively in sessions. Mrs Lee's health was visibly improving and Melanie began to talk of finding her own flat. Perhaps most significantly, they had allowed John to return to day care for two days per week, and his therapy continued for a further two years. The attachment in the family was enmeshed from the start, but therapy provided an experience of separation and individuation, thus allowing all members of the family to think about themselves as separate people.

References

Burke, P. (2004) *Brothers and Sisters of Disabled Children*. London: Jessica Kingsley.

Glasser, M. (1996) Aggression and sadism in the perversions. In I. Rosen (ed.), *Sexual Deviation* (3rd ed.). UK: Oxford University Press.

Hodges, S. (2003) *Counselling Adults with Learning Disabilities*. London: Palgrave.

Hollins, H. and Sinason, V. (2000) Psychotherapy, learning disabilities and trauma: New perspectives. *British Journal of Psychiatry 176*, 37–41.

Hopper, E. (2003) *Traumatic Experience in the Unconscious Life of Groups: The Fourth Basic Assumption: Incohesion: Aggregation/Massification or (ba) I:A/M*. London: Jessica Kingsley.

Hughes, D. (2006) *Building the Bonds of Attachment: Awakening Love in Deeply Troubled Children* (2nd ed.). Northvale, NJ: Jason Aronson.

Jeans, A. (2003) *Lost and found: How did dramatherapy provide playful space for a mother and autistic child to explore their relationship and being to separate?* MA dissertation (unpublished) Central School of Speech and Drama/Open University.

Lechavalier-Haim, B. (2001) From freezing to thawing. In J. Edwards (ed.), *Being Alive*. London: Routledge.

Parker, R. (2005) *Torn in Two: The Experience of Maternal Ambivalence* (2nd ed.). London: Virago.

Shapiro, A. (2004) *No Time for Us: Relationships between Parents Who Have a Disabled Child*. London: Contact a Family.

Sinason, V. (1992) *Mental Handicap and the Human Condition*. London: Free Association Books.

Sinason, V. (1993) *Understanding your Handicapped Child*. London: The Tavistock Clinic.

Steiner, J. (1993) *Psychic Retreats: Pathological Organisations in Psychotic, Neurotic and Borderline Patients*. London: Routledge.

Tustin, F. (1981) *Autistic States in Children*. London: Routledge and Kegan Paul.

Winnicott, D. (1962) *The Maturational Process and the Facilitating Environment*. London: Hogarth Press.

Chapter 6

'Can they see in the door?'

Issues in the assessment and treatment of sex offenders who have intellectual disabilities

Richard Curen

As J entered the therapy room and sat down, he asked me, 'Can they see in the door?' His question conveyed a mixture of almost voyeuristic excitement, as though he hoped he would be seen, and of shame – a fear of what he might reveal if he was seen. This confusion of emotion is often apparent in the sex offenders with intellectual disabilities who come for treatment and assessment at Respond.

Sexual offending and intellectual disability

Day (1988) found that offending behaviour is generally uncommon in people with intellectual disabilities. But the incidence of sexual offending by people with intellectual disabilities was found to be four to six times that by non-intellectually disabled populations. He found that sexual offending was mainly a young, male phenomenon, as it is in the general population, and that offenders tended to be solitary and functioning in the mild/borderline range of intellectual disabilities. In common with offenders without intellectual disabilities, he found that there may be a high incidence of adjustment problems at school, conduct disorder issues, a high incidence of psychiatric illness, a high incidence of organic brain damage, a family history of psychiatric disorder, that offending occurs in the context of psychosocial deprivation and that perpetrators may also have been victims.

There are a number of considerations to bear in mind when thinking about people with intellectual disabilities and sexual offending: for some the definition of 'sexual offender' will be guided by the definitions in the Sex Offences Act (2003). Others will want to include some people with intellectual disabilities who have never been near a court room and may not even be aware of having committed any offence. They may lack *mens rea* and therefore not be legally responsible for their actions in the eyes of the law but, for the purposes of accessing appropriate treatment and risk management, need to be described as sex offenders. It is also relevant to note that many people with intellectual disabilities are frequently in 24-hour supported care, and that they may have little or no time outside the sight of their carers. This means that, inevitably, their sexual behaviour is often not conducted in private and will come under the scrutiny of others in ways that that of non-disabled members of the population will not. Therefore, when a person with intellectual disabilities touches someone inappropriately or perpetrates a sexual act felt to be abusive of another, they are more likely to be discovered and punished. This does not mean, however, that they are likely to be dealt with via the criminal justice system. It may rather have the effect of making their carers more vigilant. This is especially true in cases of young people, where parents and carers often become the unpaid gaolers charged with 'imprisoning' their children/residents at home.

Thompson (2000) and Parry and Lindsay (2003) suggest that men with intellectual disabilities may be over-represented in referrals to sexual offender services due to the fact that they are more likely to be caught than other offenders because of increased impulsivity and the likelihood that professionals are already involved in their lives at some level. Thompson also found that there are significant differences in the victim profiles of sex offenders with intellectual disabilities. Most notably, their victims are more likely to have intellectual disabilities themselves. Also, offenders are less likely to be gender-specific in their victim choice.

A common theme that emerges with referrals to Respond is the unwillingness of authorities to prosecute offenders, while those same authorities expect services to provide treatment. This often leads to the unsatisfactory situation of people being referred for treatment although no proper investigation has taken place. This is doubly problematic. The (alleged) victim may feel that justice has been avoided and the (alleged) perpetrator may not have committed a crime. Also, the lack of a threat of further consequences can lead to little co-operation or compliance with treatment. This can have a damaging effect on the course of treatment as a patient may remain in a defended position throughout, while maintaining their innocence, thereby avoiding engaging more fully in the treatment.

The reasons for alleged offenders not getting to court include a reluctance to report offences, and procedural failures such as interviewing without an appropriate adult being present. Another reason might be the low expectation of conviction coupled with the implications for witnesses/victims with intellectual disabilities who might have to give evidence or appear in court.

Since the Youth Justice and Criminal Evidence Act (YJCEA) (1999) came into effect, special measures have been in place for vulnerable and intimidated witnesses. However, there is no legislation that encourages the same measures to be made available to vulnerable defendants. Along with researchers in the field (e.g. Simpson and Hogg, 2001; Burton *et al.*, 2006), I am of the view that the special measures set out in the YJCEA should be introduced for vulnerable defendants and that steps should be taken to ensure that they are aware of the meaning and consequences of their involvement in the criminal justice system.

However, the system at present would not be able to contain and treat the significant numbers of offenders with intellectual disabilities that do come into contact with it (Talbot, 2007). Talbot suggests that in a prison population of 80,000 there will be 5,500 men, women and children with IQs under 70 (about 7 per cent), and a further 16,000–20,000 people with IQs under 80 (20–25 per cent). While the use of IQ is not a concrete guide to someone having intellectual disabilities, it can be reliably used to indicate that extra support will be required by these people in order to access mainstream prison services and treatment. Researchers have found that sex offenders with intellectual disabilities may have a high incidence of family psychopathology, low specificity for age and sex of the victim, psychosocial deprivation, behavioural disturbances at school, psychiatric illness, social naivety, poor ability to form normal sexual relationships, poor self-control and low self-esteem.

The issue of whether a person with intellectual disabilities should have a chance to clear their name in a court of law is significant. Article Six of the Human Rights Act declares a 'right to a fair trial' and yet many people with intellectual disabilities are effectively denied this. We regularly come across cases where there might be a letter from a paediatrician or psychologist that states that the client is a Schedule One Offender (the term 'risk to children' is now more commonly used), but there is no other evidence on file to substantiate this claim. There is a clear risk of judgement error in this circumstance and this may have huge consequences on the life choices of the individual so labelled. Following an incident or incidents of sexually worrying behaviour, they may find themselves closely supervised and have their freedom of movement effectively restricted. Although in the best cases there will be regular professional reviews of their circumstances, these will still not have the authority of the courts behind them.

There are many instances where there is an allegation that an offence has taken place, but the police or the Crown Prosecution Service will decide that the case should be diverted (i.e. dealt with outside of the court). Unfortunately, the Home Office was unable to provide statistics relating to the numbers of diversions. In more extreme situations, it may be that an alleged offender who is felt to be too dangerous to be contained in a community setting is sent to a secure hospital or setting and detained there, often for much longer than if they had been convicted in court. It is our experience at Respond that some of the people with intellectual disabilities who are referred because of their sexual behaviour are essentially 'imprisoned without trial' and yet do not resist the supervision. If they did, it is likely that they would be detained under the terms of the Mental Health Act, where again they would benefit from legal review of their circumstances.

Sexuality and sexual offending

Sexuality and its expression are, for most people, complex areas. The expression of (a healthy) sexuality relies on an understanding of our motivation and desires. For people with intellectual disabilities this is sometimes limited or disjointed. Research has focused on why people with intellectual disabilities might be abused or offend (Walmsley, 1984; Hayes, 1991; Clare, 1993; Hames, 1993; Beail and Warden, 1995; Brown and Stein, 1997; O'Connor and Rose, 1998; Blanchard et al., 1999; Lindsay, 2005). Researchers have attempted to identify specific reasons why people with intellectual disabilities may sexually offend (Hames, 1993). Suggested factors include: the view that offences towards children are a form of sexual exploration that reflects the perpetrator's functional age; poor social skills; a lack of chances to develop meaningful peer relationships; poor impulse control; and cognitive distortions. Beail and Warden (1995) suggest that because such a large number of people with intellectual disabilities have themselves been abused, this has led to an increased number of offenders.

Being able to see the victim in the perpetrator and the perpetrator in the victim is a crucial element in our understanding and treatment of the offenders with intellectual disabilities and echoes the thinking of many contemporary forensic psychotherapy practitioners, for example Sinason (1996), Welldon (1996) and Kahr (2001).

Sinason (1996) highlights research that states that although a large proportion of people who abuse were themselves abused, a large proportion of people who were abused (13 out of 14) do not go on to repeat their abuse (Browne, 1993). Sinason describes how sexual abuse goes through the body and the mind of the victim, creating what she describes as a 'double tragedy'. The victim has to contain the despair, perversion and sadism of the abuser and, in addition, the internal fantasies and bodily responses that the trauma stirred up. Sinason states that the original hurt can petrify into a script that is repeated either through abusing (Watkins and Bentovim, 1992) or through perversion (Rosen, 1979). More recent research (Glasser *et al.*, 2001) pointed to the fact that many men attending a forensic psychotherapy service had been abused by a female relative in childhood and that they had subsequently become abusers. This finding echoes previous research (Briggs and Hawkins, 1996) that hypothesized that abuse of boys by female relatives was more likely to contribute to the victim becoming an abuser than abuse by male relatives or by those from outside the family.

Fyson (2005) connects offending behaviour with the social model of disability. She implies that changes to the way in which people with intellectual disabilities are perceived by society could reduce incidences of sexual offending. Although young people with intellectual disabilities are provided with some education at school, sometimes the specific needs of young people with intellectual disabilities who are unable to understand fully the content of what they are being taught are ignored. In addition, if personal freedoms are restricted in a highly risk-averse care culture, it is highly likely that sexual repression will find expression in self-harming behaviours, depression and other mental health problems, as well as in sexualized acting-out. Fyson concludes by recommending that professionals need to be aware of the different ways in which young people often struggle to learn the rules of social (and sexual) interaction. This leaves those that offend sexually needing to be thought of as requiring more education and appropriate treatment if further transgressions are to be avoided.

Case study: A

A 17-year-old boy with epilepsy and mild intellectual disabilities was referred by a psychologist working at a large residential boarding school for children and young people with intellectual disabilities. At the school A had been seen 'stalking' a small number of girls aged between 10 and 12. Scribbled notes of a threatening nature, written by A, had been handed to teachers. In the notes, A described wanting to force the girls to have sex with him and to hurt them. A was seen hiding in bushes and behind trees, from where he had been witnessed jumping out on these younger girls from behind. He had also crept up behind one of them and grabbed her by the neck. The girls were obviously very shaken by their experiences. The school put in place a constant monitoring system and decided to refer A for a risk assessment.

A female psychotherapist undertook this work. A revealed that he harboured sadistic fantasies that involved degrading and humiliating the young girls. He felt that these girls were contemptible, but, paradoxically, he thought that they were laughing at him whenever he saw them. By attacking them from behind, as he did, A was attempting to avoid their 'attacking' gaze and to silence them via strangulation or suffocation. The therapist noted the confusing combination of shame and sexual excitement experienced by the client.

As the assessment progressed the therapist became aware of A's deep feelings of shame and of not being the expected healthy child his parents had wanted. On exploring his parental relationships it became obvious that he was ambivalently attached to his mother. She had been treated for depression since his birth and he was his parents' only child. A's father had left his mother when A was three years old, which was very soon after his disability had been identified. A felt that his arrival was the reason for his father's leaving and he described having hateful feelings towards both his mother and father that on further exploration led to him feeling hated by them. The therapist sensed strong feelings of shame that were strongly linked to sadomasochistic enactments. The therapist also felt that the attacks on the girls were a projection of some of the feelings of humiliation that A experienced.

Soon after the assessment A started in weekly psychotherapy, initially for a period of one year, and he was seen by the therapist who assessed him. During the 12-week assessment process no new incidents were witnessed or reported. The goal of the treatment was to see if A would benefit from expressing more of his thoughts and feelings. The hope was that he might be able to contain and understand the roots of his violent fantasies. A had seemed to enjoy the assessment process and initially appeared to be very keen to attend his weekly sessions. However, after a couple of weeks A started to feign illness on the days he was due to come to Respond, or would shout at staff about not wanting to go and see 'that bloody bitch'. Around the same time A was discovered with some of the girls' underwear in his possession. This was viewed by the staff at the school as the final straw, and A was excluded permanently.[1]

It was at this time that A started to attend his sessions more regularly and he started to describe his hatred of his mother in conjunction with his feelings about how she always looked at him in a 'mean way'. On further exploration, what A seemed to be describing was his mother's murderous thoughts and fantasies. It also became clear that A's reasons for targeting these girls was a link to his belief that his mother had wanted a girl. These girls, although they too were disabled, represented a number of things to A: firstly the idealized child that he wasn't; secondly the child who hasn't developed fully yet; and thirdly the shame-inducing eyes of the mother. Although the therapist didn't share these thoughts directly with A, the case was discussed a number of times at length in supervision, and the therapist had an emerging sense of the unconscious violence and turmoil within A.

Funding for a second year of therapy was agreed following meetings with the social worker and other members of A's network. In that time A was able to develop some understanding about his acting-out and to feel some compassion for himself. He was also able to project some of that compassion towards his mother and was able to discuss what it must have been like for his mother to discover his disability and to lose her husband at the same time. The sexual acting-out did not resurface during treatment.

Forensic risk assessment

Respond has been providing risk assessments for over 10 years. The growing recognition that people are not neatly packaged into good or bad, victim or perpetrator, but are often a demanding mixture of both, led Respond to develop treatment models that could cater for abused, abuser and those that are both. The provision of forensic risk assessments has, over the years, become an important part

1   The Head's decision to exclude A might also be seen as an enactment of splitting within the team of professionals supporting him.

of Respond's service, drawing together its psychotherapeutic and investigative work.

Clients are generally referred for a risk assessment by a social worker, psychologist, psychiatrist, lawyer or probation officer. The reasons for referral are varied: a sexual offence may have been committed; there may be concerns about sexual practices in the toilet at the day centre; a keyworker in a group home may have concerns about the sexual content of his conversations with his client. If after an initial conversation it is felt that there is a compelling need for a risk assessment, referrers will be asked to gather as much background information as possible on the client, including childhood, family history, employment history, and any psychology or psychiatry assessments that may have been conducted. The therapist undertaking the assessment will then convene a professionals' meeting to discuss both the history of the case and the current areas of concern.

Our starting point is usually to ask, 'Why a risk assessment?' and 'Why now?'

Primarily, the assessment exists to take an in-depth look at the client's internal world; to consider his or her history; and to explore the reasons why sexual acting-out has occurred. Equally important is the need to look at the external world of the client. The therapist looks at the environment in which the client is housed, where they receive day care or where they work, and asks, 'Is this a setting that is able to understand this client? Can it provide safety and containment at all times or are there gaps in the safety net?' To reach answers to these questions, it is necessary to have a dialogue with those who work with the client. As well as practical issues of supervision and support, we are interested to explore less tangible issues. For example, we would want to explore how the client makes people feel, or to find out if perhaps one half of the team is feeling worried, anxious, concerned about the client, while the others feels secure with him/her, as if something is being blown out of proportion. As noted in Chapters 3 and 11, such split experiences can tell us much about what clients project onto those around them, and possibly about pre-existing family dynamics.

Once there has been an opportunity to discuss these questions, the therapist will meet with the client himself or herself for a maximum of 12 sessions. Each lasts 50 minutes; all are at the same time and in the same place each week. Nearly all sessions take place at Respond, except in cases where sessions include family members or when a home visit is made in order to see how the client functions in a more familiar setting. Respond asks a lot of the network bringing the client to it – if referrers struggle to bring a client to Respond for 12 sessions, this says something about the organization's capacity to deal with demands on it, and its ability to enact any recommendations that might be made at the end of the three months of clinical work.

In conducting a risk assessment the therapist will work against a backdrop of ethical considerations. Confidentiality is high on the list. The stance of the therapist conducting the assessment also needs careful consideration, particularly in such areas as trying to gauge when to be pushier than one would be in a therapy session, in order to get to the crux of an issue or event. Using psychotherapeutic skills in what is not a psychotherapeutic piece of work can bring up dilemmas, especially when one is confronted with a client who is deeply troubled or depressed.

Working with sexual fantasy is one of the most difficult areas to explore, enmeshed as it is within the client's sense of himself/herself as a private and sexual being. The assessment is spread across only 12 sessions, and therapist assessors must always be mindful of the dangers of dismantling people's carefully erected defences if there is not time to think about what could take their place.

Most risk assessments, because of their length and because they take place in a therapy room with a trained therapist, will almost certainly have therapeutic elements. It is important not to isolate any of the content of what emerges during the assessment. The experience of hurting others through sexual aggression will rarely be found to be a behaviour that does not have its roots in earlier trauma. The risk assessment is likely also to consider the impact of the client's sense of himself or herself as a person with a disability, as questions of self-identity will be significant to their view of their offending behaviour. The risk assessment must then incorporate explorations of disability, both the primary organic deficit and 'secondary handicap' (Sinason, 1992) which, as earlier chapters have described, can be employed as a defence against trauma – sometimes the trauma of being abused, sometimes the trauma of disability. The more the therapist assessor is able to consider these issues with clients, the less restricted formulations will be, and the more useful recommendations will be in terms of long-term risk management.

At the end of the assessment a report is produced and another professionals' meeting is held to discuss the findings. The report will cover such issues as family history, childhood, attachment history, education, sexual history, offending history and an analysis of any offending cycle (Wolf, 1984). It ends with a list of conclusions and a further list of recommendations of steps to be taken by referrers to manage the level of risk. There is then a final professionals' meeting which is an opportunity to look in detail at the recommendations and to think about the current and future needs of the client. The report serves as a snapshot of a particular time in the client's life and the picture that emerges is often both illuminating and life-changing. In some cases Respond may recommend (in addition to individual treatment for the client) a parallel process for the team in which issues such as splitting and division can be considered.

Risk assessment case study: M

[In order to give a flavour of a risk assessment and the final report I have used some of the headings that would appear in a risk assessment report.]

Client M, aged 19 years, was referred because staff in his care home had anxieties regarding behaviour towards some local boys. There had been a number of incidents in which M had attempted to befriend them and at times attempted to touch them. Some staff felt that M's tendencies were 'an accident waiting to happen'.

Although M's parents were not the actual referrers, they were actively involved in the referral process. They wrote a long detailed letter recognizing that sexual activity was very much alive in M's mind and that if M was a risk to others then this needed to be quantified, managed and treated.

The assessment started and when M was questioned about why he was coming to Respond, he seemed to be unclear. The assessor tried on a number of occasions to explain the reasons to him, mentioning that concerns had been expressed about some of his behaviour and some fears about what he might do to young boys. However, M was unwilling or unable to consider his risk during the early sessions.

The first few sessions were devoted to establishing a good working relationship through gradually building up trust in the assessor and in the process. M facilitated this process by quickly forming a positive relationship to the assessor. His presence seemed to evoke caring and sympathetic feelings and the assessor regularly found himself 'moved' by his communications and descriptions.

Having established a facilitative working environment, the assessor attempted to enter some of the emotionally difficult and behaviourally problematic areas of M's life. However, although M was prepared to explore some highly personal areas such as his sexuality, his self-harm and previous abusive experiences, it became clear that he was reluctant to speak about anything related to possible inappropriate behaviour on his part. When the assessor touched on such areas he would often attempt to change the subject or he would state explicitly that he did not want to talk about such matters. The assessor was able to obtain some material for consideration of risk through indirect means and through an understanding of such avoidant behaviour. Of great use were the reports from psychiatrists and psychologists, along with reports from residential care homes, concerning disclosures of M's own abuse and his paedophilic thoughts concerning boys.

Sexual history and sexuality

M mainly talked about homosexual abusive encounters. At one point he seemed to suggest that he had had heterosexual sex with his 'girlfriends', although it was conveyed to us by his mother that he had never had sexual intercourse.

The various comments that M made relating to his sexual inclinations and preferences were rather intriguing. When he first brought up the matter of sexuality – and this occurred spontaneously without questioning or prompting – he insisted that he was gay and that he had every right to be so. Nevertheless he went on to mention 'girlfriends'. Some sessions later he described himself as being straight. It seemed that this coincided with a gay home manager going on holiday. Knowing about his strong identifications with this worker and the importance of his relationship to him, the assessor tentatively suggested that maybe his worker being away had freed him to express himself in this way. M affirmed this.

In the consulting room, M often expressed curiosity about how the assessor felt towards him as well as openly wondering what the assessor's sexual preferences were – M speculated that the assessor was heterosexual. He would often touch the assessor through handshakes and hugs and would sometimes attempt to kiss. None of this had a sexual feel but he would occasionally purse his lips as if to blow a kiss and that had a sexual charge to it. However, when asked about this, M would deny any sexual intent on his part.

When questioned, M eventually admitted that he was interested in boys but refused to acknowledge any attraction to girls even though he had previously expressed such feelings. He seemed to 'blame' this interest on a voice in his head encouraging him to be so inclined. According to him, the voice belonged to a previous keyworker.

Abuse

Right at the end of one session – in fact, as he was walking out the door – M said that he had been raped in the past. This somewhat dramatic disclosure (in terms of the way it was announced) was obviously taken up in the following session, where M said that it had happened at school and was perpetrated by someone who was supposed to be a friend. From his descriptions it was difficult to formulate a consistent picture of what might have happened. In the final session he spoke about a previous worker of his raping him as well as being raped by another keyworker, who was someone about whom he had previously made disclosures.

M also described (virtually from the beginning of the assessment) being abused in various ways (including emotionally and physically). However, it is important to mention that M used the word 'abuse' in a somewhat idiosyncratic, broad way. For example, when the assessor arrived very late for one session, M described this as abusive. Similarly, his not being invited to the referrers' meeting in the course of the assessment was described as a form of abuse. The use of the term may partly be an indication of the high emotional impact on him of such experiences.

Sexual abuse

It was difficult to get a consistent picture of the details of the sexual abuse M had suffered. However, whether or not the details of his descriptions and in his previous disclosures are accurate, what can be stated categorically is that elements of abusive behaviour (including rape) existed in his mind. When he described abusive episodes he was asked if such experiences made him want to do similar things to others and he was emphatic in saying 'no', and pointing out that it would not be right. However, one might well ask what impact those abusive experiences have had on his own proclivities and whether and where there had been any processing of the abuse (see above).

Offending history

While it was clear that M had paedophilic thoughts, and he felt compelled to seek out and then to touch young boys, he had never actually been reported to the authorities and there had therefore been no police involvement. In this case, like many others at Respond, the 'offending' that is assessed is a 'potential' to offend, and the anxiety that this potential stimulates in carers and professionals is of a different quality to that of a client who has been convicted of an offence, or a client who admits to wanting to harm others, but who has never hurt anyone previously. M fits into a group of people with intellectual disabilities who have not committed an offence (and may never do so) but, due to what their carers know about their thoughts and motivations, are supervised in various ways and with differing intensities.

Avoidance of problematic areas

As mentioned above, M was reluctant to discuss his feelings and behaviour relating to matters that might be considered inappropriate. He avoided any mention of his inclinations towards children until the issue was raised by the therapist and even then he was hesitant and deflective. It is possible that M's reluctance and avoidance were partly due to having had to speak about such matters to professionals in the past and not wanting to go over understandably uncomfortable material. Another factor to bear in mind is that having established a good, 'friendly' relationship with the assessor he did not want to jeopardize that relationship through admitting things that he might have imagined would cast him in a negative light. However, even taking these points into consideration his avoidance would have to be taken as a negative element in terms of risk. The existence of 'no-go' areas would suggest that he was consciously and/or unconsciously keeping certain matters hidden.

Inconsistencies in description

One of the problems that arose in regard to an understanding of risk was that M regularly seemed to change certain details when speaking about emotionally charged areas. Some of this may have had to do with difficulties in understanding his speech, or to misinterpretation, but given his clarity and accuracy in emotionally 'easier' areas such inconsistencies again made the assessor feel uneasy in relation to risk.

Masturbation fantasies

At one point in the final session M stated that he masturbated every night to thoughts about boys. In fact, he initially said 'girls and boys' and then changed that to 'boys'. When asked about their ages he stated that they were his own age and then used the term 'men' to refer to them but slipped back into the description 'boys' a little later. If one takes his initial statement to be the truth with the other comments as attempts at avoidance then the clear implication is that he gets sexually aroused on a regular basis at the thought of boys and girls.

Conclusions

The above factors mentioned were all of a concerning nature in terms of risk. Taken together, the indications are that there is the potential for further inappropriate sexualized behaviour. The nightly masturbatory activity with the corresponding thoughts of boys and girls, and the obsessive thoughts about the local boys and his attempts to touch them, can be seen as particularly worrying. However, it has to be stated that there is very little conclusive evidence that M has acted out these risky or harmful potentials or that he has significantly overstepped social boundaries or restrictions in order to achieve what might be his aims. M's mother pointed out that even the incidents that came to light and were investigated either were dropped due to insufficient evidence or contained some ambiguity in their interpretation.

However, is it right to use the legal notion of 'innocent until proven guilty' when thinking about risk assessment and risk management? Until it is possible to obtain sufficient understanding of the state of M's internal world, preferably via psychotherapeutic treatment, it is hard to obtain reassurance that he will not act on the various inclinations that were presented during the assessment.

Recommendations

Residential arrangements, supervision and care

The current residential, supervision and care arrangements appeared to be satisfactory and appropriate. Based on the considerations mentioned above it was suggested not to relax any of the supervisory restrictions in place at that time. However, it was felt that if the recommendation for psychotherapy in conjunction with continued risk assessment reporting was followed, it might have been possible to obtain sufficient reassurance in the future to suggest the lessening of such constraints.

Psychotherapy (with ongoing risk assessment component)

The assessor believed that psychotherapy would be of significant benefit for M for a number of reasons, as follows.

- In the course of the risk assessment (which almost inevitably has therapeutic elements) he liked being listened to and seemed to value the space for expression and exploration. M welcomed the opportunity to form a relationship where there was some focus on attempting to understand his inner world. The assessor obtained feedback that his behaviour outside the sessions during the assessment displayed increased calmness and reflection.
- The assessor believed that there was much pain that M needed to work through ranging from his relation to aspects of his intellectual disability to that arising from difficult (and possibly abusive) relationships from his past.
- If one were to believe M's statements about being abused and raped then it was important that he be given an opportunity to process and work through such experiences therapeutically. Even if the details he gave were not wholly true it made sense to explore why such incidents *did* then exist in his mind.

The assessor recommended once-weekly psychodynamic therapy for a period of at least one year. In conjunction with this it was suggested that the therapist produce six-monthly reports reviewing M's risk. Although there were potential complications in attempting to combine psychotherapy (with its high level of client confidentiality) with ongoing risk review (where session material will inform the reporting to the referrers), the assessor believed that this would have been the only way to obtain a more definitive assessment of M's risks in society. There had to be an extended exploration of his inner world in order to appraise more accurately how it might impact on his external life.

Forensic psychotherapy and links with intellectual disabilities

Forensic psychotherapy can be broadly described as the psycho-dynamic treatment of offenders and victims. Forensic psychotherapy is conducted by psychologists, psychiatrists, psychotherapists and psychiatric nurses in both the community and a range of secure settings. It is understood to be a treatment that uses the therapeutic relationship to consider offending behaviour and thence to change that behaviour. Attention to the transference and countertransference experienced in the consulting room is central to the treatment. An understanding of developmental theory and attachment theories is also of benefit when one is considering the aetiology of offending behaviours. Forensic psychotherapy is essentially an attempt to grapple with the core issues of aggression, perversion and hostility and their manifestation in behaviours and in the consulting room.

In the field of intellectual disability there is a need to provide a service for men and women who may have engaged in behaviours that put others as well as themselves at risk. These range from what one might describe as 'sexually inappropriate' behaviour – for example, masturbating in public – to serious sexual assaults and paedophilia and those that rely on fetishistic enactments that might put themselves or others at risk, for instance auto-asphyxiation or frottage.

Case study: H

H, aged 38, was referred to Respond for individual psychotherapy following an attempted rape he experienced while looking for sex in a well-known homosexual cruising area. H has a moderate intellectual disability and lived in a small group home with three other men. He has a history of sexual abuse from his early childhood. He also has a history of sexually inappropriate behaviour and of sexually assaulting young men with intellectual disabilities. H, like many other intellectually disabled men, was lonely and craved a sexual relationship. For many years he had allowed himself to be picked up by men for sex. This had led to him having been assaulted on a number of occasions. Support staff struggled with decisions about whether H should be allowed to go out on his own late at night. It was decided to refer him for psychotherapy as a way for him possibly to make some connection between his early childhood experiences and the 'dangerous' behaviour he was engaging in.

In the early sessions H focused on his loneliness and lack of a sexual partner. He formed a strong attachment to his male therapist and would sometimes be flirtatious and at other times condescending and officious. H would complain about the other clients in the waiting area, specifically about their clothes and their smells. The therapist concentrated on these feelings and helped H to explore them. It became apparent that H was defending against his own feelings of inadequacy and low self-esteem. H thought of himself as not having intellectual disabilities, and his feelings of superiority in the waiting area and elsewhere in his life were his way of coping with profound feelings of inferiority. His mother had left him in the care of her parents after his birth. She had been sexually abused by her father and mother, yet was unable to care for H herself and reluctantly surrendered him to their care. His early childhood was marked by severe neglect and sexual abuse via his uncles and grandparents.

H described terrible scenes of a violent sexual nature and it was hard for the therapist to contain his shock and horror about what was described. The therapist worked on his countertransference feelings and in supervision it was suggested that in subsequent sessions he might try to help H to explore the apparent dichotomous presentations of contemptuousness and flirtatiousness. The following sessions were marked by an increase in the presentation of these polarities. H asked the therapist more probing and personal questions and was more flirtatious than previously. The therapist's interpretations were met with barriers of words – H would talk incessantly over the therapist. However, the therapist was able to explore these defences. This seemed to have the effect of shifting H's defended way of thinking about the therapist as either a person who wanted to abuse him or someone who hated him too. It was the experience of being seen as a person and not as a sexual or hated object that made a difference to H.

The treatment continued for five years with no known incidents of assault taking place during or after the treatment, and the therapy ended by mutual consent.

Relevant ideas and theories

A number of psychoanalytic ideas have been helpful in our understanding of therapy and assessment with people with intellectual disabilities, most notably theories of perversion (Freud, 1905;

Glasser, 1996; Welldon, 1988) and delinquency (Winnicott, 1956; Campbell, 1989).

Freud (1920) wrote that 'perverted sexuality is nothing more than infantile sexuality magnified and separated into its component parts'. In 'A Child Is Being Beaten' (1919) he saw that sexual perversions can be regarded as defensive formations rather than more simply as components of infantile sexuality that have avoided defence.

Glasser's (1996) core complex has been a helpful tool in advancing our understanding of intellectually disabled clients. Glasser suggests that the offender client has two apparently contradictory emotions: one is aggression in response to perceived threat and is concerned with survival; the other is a profound longing for complete merging with the object. However, since the object is invariably regarded as potentially engulfing, the client fears that the loss of separate identity will inevitably follow in its wake. One of the reactions to this threat is self-preservative aggression directed against the very object that is longed for as a source of intimacy and the gratification of his needs, security and containment. This poses irreconcilable conflicts. The client's solution to this is the employment of sexualization which converts aggression to sadism. Here, the intention to destroy is converted into the wish to hurt and control. In this way the object is preserved and the viability of the relationship is ensured, albeit in sado-masochistic terms.

Campbell (1989) has related Glasser's theory to children and suggests that, in the child, these double annihilation anxieties of engulfment and abandonment mobilize a self-preservative aggression – an aggression that attempts to destroy threats to physical or psychological survival. For the child the threat to its survival and its mother are impossible to tell apart, hence the child is in a bind: it cannot afford to destroy the object that threatens its survival, as this is the same object on which it depends for survival. Glasser and Campbell agree that the way out of this bind lies in changing the aim of the child's aggression from eliminating the mother to controlling her by sexualized aggression (sadism). There may also be a link between the core complex and the 'disorganized' attachment category (see Chapter 4), seen in situations where the child's abuser and primary carer are the same person.

Hopper (2003) describes 'difficult' patients as having a distinguishing feature – a fear of annihilation in response to severe trauma. This manifests in helplessness and powerlessness arising from loss, abandonment and damage within the context of the trauma. The fear of annihilation permeates the human condition, as does trauma itself, but the experience of severe trauma, as a function of either the degree of immaturity of the ego or of the severity of the calamity, is a variable. Hopper suggests that this fear of annihilation is closely connected with the fear of separation. Separation from an object with whom one has fused is like losing a part of one's self, and because one is most likely to fuse with an object one has lost prematurely, this is when it is difficult to hold in mind representations of the object.

In order for life to continue, the separation or loss experience is often petrified and thrown into the deeper recesses of the mind. This is characterized in patients by an all-encompassing silence concerning the loss and gaps in the necessary developmental stages. Hopper continues by describing patients who have had these traumatic experiences as having forms of self-protection that are either 'crustacean' or 'amoeboid' (Tustin, 1981) or 'contact shunning' and 'merger hungry' (Kohut and Wolf, 1978). I am struck by how many of the traumatized patients treated at Respond have used crustacean imagery to describe themselves. It is as if the idea of a shell/barrier has been internalized in order to protect from further abandonment. These are clients whose experiences of separation and of loss mean that issues of relating to others are mixed with feelings of anxiety and of depression.

A treatment of choice

There is agreement in the literature that prison settings are fundamentally unable to address the treatment needs of this group (Coffey et al., 1989; Reed, 1989). The problem can be traced to the criminal justice system's inability to identify inmates who are developmentally disabled. In addition to this absence of resources and knowledge among prison staff, there is a lack of inter-agency agreement and co-operation (Coffey et al., 1989; Reed, 1989; Swanson and Garwick, 1990; Davison et al., 1994; Holland et al., 2002).

In their examination of the effectiveness of probation for sex offenders with intellectual disabilities, Lindsay and Smith's (1998) research led them to recommend two-year probation orders over one-year probation periods, as the shorter term was not long enough for any sex offender programming to take effect. Group-based therapy, as described by Swanson and Garwick (1990), has been discussed for its potential in providing effective treatment. Firth *et al.* (2001) also found that long-term engagement in art therapy together with cognitive-behavioural therapy proved to be particularly effective in helping a victim of sexual abuse who went on to perpetrate abuse to recognize abusive thoughts. Indeed, the prevailing model for treating most offenders is a cognitive-behavioural one. Riding (2005) points to the work of Clare *et al.* (1992) and their adaptation of cognitive-behavioural techniques to make them more accessible for offenders with intellectual disabilities. He also points to the lack of empirical data to support the efficacy of psychodynamic psychotherapy as a treatment model for this group. Much more work needs to be done in this area, and until findings are made available we rely on our clinical judgements and experience to guide our decision-making in matters such as the length of treatment and a patient's suitability for this type of intervention.

A central aim of psychotherapeutic treatment is to lessen the negative or unhelpful defences against internal conflict by supporting the client to identify and address unconscious dynamics. As Hodges (2003) writes, 'this aim is hopefully achieved by making internal objects, inner worlds and their workings more available or accessible to the client'. She goes on to state that a careful exploration of the meaning in the client's behaviours can lead to a more useful expression of feelings.

Clearly, more research needs to be done, but experience so far suggests that interventions of this kind can provide a thoughtful and containing space, for both the client and those who work with the client, supporting and supervising him or her in the community. Sex offenders who have intellectual disabilities may find themselves beyond the reach of the criminal justice system and attendant treatment programmes. They are therefore highly dependent on care providers to offer imaginative and thoughtful interventions that respect their human rights and also recognize the impact of early trauma and of the lived experience of disability. These interventions and treatments must, of course, ensure the safety of others but should also allow for the personal growth and development of the offender and for the possibility of change in his or her dangerous behaviour.

Adams (2003) recommends that, while not all sexual offenders are themselves victims of sexual abuse, the field of sex offender treatment would benefit from more research on the relationship between early victimization and later sexual offending. Adams expressed regret that there is little apparent interest in applying the lessons gained from trauma theory, despite the overwhelming evidence that most sex offenders are trauma survivors. What has also become very clear from our work at Respond is that it is extremely difficult for a perpetrator of abuse to feel empathy for his/her victim if they feel no empathy for the victim in themselves. How can we expect the perpetrator who dissociated from his own experiences of abuse to be able to understand the feelings of his/her victims? It is our view that psychotherapeutic treatment that is informed by psychoanalytic thinking with perpetrators of abuse, and that focuses on early trauma experiences is more likely to lead to an understanding of the effects of abuse on self and others, and that this in turn will lead to a diminishing of acting-out and damaging behaviours.

References

Adams, M. J. (2003) Victim issues are key to effective sex offender treatment. *Journal of Treatment and Prevention 10*(1), 79–87.

Beail, N. and Warden, S. (1995) Sexual abuse of adults with learning disabilities. *Journal of Intellectual disability Research 39*(5), 382–387.

Blanchard, R., Watson, M. S., Choy, A., Dickey, R., Klassen, P., Kuban, M. and Ferren, D. J. (1999) Paedophiles: Mental retardation, maternal age, and sexual orientation. *Archives of Sexual Behavior 28*(2), 111–127.

Briggs, F. and Hawkins, R. M. F. (1996) A comparison of the childhood experiences of convicted male child molesters and men who were sexually abused in childhood and claimed to be non-offenders. *Child Abuse and Neglect 20*, 221–233.

Brown, H. and Stein, J. (1997) Sexual abuse perpetrated by men with intellectual disabilities: A comparative study. *Journal of Intellectual Disability Research 41*(3), 215–224.

Browne, K. D. (1993) Family violence and child abuse. In C. J. Hobbs and J. M. Wynne (eds), *Baillière's Clinical Paediatrics*. London: Baillière Tyndall.

Burton, M., Evans, R. and Sanders, A. (2006) *Are special measures for vulnerable and intimidated witnesses working? Evidence from the criminal justice agencies*. Home Office Online Report 01/06, p. 69. Retrieved April 9, 2008, from www.homeoffice.gov.uk/rds/pdfs06/rdsolr0106.pdf.

Campbell, D. (1989) A psychoanalytic contribution to understanding delinquents at school. *Journal of Educational Therapy 2*(4), 50–65.

Clare, I. C. J. (1993) Issues in the assessment and treatment of male sex offenders with mild learning disabilities. *Sexual and Marital Therapy 8*(2), 167–180.

Clare, I. C. H., Murphy, G. H., Cox, D. and Chaplin, E. H. (1992) Assessment and treatment of fire-setting: A single-case investigation using a cognitive-behavioural model. *Criminal Behaviour and Mental Health* 2(3), 253–268.

Coffey, O., Procopiow, N. and Miller, N. (1989) *Programming for Mentally Retarded and Learning Disabled Inmates: A Guide for Correctional Administrators.* Washington, DC: U.S. Department of Justice.

Davison, F. M., Clare, I. C. H., Georgiades, S., Divall, J. and Holland, A. J. (1994) Treatment of a man with a mild learning disability who was sexually assaulted whilst in prison. *Medicine, Science and the Law 34*(4), 346–353.

Day, K. (1988) A hospital-based treatment programme for male mentally handicapped offenders. *British Journal of Psychiatry 153*, 635–644.

Firth, H., Balogh, R., Berney, T., Bretherton, K., Graham, S. & Whibley, S. (2001) Psychopathology of sexual abuse in young people with intellectual disability. *Journal of Intellectual Disability Research 45*(3), 244–252.

Freud, S. (1905) Three essays on the theory of sexuality. In J. Strachey (ed.), *The Standard Edition of the Complete Psychological Works of Sigmund Freud, Vol. 7.* London: Hogarth Press.

Freud, S. (1919) A child is being beaten (a contribution to the study of the origin of sexual perversions). In J. Strachey (ed.), *The Standard Edition of the Complete Psychological Works of Sigmund Freud, Vol. 17.* London: Hogarth Press.

Freud, S. (1920) Beyond the pleasure principle. In J. Strachey (ed.), *The Standard Edition of the Complete Psychological Works of Sigmund Freud, Vol. 18.* London: Hogarth Press.

Fyson, R. (2005) *Young people with learning disabilities who show sexually inappropriate or abusive behaviours.* Nottingham, UK: Ann Craft Trust Report.

Glasser, M. (1996) Aggression and sadism in the perversions. In I. Rosen (ed.), *Sexual Deviation* (3rd ed.). Oxford, UK: Oxford University Press.

Glasser, M., Kolvin, I., Campbell, D., Glasser, A., Leitch, I. and Farrelly, S. (2001) Cycle of child sexual abuse: Links between being a victim and becoming a perpetrator. *British Journal of Psychiatry 179*, 482–494.

Hames, A. (1993) People with learning disabilities who commit sexual offences: Assessment and treatment. *NAPSAC Newsletter 6*, 3–6.

Hayes, S. (1991) Sex offenders. *Australia and New Zealand Journal of Developmental Disabilities 17*(2), 221–227.

Hodges, S. (2003) *Counselling Adults with Learning Disabilities.* Basingstoke, UK: Palgrave.

Holland, T., Clare, I. C. J. and Mukhopadhyay, T. (2002) Prevalence of 'criminal offending' by men and women with intellectual disability and the characteristics of 'offenders': Implications for research and service development. *Journal of Intellectual Disability Research 46*(1), 6.

Hopper, E. (2003) *Traumatic Experience in the Unconscious Life of Groups.* London: Jessica Kingsley.

Kahr, B. (2001) Introduction. In B. Kahr (ed.), *Forensic Psychotherapy and Psychopathology: Winnicottian Perspectives*. London: Karnac.

Kohut, H. and Wolf, E. S. (1978) The disorders of the self and their treatment: An outline. *International Journal of Psycho-Analysis 59*, 413–425.

Lindsay, W. R. (2005) Model underpinning treatment for sex offenders with mild intellectual disability: Current theories of sex offending. *Mental Retardation 43*(6), 428–441.

Lindsay, W. R. and Smith, A. H. W. (1998) Responses to treatment for sex offenders with intellectual disability: A comparison of men with 1- and 2-year probation sentences. *Journal of Intellectual Disability Research 42*(5), 346.

O'Connor, C. R. and Rose, J. (1998) Sexual offending and abuse perpetrated by learning disabilities: An integration of current research concerning assessment and treatment. *Journal of Learning Disabilities for Nursing Health and Social Care 2*(1), 31–38.

Parry, C. J. and Lindsay, W. R. (2003) Impulsiveness as a factor in sexual offending by people with mild intellectual disability. *Journal of Intellectual Disability Research 47*(6), 483–487.

Reed, E. (1989) Legal rights of mentally retarded offenders: Hospice and habilitation. *Criminal Law Bulletin 25*, 411–443.

Riding, T. (2005) Sexual offending in people with learning disabilities. In T. Riding, C. Swann and B. Swann (eds), *The Handbook of Forensic Learning Disabilities*. Oxford, UK: Radcliffe.

Rosen, I. (1979) Perversion as a regulator of self-esteem. In I. Rosen (ed.), *Sexual Deviation* (2nd ed.). Oxford, UK: Oxford University Press.

Sexual Offences Act (1993) London: The Stationery Office.

Simpson, M. K. and Hogg, J. (2001) Patterns of offending among people with intellectual disability: A systematic review. Part I: Methodology and prevalence data. *Journal of Intellectual Disability Research 45*(5), 384–396.

Sinason, V. (1992) *Mental Handicap and the Human Condition: New Approaches from the Tavistock*. London: Free Association Books.

Sinason, V. (1996) From abused to abuser. In C. Cordess and M. Cox (eds), *Forensic Psychotherapy: Crime, Psychodynamics and the Offender Patient*. London: Jessica Kingsley.

Swanson, C. K. and Garwick, G. B. (1990) Treatment for low-functioning sex offenders: Group therapy and interagency coordination. *Mental Retardation 28*(3), 155–161.

Talbot, J. (2007) *No one knows. Identifying and supporting prisoners with learning difficulties and learning disabilities: The views of prison staff*. Prison Reform Trust Report, London.

Thompson, D. (2000) Vulnerability, dangerousness and risk: the case of men with learning disabilities who sexually abuse. *Health, Risk & Society 2*(1), 33–46.

Tustin, F. (1981) *Autistic States in Children*. London: Routledge and Kegan Paul.

Walmsley, R. (1984) Recorded incidence and sentencing practice for sexual offences. In M. Craft and A. Craft (eds), *Mentally Abnormal Offenders*. London: Baillière Tindall.

Watkins, B. and Bentovim, A. (1992) The sexual abuse of male children and adolescents: A review of current research. *Journal of Child Psychiatry and Psychology 33*, 197–249.

Welldon, E. V. (1988) *Mother, Madonna, Whore: The Idealisation and Denigration of Motherhood*. London: Guilford Press.

Welldon, E. V. (1996) Contrasts in male and female sexual perversions. In C. Cordess and M. Cox (eds), *Forensic Psychotherapy: Crime, Psychodynamics and the Offender Patient*. London: Jessica Kingsley.

Winnicott, D. W. (1956) The antisocial tendency. In D. W. Winnicott, *Collected Papers: Through Paediatrics to Psycho-Analysis*. London: Karnac Books.

Wolf, S. (1984) *A multifactor model of deviant sexuality*. Paper presented at 3rd International Conference on Victimology, Lisbon, Portugal.

Youth Justice and Criminal Evidence Act (1999) London: The Stationery Office.

Chapter 7

Going on down the line

Working with parents who have intellectual disabilities

Chris Neill and Tamsin Cottis

Ordinary life principles, and values of inclusion and empowerment, currently dominate the culture of services for people with intellectual disabilities (Department of Health, 2001). Yet it is still rare to see parenthood actively promoted as a life choice for people with intellectual disabilities. The perception may be largely unspoken, but the demands of parenthood are perceived to be too great for very many people with intellectual disabilities. Instead, if pregnancy occurs, services tend to be reactive, with large numbers of professionals dedicating many hours of time and large quantities of money to ensure good outcomes for the children of parents who have intellectual disabilities. As Booth and Booth (1994) have described, precise data on the numbers of parents with intellectual disabilities is difficult to find, but we can assume that, with increased care in the community and with policy-driven efforts to enable people with intellectual disabilities to lead lives of their own choosing, the incidence of people with intellectual disabilities becoming parents is likely to increase. Service interventions after the birth of children will generally involve personnel from intellectual disability services as well as those from child protection. The differing values bases of these two branches of the service tree may make it difficult for constructive work to take place. The needs of the child are paramount and the parent who has intellectual disabilities, as well as their carers and advocates, may find it shocking that they have no rights *per se* to be parents. There may, additionally, be conflict between the rights of the child for good enough care, and the stated aim of the Children Act (1989) that the child must be maintained in their family of origin wherever possible.

At the point of referral of one case to Respond, where two children had been taken into care, there were (and this is not untypical) at least 14 different professionals, from the fields of intellectual disability, child protection, family courts and education, actively involved in the case. In addition, three separate parenting assessments had already taken place.

It seems sensible to ask, when considering this spider's web of involvement and concern, what might be the aim and value of a therapeutic assessment, or indeed long-term psychotherapy, for the parent? We have found that reasons for referral vary considerably from case to case. There may be a request from social services or another interested party in a case before the family court (a solicitor or guardian *ad litem*, for instance) for an assessment of a parent (or two parents in partnership or a family as a whole), regarding their ability to provide good enough care for children. A referral may be made for Respond to provide support to a parent or parents who have ongoing care of children, with a view to raising awareness and confidence or providing containment and a space to talk through difficulties. Or it may be that parents whose children are in foster care or have been removed for adoption require help to come to terms with this situation and deal effectively with the process of separation or managing the often very stressful and challenging experience of maintaining a routine of contact with children who are looked after away from the family home. At one end of the spectrum, intellectually disabled parents may be facing a situation similar to that faced by parents without intellectual disabilities whose childcare abilities have been questioned. At the other, we might be dealing with a quite special experience of loss: a number of Respond clients were abused and made pregnant while living in long-stay institutions. Their babies were removed from their care immediately and then adopted. The terrible losses associated with this experience may never have been recognized or mourned. Audrey, whose daughter, Joy, had been born 35 years previously, came to Respond aged 64. Audrey would repeat, perhaps 30 times in a single session, 'Where's my Joy? See Joy? Where is she? Where's she gone?' Staff who had known Audrey for many years had become inured to the repetitious nature of her communication and it was only the arrival of a new social worker, attuned to Audrey's underlying distress, that precipitated the referral for psychotherapy.

In most situations it is likely that Respond's task will involve some combination of assessment and support. It would be unrealistic, wrong and contrary to legal principles to suppose that, even in the confidential setting of personal therapy, support for parenting can be provided without regard to the ongoing safety of the children being parented and without the possibility, if necessary, of communication and collaboration with other services responsible for the well-being of the children. Equally, according to the principles that guide Respond's approach, it will be ineffective and ultimately counter-productive to undertake an assessment task, even in such cases where parents themselves are reluctant to engage in the process, without also adopting an empathic stance that can provide support and understanding.

Whatever the precise circumstances, a psychotherapeutic frame of reference is held. Mary Main's development and implementation of the Adult Attachment Interview (Main *et al.*, 1985) has enabled researchers to explore the link between attachment patterns in the parents and those of their children. Fonagy *et al.* (1991) found a 70–80 per cent correlation between the attachment states of parents and those of their children. At Respond, we assume that a parent's own experience of being parented will have contributed to the for-mation of their parenting style and patterns of response to their children. We also recognize that numerous factors arising from their past, and present, personal experience, potentially including trauma, neglect, discrimination, exclusion, deprivation and insecurity, will be as significant in affecting their parenting ability as the intellectual disability that may appear to be at the forefront of issues to be assessed and dealt with. We assume that adopting an approach in which the worker seeks to stand alongside the client, to enter and appreciate their own frame of reference, and to communicate that they are valued as a person with an emotional sensitivity and a mean-ingful inner life, whatever the degree of intellectual ability or chal-lenging behaviour, may be healing and restorative in itself. This is not to say that we can be anything less than robust in upholding the paramount rights and needs of children for good enough care and nurturing. We are equally robust in communicating this to parents and all others involved in a case, and in making decisions and recommendations, in the case of assessment, accordingly. But we know that to approach the task of 'working with' parents without keeping their own experience at the centre of the process will be to risk simply compounding the damage of past traumas, will be of little or no benefit to any children, and may potentially increase the family's burden of suffering and the pain of misunderstanding, rejec-tion and failure, leaving it to be passed on to another generation.

As Booth and Booth (1994) have discussed, intellectual disability in itself is not an automatic disqualification or obstacle to parenting. However, research for the Plymouth Health Action Zone (Hodgetts and Power, 2002) showed that 50 per cent of parents with intellectual disability in that region had their children taken into care. This is of course far higher than the rate for parents in general, and it is the case that an intellectual disability may give rise directly to circumstances that do impinge significantly on a child's sense of well-being. As Winnicott (1962) describes, harm to a child's sense of 'going on being' may be caused by accumulated minor impingements as well as by major trauma. Details matter. It is important for a parent to be able to understand and act upon a child's need for careful handling and regular feeding, to be able to respond thoughtfully to a child's crying or signs of illness, and to be capable of attunement with a child's developing sensitivities and interests, to be able to communicate to the child about the child's own developing experience. All of these capacities, and the attendant requirements for appropriate patience, judgement and communications skills, may be negatively impacted by an intellectual disability.

And yet there are many parents with intellectual disabilities for whom the capacity to be what Winnicott refers to as a 'good enough' parent in this way is not at issue, intellectual intelligence level being only one of a number of variables that contribute. Indeed, Hodgetts and Power (2002) found that in families in which both parents had intellectual disabilities, parents did better in keeping care of their children than in families where a single parent had intellectual disabilities or only one parent had intellectual disabilities. There are others for whom the capacity to do well enough in this way seems to vary considerably from time to time or from situation to situation – depending, for instance, on whether there are anxieties about other events or issues, on who is being supportive or not supportive or perhaps on who is observing or not. Once actual capacity is established (for instance: the parent does know how to sterilize bottles and does have the planning skills to carry out a routine; they evidently can differentiate what children are communicating and can respond varyingly with tenderness, firmness or humour as appropriate), we can say that variations in it are most likely due not directly to a person's intellectual disability as such, but to a complex interplay of other, psychological factors, including their own or others' attitude to their intellectual disability. In other words, the failure to provide good enough parenting may arise not from an innate incapacity but from the parent's experience of themselves, and therefore belief about themselves, as not good enough, and the creation or reinforcement of this belief by others, in the past or in the present.

Of course, the experience of feeling or being made to feel not good enough in the past will almost certainly be projected into present relationships. Where helpers, family centre workers, support workers and social workers have taken great care not to give this message to a parent with an intellectual disability they may then be bewildered and frustrated to experience that, nevertheless, a chronic lack of self-belief and confidence persists and is framed, perhaps, by the parent as being the result of others' lack of faith in them.

What this points to is the need to go beyond what appears on the surface to the underlying or inner experience of the parent. As the work of Winnicott (1962), Bowlby (1969) and others describes and affirms, a child needs to experience a quality of attention to their being that is ongoing and at depth. This is achieved partly through physical (surface) handling and care but the security of attachment and sense of confidence in self, or 'holding', in the Winnicottian sense of being 'held in mind' and the ability to manage life that arises as a result, are actually experienced at depth. By the same token, our attempts to address the chronic lack of security and self-confidence experienced by many people with intellectual disabilities need to be from this context and perspective.

It is not at all unusual, in cases concerning parents with intellectual disabilities, to hear a parent complain that they have not had enough help. This is usually taken to mean, and probably con-sciously intended to mean, help with learning practical skills, with gaining knowledge, with building awareness – the context may be anything within a wide range from setting boundaries with a chal-lenging toddler to overcoming anxiety about changing nappies or giving feeds, or the parent developing the necessary assertiveness to protect themselves and their child from other adults who may harm them. Those in the helping role in these situations – usually the local authority social services department or an agency such as a family centre operating on their behalf, or maybe school or nursery staff, will often quite reasonably argue that, by normal standards, a lot of help has been given. There, may, for instance, have been several pro-grammes of work lasting weeks or months at family centres provid-ing ongoing instruction in childcare techniques alongside assessment and practical support. There may have been financial grants for equipment or redecoration to improve the home environment. There may have been attempts at reconciliation in a residential centre between parents and children previously separated. All this seems like a 'lot of help' and yet the workers report that very little change or improvement is made or else that each new programme of help or helping relationship produces an initial improvement that is then not sustained.

The capacity to make use of help is as significant as the provision of help. When assessing, we are concerned to find out if a difficulty in putting learning into practice arises from cognitive difficulties or from psychological ones. Being able to have some trust and confidence in the helper is crucial. People whose parents abused or neglected them, for example, may experience enduring difficulties in doing this (Hughes, 2000). One important consideration, of course, is that the actual amount of help required by a parent who has intellectual disabilities may well be more than that required by a parent without intellectual disabilities. Things need to be repeated or need to be gone through more slowly or in a simpler way. The client needs more time to absorb and integrate information and ideas. This may be partly because of intellectual impairment but often, also, partly because the client's anxiety about the task of learning, and fear of being judged for not meeting required standards, may well be so high as to be an obstacle in itself to learning.

But this does not seem to be the whole explanation. Many helping agencies – not all – have progressive policies and an understanding about how procedures for supporting or educating a person with intellectual disabilities might need to be adapted in order to be effective. A deeper reason for the failure of progress to expected levels and rates, underlying the discrepancy between what client and worker see as 'enough' help and fuelling the disappointment and frustration of both, is often that the wrong sort of help is being given, and/or that it is directed towards the wrong areas of a client's life.

Case study: Family S

Family S had been the recipients of a large amount of 'help' from their local social services department. This focused particularly on giving advice to the parents about how to discipline their four unruly children, and on providing money and personnel to improve hygiene and safety in the home. Each new initiative in either area produced an initial surface improvement that was not sustained. The house remained a health hazard – dirty, full of broken or dilapidated furniture and overcrowded with pets – and the children continued to present very challenging and often disturbing behaviour in school. Significant and sustained change began to occur when both parents, individually and together, were provided with therapy sessions in which they could build relationships with people whom they began to trust, and in which they could begin to explore some of the issues that appeared to be underneath the surface – including especially the abandonment and sexual abuse of the mother in her own childhood and the father's chronic addiction to gambling, the cause of much hidden conflict in the parents' marital relationship. These issues, suspected or half known about before, had never been brought to light or addressed directly in this way either by the parents themselves or by professionals working with them. Gradually, the house got cleaner, and stayed cleaner, and the children's health, behaviour and capacity to relate to others improved significantly. There were setbacks and relapses, but it came to be understood by all concerned that these were related much more to the mother's recurring sense or fear of abandonment and the anxiety or anger that arose in all family members if the father spent the housekeeping in the bookmaker's than to the degree of knowledge held by family members about, for example, which cleaning fluids to use, how often to Hoover, or how to discipline the children. Essentially, we might say that the help that Family S needed was listening – carefully and over time, not only to what the parent was saying about what was obviously happening at the time, but also about what had happened to them in the past and what this meant to them.

There will of course be occasions when a failure to buy food instead of alcohol, to keep away from abusive acquaintances, or to manage a violent temper, indicates an incapacity to learn or change or a simple unwillingness to do so (perhaps because the parent simply cannot face the pressure of parenthood). But, as with any symptom presented for treatment, it is important to see beyond or beneath the surface appearance to look for the root cause. We are not averse to accepting that a stomach ulcer is the result of stress or that alcoholism arises from dysfunction in the family of origin of the sufferer. We should also be open to the idea that not being a good enough parent is the result of past or hidden events. It may be that such a degree of difficulty or evident need for help with childcare is, in fact, the only way in which the client, albeit unconsciously, can bring past trauma to attention. For many people with an intellectual disability, as for others whose life circumstances have caused them to suffer deprivation, exclusion and impoverishment on many levels, and who have experienced failure and repeated rejection, the conception and birth of a child is a particularly highly treasured experience of successful creativity. It may reasonably be thought that such an experience marks a very crucial juncture in life – where it is perhaps inevitable not only that a parent's own experience of childhood will be reactivated in unpredictable and unknowable ways but also that such a rare experience of success will create, alongside pleasure, a great deal of pressure related to anxiety about potential loss and disappointment.

So we need this context in order to understand what a parent may mean when they say they haven't had enough help. For a person who has intellectual disabilities, what is being brought to attention may be, as referred to many times in this book, very traumatic experiences of neglect, abuse and rejection. The parent who has intellectual disabilities may well, from childhood, have been seen, or perceive themselves to have been seen, as variously over-demanding, difficult, disappointing, embarrassing – an awkward nuisance necessitating explanation and apology or, worse, a source of deep shame. And to an experience of suffering within the family, we may well need to add the experience of feeling rejected within the wider community, giving rise to low self-confidence and self-esteem, feelings of inadequacy and intense shame. A Mencap survey (2000) found that nine out of ten people with intellectual disabilities had experienced bullying in the community in the previous year.

Case study: Family K

David, the father in family K, visibly carried such a sense of himself into therapeutic assessment sessions. His expectation that he would be unwelcome or judged as inadequate or somehow 'not OK', essentially that he would be disliked and rejected, was apparent in how he moved, stood and sat and in how he spoke and what he said. His entry into the therapy room was made with a stooping, almost flinching, posture as if he expected attack or reprimand simply for being there. He would at first perch on the edge of his seat and then, later in the session, edge his body more fully into the chair slowly and tentatively, as if he felt it could not bear to touch him. His repressed anger about this seemed apparent in his affect, particularly his eyes. This might have been interpreted as menace, although a closer relationship with David uncovered sadness and fear about what had been done or might be done to him. He described a family and home environment in which, while basic physical needs were met approximately, any sense of security and safety was at best highly unpredictable. A physically ailing mother who suffered bouts of severe depression that were covered up by David's elder, more able siblings, had few resources to meet adequately David's needs for emotional security and a sense of continuing well-being. His brother and sister's attempts to look after him in his mother's absence told him that he was cared about, but the sporadic nature of this as they inevitably struggled themselves to grow up successfully let him know that care was conditional and unreliable. His father, always an only occasional and flimsy presence in the family, eventually abandoned it altogether and this seems to have left David much more exposed and unprotected. Although David was established by this time in a special school that gave him some support for his mild/moderate intellectual difficulties and some sense of safety during school hours, the integrity of family structure deteriorated further as David's older siblings sought their own peer groups and their mother's mental health took a sharp decline.

David either cannot recall or chooses not to talk about incidences in which he suffered direct abuse within the family itself, although experience tells us that it is very unlikely that this did not occur. What he does remember and describe is a household that was very isolated and vulnerable within the wider community. The children were frequently subjected to harassment and bullying in the neighbourhood and the family generally were held in low regard due to neighbours' judgements about standards of hygiene, the children's unruly behaviour, the mother's depression and lack of social confidence. David, as a child with intellectual disabilities within this family, became a particular target for victimization and humiliation outside it. The feelings of low self-esteem, inadequacy, loneliness and exclusion that David already experienced within the family simply on account of his intellectual disabilities were magnified outside it. Feeling himself habitually treated as a lesser person, he began to feel he was regarded, as he described it, as 'some sort of monster'.

David was also aware of repeated intrusions into the family, in the form of physical and sexual assaults upon his mother and sisters by men in the local community and, whether or not he was directly abused, it is clear that David was at least indirectly heavily impacted by this lack of proper boundaries that could be seen to determine his or his family's safety or to limit or restrict male behaviour. As he grew older and continued to struggle to find place and identity in the world, where there might be a sense of security and a feeling of being valued rather than rejected and powerful rather than powerless, it is not surprising and perhaps inevitable that he gravitated towards other family groups whose members were vulnerable – families with poor boundaries, with children and/or parents with social difficulties or disabilities of some kind, where David found he could assume the role of protector.

Although there had been a number of interventions and offers of support to David's family of origin, his and their experience had been that this was inadequate to deal with the real issues in any depth. With no culture or history of trust in community and services to build upon, and afraid of the consequences of revealing the reality of family problems (the family being split up, friends whom they relied on for support being punished, people they were already afraid of hurting them more in revenge for reporting them, etc.), they had done what many families in trouble do and accepted the kinds of help that would scratch at the surface of the layers of difficulty and they kept the more serious issues as much out of sight as possible.

As David eventually developed a new family life of his own, with himself in the role of father-figure, this pattern was continued. He and his partner, a woman also with a mild intellectual disability who already had a young child by another man, established themselves as a family unit. When the child's behaviour and presentation began to raise serious concerns in staff at his nursery placement, David and his partner Julie responded to these concerns not as an opportunity for them to receive help but as a threat to the integrity of their family. Having each survived extremely difficult, dysfunctional family circumstances as children and teenagers and suffered intense feelings of rejection, loneliness and shame in attempts to forge social and personal relationships with peers, they had now invested heavily in an idealized concept of their own relationship and family unit as offering hope for the future and redemption of the past. David displayed intense symptoms of stress and Julie experienced bouts of depression. These difficulties resulted in discord between the two (exacerbated rather than alleviated by unhelpful advice from wider family members), which weakened an already fragile family structure.

By the time that they were referred for assessment, a pattern of defensiveness, resistance, collusion and deception was very well established. Accustomed from their own very early years to harassment, victimization and the unfair presumption of incompetence, and suffering a chronic lack of self-esteem and self-confidence, their situation was further worsened and complicated by financial poverty, by the lack of adequate informal support systems from family and neighbours, and by physical health problems for them and their child. None of these issues, it might be noted, are directly attributable to the intellectual disabilities of either David or Julie.

It is in this context, if we are to make any meaningful intervention in such a situation, that we need to consider the idea of what 'help' might actually usefully consist of. Professionals, who feel that they have tried very hard and perhaps drawn deeply on their resources of sympathy and patience, may become exasperated. If this is communicated in such a way that the parents perceive increased criticism, then the existing feelings of low self-esteem and low self-confidence and the expectation of judgement and failure are compounded.

In fact, key to beginning actually to help is to build a relationship with the parents, based not around what the parents do, or on how effective they are as parents, but first and foremost on a simple valuing of them as people. Their children, their children's progress or lack of progress, successes or problems, will certainly be a subject around which it is possible to build a rapport and a relationship with the parents, but this relationship needs nevertheless to be with the parents as people with feelings, deep motivations, thoughtfulness and a meaningful inner life that is directly relevant to the way they think about and behave towards their children. It is crucial that the parent can be seen as separate from their child, as well as responsible for their child. Our experience is that when people with an intellectual disability begin to feel really met and understood in this way they may begin, in just the same way as other people do, to connect with their own inner creative resources in a way that leads naturally towards the resolution of problems and difficulties – whether these problems and difficulties are in the area of learning new skills, communicating more effectively, having more harmonious relationships or getting round to cleaning the house! Of course, this is neither a simple nor a short process but it remains the case, in our view, that an intervention that addresses the inner emotional/psychological experience of the client/parent will be far more cost-effective in the long term than one directed primarily at the outer events and behaviour.

Case study: Jess

Jess had three children – a son aged 13 and two daughters aged 10 and 8. All three had been removed from her care two years before her referral to Respond. Her elder daughter alleged to a teacher that she had been sexually abused by a male friend of Jess's, though Jess did not believe her daughter and an investigation was inconclusive. A neighbour had reported to social services that she had seen Jess hitting her son with a shoe, but Jess denied this. The children had also been on the Children in Need 'At Risk' register from the time of the birth of the second child, on the grounds of risk of neglect and emotional abuse.

Jess was now engaged in a lengthy, painful and, ultimately fruitless, battle with social services to have her children returned to her care. As with many other parents in this situation, the struggle to get back her children had become the focus of her life. Her relationship with the children's father was over. It had been characterized by his lack of commitment to, and now total abandonment of, Jess and the children, after the birth of the third child.

It is worth noting, in relation to this case, that research (Hodgetts and Power, 2002) also found that 'Some young women [with learning disabilities] meet young men, also with a learning disability and together form stable relationships based on shared aspirations. They have an improved chance of bringing up their children. Others make unwise, and sometimes repeated relationships with unstable men that are stressful and frequently break down. Their children are more likely to be placed in substitute family care through adoption or fostering' (summary, paragraph 3).

Jess talked very movingly about the joy of the early days of her relationship and of how the birth of her eldest child in particular had been her first experience of success. 'I felt I was normal', she said. In her own childhood, Jess had experienced intense verbal and physical abuse by her father who expressed his constant disappointment in her and told her she was 'stupid and would never amount to anything'.

At first, Jess only consented to therapy because she thought it might help her get her children back. This is often the case and casts a very specific and potentially damaging dynamic over the therapeutic work with parents who have intellectual disabilities. Ideally, of course, clients will consent to therapy for its own sake – to have some sense that it may be helpful on an internal, personal level – not as a means to an end. It is a challenge to establish a therapeutic rapport in circumstances in which the client experiences life as a battle, where each person encountered is characterized as either against or in favour of them being allowed to care for their own children, if one cannot also explicitly support their bid to be allowed to care for their own children.

Jess, like many parents in her position, did not at first see any value in talking about 'the past', except for the perceived past mistakes of social services in their handling of the care proceedings. She professed to be concerned only with the present and the future. She also knew, though perhaps unconsciously, that any exploration of her past would force her to confront painful childhood experiences as well as her inadequacies as a parent. However, the therapist's view was that only by looking at Jess's own experiences of being parented would she achieve any understanding of what professionals around her meant when they talked about 'emotional abuse'. As Fonagy and Target (1997) found, there is evidence of an association between the quality of attachment relationship and reflective function in the parent and the child, and key to this is the caregiver's ability to communicate understanding of the child's intentional stance. Jess's childhood experiences had impaired her own capacity to help her own children to 'mentalize' and to develop a theory of mind; all three were themselves experiencing social and educational difficulties.

Jess was angry and hostile in her encounters with professionals. She told me that she felt she was misunderstood and that 'whatever I do is wrong'. Jess had mild intellectual disabilities and was well able to learn practical care skills and abide by basic home safety procedures. Problems arose rather because she had difficulty in understanding that her children had emotional as well as physical needs. Jess found it difficult to understand that a child might not behave rationally, and she would quickly become enraged when her children did not do as they were told. She had no concept of behaviour as an expression of emotional disturbance. Her own childhood had lacked empathy and understanding. It was the therapist's view that for affective change to occur, Jess had to feel understood by another person, to reflect on as well as internalize that experience, and thus be able to recognize her own children's need for such understanding. The therapist was aware that it was unlikely she would experience enough change internally in time to regain care of her children. However, there was hope that she might experience some relief from the torment of, quite literally, not understanding why they had been removed from her care. She was, on referral, cut off from the impact of her own traumatic childhood. Over time, however, this began to change. She began to express signs that positive attachment to her therapist was forming – becoming furious at breaks, for example, and also requesting that therapy be continued beyond the initial 12-month treatment period.

The therapist spent time talking with Jess about her battles with the social services – for this was the material she brought to sessions. However, the underlying dynamics was also emphasized – for example, her sense of being misunderstood, of being under siege, of being unable ever to get it right – and these thoughts were linked to her childhood experiences rather than to the minutiae of the battle itself. The work was extremely difficult and infuriating at times, as Jess's ignorance of the children's needs and refusal to acknowledge that the local authority might have had any grounds for removing the children was so absolute. It was hard for the therapist to resist becoming yet another critical, and so bewildering, voice. Work with Jess led to many conflicting feelings: sadness for her children, relief that they were no longer in her care, alongside great sadness that Jess herself had been so harshly treated in her own childhood. In addition, Jess would frequently be angry and abusive towards the therapist.

However, through well-supervised, regular and long-term therapy, the therapist demonstrated an attentive and respectful commitment to Jess. As her trust in the therapy grew, she began to talk more about her own past. Her childhood shame and humiliation had been compounded by the failure of relationship with the children's father who had himself deceived and abused her and then exacerbated further by the horror of her failure as a parent. It was only after two years of work that she was able to recall the extent of her father's abuse and to cry at the memory of it. One week, she brought in a letter that she had written to him, detailing all the things she would like to say to him if he were still alive.

After three years of work, with her children apparently further away from her care than ever (having been either adopted or placed in long-term foster care), Jess was able to say that, 'I don't think I put [my son's] needs in front of my own. I was too selfish.' Her solicitor began action on her behalf to allow for increased contact with the two children who had not been adopted and, as the process had been so protracted and her son was now in adolescence she began to see that, as he got old enough to make his own decisions, some kind of relationship with him might be possible in the future. We know from the work of Booth and Booth (1998) that attachment bonds between children and their parents who have intellectual disabilities are no less tenacious and enduring than between any parent and child. Jess had retained her contact with the children as far she was legally able to do. When therapy ended after three years, the hope of the therapist was that the relationships she was able to build with her children would be better ones. Through therapy, Jess had also had the opportunity to have the pain and trauma of her own childhood witnessed and to begin to process it. To her lifelong struggle for normality and her extraordinary and enduring strength and persistence now was added insight and a level of empathy hitherto absent.

Psychotherapy with parents who have intellectual disabilities perhaps involves some of the most difficult work we do, and nearly all of the parents referred have histories of terrible abuse and trauma. Many have also harmed their children, and as therapists exploring their experiences we have to absorb that pain too. It involves us working alongside a host of other professionals, whose views and values may not accord with our own. Client confidentiality, and therefore therapeutic rapport, can be extremely difficult to attain (although a case management approach as described in Chapters 3 and 11 may help to ameliorate this). As with our work with offenders, we operate with the knowledge that our work is more than usually likely to come under the scrutiny of a court process. However, we have found that (as with the process of risk assessment described in Chapter 6) a psychotherapeutic approach can make the experience of a parenting assessment less damaging and emotionally fraught for a parent who has intellectual disabilities. It can inform the process by which parenting difficulties are understood. It can also help people who may have lost their children many years ago.

For many of our clients, the experience of becoming parents has been a rare source of joy and pride and yet too often, it has gone wrong and they find their children are lost to them. The experiences of loss frequently leave them humiliated, ashamed and terribly sad. Most parents who are referred want their child back and we have to accept that although in some cases an opportunity for a parent to be bolstered by a recognition of her own needs in therapy can help them manage their parenting role more successfully, for many, the application of therapy will not restore the child to the parent. In such cases the value of the therapy is to help the parent understand what has happened and why, as well as providing an opportunity for the healing of wounds of past abuse and trauma. Parenting issues are often so difficult as to lead to damaging splits between all concerned. Psychotherapy, in these circumstances as in others, allows for a thoughtful and productive exploration of highly complex, apparently intractable, and desperately painful situations at an individual, professional and policy level.

References

Booth, T. and Booth, W. (1994) *Parenting under Pressure: Mothers and Fathers With Learning Difficulties*. Buckingham, UK: Open University Press.

Booth, T. and Booth, W. (1998) *Growing Up with Parents Who Have Learning Difficulties*. London: Routledge.

Bowlby, J. (1969) *Attachment and Loss, Vol. 1: Attachment*. London: Hogarth Press.

Department of Health (1989) *The Children Act 1989*. London: Department of Health.

Department of Health (2001) *Valuing People: A New Strategy for Learning Disability for the 21st Century*. London. Department of Health.

Fonagy, P., Steele, M., Steele, H., Moran, G. and Higgins, A. (1991) The capacity for understanding mental states: The reflective self in parent and child and its significance for security of attachment. *Infant Mental Health Journal 12*, 201–218.

Fonagy, P. and Target, M. (1997) Attachment and reflective function: The role in self-organization. *Development and Psychopathology 9*(4), 679–700.

Hodgetts, A. and Power, M. J. (2002) *Factors influencing the ability of parents with a learning disability to bring up their children*. Health Action Zone Report, Plymouth, UK.

Hughes, D. (2004) In conversation with L. Hughes in *The Impact of Trauma on Children and How Adoptive and Foster Families can Help Them*. A Ponderous Production Training Video for Family Futures Consortium, London.

Main, M., Kaplan, K. and Cassidy, J. (1985) Security in infancy, childhood and adulthood. A move to the level of representation. In I. Bretherton and E. Waters (eds), Growing points of attachment theory and research. *Monographs of the Society for Research in Child Development 50*, 66–104.

Mencap (2000) *Living In Fear: The Need to Combat the Bullying of People with Learning Disability*. London: Mencap.

Winnicott, D. W. (1962) *The Maturational Processes and the Facilitating Environment*. London: Hogarth Press.

Chapter 8

Differences, differences, differences

Working with ethnic, cultural and religious diversity

Shahnawaz Haque

> O mankind! Behold, We have created you out of a male and a female, and have made you into nations and tribes, so that you might come to know one another.
>
> (The Qur'ān 49:13)

It is probably the case that many people who seek psychotherapy feel a little different from the rest of society in some way, if only perhaps by dint of the fact that their problems or their suffering have led them to take the step of seeking professional help. However, the differences from others that might be perceived by our clients at Respond are potentially profound and difficult. The dual characteristics, common to Respond clients, of struggling with intellectual disability and having experienced sexual trauma are significant factors in creating such perceptions of difference. In some cases there is the added contribution of belonging to a minority ethnic, cultural or religious group.

This chapter is a description of the attempts made at Respond to address – principally though its Equal Access Project (EAP) – issues related to differences of ethnicity, culture or religion. It is also an exploration of the struggles in working psychotherapeutically with such a concentration of difference as described above. As the nature of the EAP issues required a fair amount of soul-searching and self-reflection, much of what follows is a somewhat personal account. The ideas and procedures outlined are not meant to be prescriptive, nor are the conclusions drawn claimed to be definitive. However, I believe that the structures that were set up and the processes gone through might well be of some benefit in any organization seeking to address such issues.

Background to and birth of the Respond Equal Access Project

In the late 1990s there emerged and developed a commitment within Respond to address and examine issues of ethnic and cultural diversity. This was partly motivated by awareness of the striking fact at the time in the organization that despite many of the clients being of Black or Asian origin, all the clinical and administrative staff as well as the trustees were white.[1] It was decided that something proactive should be done about this and it was in this context that the EAP was conceived and eventually how I came to be employed at Respond.

As stated in the Respond EAP proposal document (Respond, 1997, p. 1), the basic aim of the EAP was 'to provide greater access to treatment of equal quality for clients from ethnic minorities'. The planned means by which this was to be achieved was firstly to employ a psychotherapist from an ethnic minority community who would then carry out EAP developmental and clinical work.

At the time I was a trainee psychoanalytic psychotherapist in the post-curricular part of my training. I was keen to find work as a psychotherapist but I had little experience of working specifically with people with intellectual disabilities and no significant inclination to do so. However, I did have some experience of therapeutic work with sexual abuse. The fact that the Respond job advertisement stated that applications from ethnic minorities were especially welcome gave me some hope – I was aware of how few psychotherapists or even psychotherapists-in-training there were from minority ethnic groups. I was called for interview and liked what I saw of the organization and the staff, and so was delighted when I was eventually offered the post. I had secured myself a psychotherapy job and Respond had employed a Muslim, Bangladeshi-born, British, part-time honorary Imam as the new EAP psychotherapist and developmental worker!

Development of the Equal Access Project

On paper, my function as the EAP psychotherapist was a dual one: there was to be a clinical aspect – basically my being available as a

---

1   I find it difficult to know which terms to use while maintaining accuracy and flow. We come across the terms minority ethnic, ethnic minority, black, Black and Asian, Afro-Caribbean, white etc. In this chapter I have not attempted to be rigidly consistent and this reflects the diversity of the terms used.

psychotherapist for both white and minority ethnic clients – and a developmental one. The latter included making contacts with other organizations working with people with intellectual disabilities and also arranging regular EAP seminars within Respond.

However, there was a third function which, though not formally described, was nevertheless sensitively recognized by the originators of the EAP and which I soon came to appreciate. This aspect of my position did not really require me to do anything specific – it basically involved my simply being there. In other words, it just needed my physical presence at Respond.

In order to try to explain this and convey the possible impact of the presence of a Muslim, Asian man in an otherwise white organization, I would like to suggest two scenarios. Firstly, we can imagine Black or Asian clients coming to Respond and noticing – perhaps consciously or possibly at a more subliminal level – that all the therapeutic and administrative staff were white. They might see other clients or escorts in the waiting area where there would be a mixture of ethnic groups, but the fact would remain that wherever they looked they would see only white Respond faces.

Now, if we insert in that picture a recognizably Muslim, Asian man who is one of the 'professional' team, the asymmetry is noticeably broken and we change the 'feel' of that original scenario significantly. I believe that the shift in perception would not have been restricted to the client group. Escorts, carers and referrers would also have had very different experiences in the two situations. So too, of course, would the Respond team members.

As mentioned above, the developmental aspect of my EAP role included work both with outside organizations and within Respond (partly in the form of arranging regular in-house seminars). When I joined Respond I had been training as a psychoanalytic psychotherapist for a number of years. So it was hardly surprising that in organizing my activities in the EAP I found myself inclining more to exploring internal processes in the sense of what was going on within myself and within the Respond team in relation to EAP matters, rather than the 'external' contact-forming work. Although the latter proved to be quite fruitful, with a number of referrals, training requests and invitations to speak at conferences resulting, looking back it is clear that I was devoting more energy to thinking about and reflecting on what might be described as 'inner considerations'.

EAP seminars

For me, the in-house seminars were one of the most interesting and exciting aspects of the developmental work of the EAP. These seminars offered a regular space where the Respond team could openly explore and reflect on both theoretical and clinical issues related to the EAP. Again, my physical presence in the team probably had a significant impact. A group of white, relatively culturally homogeneous, well-meaning people discussing matters of ethnic, cultural or religious diversity is one thing, but having within their midst someone who is noticeably ethnically, culturally and religiously different is potentially quite another experience.

I was given overall responsibility for organizing the seminars and on the first few occasions gave presentations at the beginning to help stimulate thought and discussion. However, it was soon agreed that other Respond members might also conduct seminars and give presentations themselves. It was generally felt that the development of the EAP was a shared endeavour for the Respond team and that I should not – especially as the sole member of the team from an ethnic minority community – be carrying too much of the burden of responsibility for its activities and implementation. On a couple of occasions we also invited guest speakers from outside Respond to contribute.

Originally one of the ideas for the seminars was that the team would perhaps learn more about different cultures or ethnic groups and that this would inform our work with clients from such groups. Although there was some activity of this nature (including clinical presentations given by Respond therapists working with clients from ethnic minorities) we found that we very soon moved into more personal and challenging areas relating to our own identities and attitudes and not just theoretical considerations or material relevant to our clients. There was a fluidity to the seminars that facilitated such movements. There was also some tendency for EAP seminar material to spill into other spaces and other times, not just in terms of application of ideas but also in terms of discussion in smaller groups and between individuals. In short, the seminars seemed to have an energy that suffused the organization and created a profound 'buzz' with far-reaching consequences.

Part of the reason that the EAP issues tended to generate much 'heat' was that they often touched on, as alluded to above, very personal and sometimes difficult areas such as matters of identity;

our own belief systems; assumptions we made about others; and even prejudices we held. As psychotherapists we may well be theoretically aware of mechanisms and defences such as splitting and projection and their part in, for example, racism, but to be able to recognize and face the existence of such processes within ourselves is not always an easy matter. However, for most of us the climate at Respond was experienced as sufficiently safe, holding and containing to 'take risks' in such areas and it proved to be the case that the relationships within the team were strong enough to withstand the challenges faced and to facilitate constructive exploration.

So what exactly did we talk about and explore in the EAP seminars? In a chapter of this length it will not be possible to go into too many specific details. However, I would like to describe here various themes which emerged and some of the more interesting or striking features.

With their interest in the internal world and intrapsychic conflicts, psychoanalysts and psychoanalytic psychotherapists are sometimes caricatured as not being at all concerned with external realities. Although this position did not exist in the Respond team, an opinion was expressed – albeit by a single member of the clinical team – that considerations of ethnic or religious diversity were not entirely relevant to the nature of the therapeutic work. This attitude was somewhat problematic as it rather undermined the *raison d'être* of the EAP and the active attempt to employ a psychotherapist from an ethnic minority, but it provided a healthy (though sometimes frustrating) counterpoint to the majority opinion. A lesson that was learned from this and from subsequent significant differences of opinion was that very little could be taken fully for granted in terms of shared values and understandings – like it or not, differences within the team itself did actually exist.

The dominant thinking at Respond, however, continued to be that ethnic, cultural and religious differences needed to be addressed and understood at least in the minds of the therapists. As an example of this it is interesting to note that in 1978, Jafar Kareem, the founder of Nafsiyat – the intercultural therapy centre – attempted to formulate a definition of intercultural psychotherapy thus:

> A form of dynamic psychotherapy that takes into account the whole being of the patient – not only the individual concepts and constructs as presented to the therapist, but also the patient's communal life experience in the world – both past and

present. The very fact of being from another culture involves both conscious and unconscious assumptions, both in the patient and the therapist.

(Kareem and Littlewood, 1992, p. 14)

This seems natural and sensible and generally very much in keeping with the work of the therapists at Respond.

Another area where assumptions were challenged was the following: implicit in the formation of the EAP was respect for cultures and races other than the dominant or majority one. However, was this respect to extend to all situations and at all times or were there limits to, for example, the toleration of behaviour on the grounds of cultural appropriateness?

This question arose powerfully when, in a presentation of a case to members of the Respond clinical team, the behaviour of a mother in relation to her intellectually disabled teenage daughter was thought to be clearly intrusive and sexually inappropriate. It involved among other things physical examination of her daughter's breasts, genitals and bodily curves (in the shower) and related comments on the latter's development as a woman. The referrers – who were aware of these practices of the mother – explained that they had been informed by the client's parents that this sort of behaviour was culturally acceptable and common in their community. We were not able to ascertain the truth of the parental assertions – it being a very small minority ethnic group in London – but in terms of our understanding of the client's sexual development we essentially treated the relationship with her mother as containing inappropriate, abusive elements and we thought in terms of the potential pathological impact of such experiences. However, had we discovered that it was indeed a prevalent practice in that minority community some difficult questions would have been raised – in fact, they were raised but we had the luxury of not having to resolve them practically. For example, surely – some might say – abuse is abuse whether culturally, racially or religiously sanctioned or condoned? But whose definitions of abuse are we using? We might make recourse to legal definitions but we then still have the question of why the law of one land, i.e. ours, should contain more accurate descriptions or be closer to 'truth' than the law of another.

Another interesting dilemma arose in relation to racism. At Respond there were various anti-racist, anti-discriminatory practices in force (with, at one time, even posters on the walls to remind both staff and clients of the prevailing attitudes). However, in psycho-analytic psychotherapy there does, of course, exist the principle of free association and we often invite our clients to say whatever occurs to them or comes in to their heads without censorship or suppression. We wondered if this would extend to clients using racist, abusive language in sessions, especially if directed at their own therapist. Would this be or could it be tolerated in the interests of the therapeutic work? Again this might have been an interesting hypothetical question but was possibly potentially much closer to being a practical realistic problem with my arrival at Respond. (Of course, it is not the case that invoking free association gives *carte blanche* to absolutely anything being said in sessions. Boundaries are a crucial part of the treatment, and client material could be used to work with these.)

In actuality the above problem never materialized in my own sessions at Respond. However, for example, a (white) colleague had to deal with the following experience when working with a white client with significant intellectual disabilities who was on the autistic spectrum.

The client had been verbally and physically abused in a residential home by a member of staff who was black. In exploring her experiences, this client said that she thought the abuse had occurred, 'because [the abuser] was dark'. This was heard as clearly a racist sentiment. Initially, the therapist reflected the comment back to the client, to show that her feelings had been heard, but then challenged the client in quite a conscious way, which the therapist thought was perhaps antithetical to the process of free association. The client had other carers who were black – whom she trusted and who were not abusive to her. The therapist pointed this out while also recognizing the very real fear that the client had of the abusive worker's apparently otherwise inexplicable behaviour.

Clinical discoveries, surprises and reflections

I would now like to describe some of the clinical discoveries made and surprises encountered both in the course of the EAP and in subsequent work. I should mention that in the clinical vignettes that follow and even in the longer accounts I make little reference to the 'bread-and-butter' therapeutic work. This is because this chapter is not about psychotherapeutic work with people who have intellectual disabilities – descriptions of many aspects of which may be found elsewhere in the book – but is more concerned with the extra dimensions and issues arising from cultural, religious and ethnic differences.

Ethnic composition of Respond client group

One of my early tasks in terms of the developmental work of the EAP was to gather information on the ethnic composition of clients referred to Respond. For me the results proved to be rather surprising. One might have expected – in keeping with research and anecdotal knowledge – that the numbers of clients from ethnic minorities referred for psychotherapy would be low in comparison to their proportions in the general population.

However, what we discovered was very different. The proportions of clients from Black and Asian groups at Respond were actually higher than their proportions in the general population. How were we to understand this? Well, in fact, this had already been noticed in the planning stage of the EAP and there it was interpreted in the light of there being in the wider population disproportionately more perpetrators and victims of crime from such minority ethnic groups. It was understood that the figures at Respond simply reflected this.

Racism

In the original proposal for the EAP one of the areas that was described as needing to be addressed was that of possible racism experienced by clients in their lives, in order 'to work therapeutically with the additional and deep damage done to Black clients by experiences of racism and by internalised racism' (Respond, 1997, p. 3).

In the wider community the trauma of racist experiences is nowadays generally recognized and taken relatively seriously. Given the terrible experiences in other areas in the lives of many of our clients at Respond, we might have expected sessions to be replete with descriptions of traumatic racist experiences. However, in my experience and, from what I have observed in supervision, in the experience of most of my colleagues such incidents did not feature significantly in the material of clients – I am not stating that descriptions of racist experiences did not arise at all; it was just that they did not seem to have taken on the sort of significance that I have heard non- disabled clients convey.

How do we understand this? Perhaps, somewhat paradoxically, the horrors of the experience of being a person with intellectual disabilities who has also been sexually traumatized simply overshadow the impact of racism.

Case study: Bilal

Bilal, a North-African man with mild intellectual disabilities – but with physical features making his disabilities immediately apparent – developed phobias of certain places or situations. As a boy, he had been anally raped on a number of occasions by a male lodger (of similar descent) in his parents' home. He also described having had a number of experiences with racist connotations with white people in various situations as well as verbal abuse resulting from people's perception of his disability. However, his sessions were dominated by his descriptions of his feelings related to the sexual abuse and his anxieties of ever meeting his abuser again. What was striking in listening to his accounts was the contrast between the emotionally powerful descriptions of the sexually abusive incidents with the complex set of associated feelings that were expressed and the almost matter-of-fact way he described the other abusive experiences. It appeared that in comparison to the humiliation, betrayal (prior to the abuse his abuser had been friendly to Bilal), confusion (his abuser continued to be friendly to him at other times), and pain he felt (both psychic and physical) in relation to the sexual abuse, the racially abusive experiences almost paled into emotional insignificance. The comments relating to his intellectual disability probably came somewhere between the two in terms of adverse impact on him. (We discovered in the course of his sessions that the phobias were connected solely with the possibility of meeting his abuser, and in fact the fears subsided to a significant extent with therapeutic time.)

The thorny question of 'matching'

The idea that matching – that is, providing a client with a therapist of similar ethnic, cultural or religious background – is in some way beneficial or appropriate was an implicit assumption in the formation of the EAP. Although there were various (and valid) reasons as outlined above for employing a psychotherapist from an ethnic minority group, one belief was that the availability of a Black or Asian therapist for a Black or Asian client was for some reason to be welcomed. The matter is a highly complicated one, however.

For example, we have the following quote from Nafsiyat relating to its practice:

> It should not be concluded, however, that the patient should invariably be matched with a therapist from the same racial and cultural group ... [Therapists] learn to work cross-culturally and to constantly examine their practice as a part of a dynamic and growing process.
>
> There is a great need for more working psychotherapists, indeed more professionals in all fields, from black and ethnic minority groups. They should not, however, be deployed to work exclusively with people from their own cultural group. Matching done purely on the basis of race or colour can imprison both the professional and the client in their own racial and cultural identity. It also diminishes the human element which must be an integral part of all professional encounters.
>
> (Kareem and Littlewood, 1992, pp. 23–24)

And here, with somewhat different emphases, is a description by Mohamed and Smith (1997) of the policy of the Women's Therapy Centre:

> We needed to understand what it means for a Black woman or woman of an ethnic minority to come for therapy within the context of her experience, and to be aware of issues which might make it hard for her to engage fully in the therapy. As we have mentioned, the first hurdle to overcome is the fear of stigma. It is difficult for a Black client to take the step of seeking therapy when she fears being misunderstood, labelled mad or, worse still, sectioned into a psychiatric hospital, so to facilitate the process of entering therapy, it is essential to establish *trust* and build a positive therapeutic alliance. One way of doing this was to offer an initial consultation with a Black therapist. Women had repeatedly talked of their experience of institutions with which they could not identify, so we hoped that having their first consultation with a Black therapist would offer Black women an opportunity to explore what their needs were in a safe space, thus encouraging more women to use the service. Wherever

possible, if a Black client asked to continue working with a Black therapist, this was accommodated.

(Mohamed and Smith, 1997, pp. 145–146)

Respond did not – and does not – have fixed policies in relation to matching. In the course of the EAP and subsequently, I have been referred white clients and clients from ethnic minorities in virtually identical proportions (if we include both psychotherapy and risk assessment clients).[2] Here I would like to reflect on some of the experiences we have had and discoveries we have made in the course of our work.

Firstly in order to match a client to/with a therapist there must be some perceived similarity or identity between the two in the mind(s) of the assessor(s). What seems to be crucial to the therapeutic process is the client's perception of the identity and his/her relationship with that identification. Depending on how the client relates to perceived similarity or identity, various projective mechanisms can come into play and the initial therapeutic alliance can be strengthened or weakened. (Of course, the therapist's perceptions of similarity or identity also play some part in the therapeutic relationship and process but here I am more concerned with the client's perspective.) There are all sorts of possibilities – as we have discovered over the years.

Positive consequences of perceived identifications: Thao

This experience occurred with a potential client for a risk assessment (see Chapter 6 for more information about this process). I was informed by the referrers at the pre-assessment professionals' meeting that because of his shyness and general reticence it was extremely unlikely that Thao, a young Vietnamese man, would say much at all in the first few sessions. Thus, I was very surprised when he spoke expansively from our first moments of meeting, delving into areas that I was led to believe would remain untouched for many sessions.

2 I was somewhat surprised to discover this when I actually carried out a head-count. Had I been asked to guess what the proportions were I would have estimated that the majority were in the ethnic minority group. In trying to understand this distortion in perception I came to realize that in my mind in some sort of vague way, at some level, the clients from ethnic minorities stood out as different and were perhaps thus more prominent. In other words, I was unconsciously taking 'white' as the norm and therefore such clients were less noticeable.

For example, he voluntarily mentioned his sexual predilections and his feelings relating to his sexually inappropriate behaviour. At first I did not fully understand what had happened, but as the assessment progressed it became clear that he was employing a splitting mechanism whereby he basically divided the people of the world into the categories of Vietnamese or English and correspondingly in his mind into good or bad and friend or foe, respectively. (At the time I thought that the reason for the occurrence of his splitting and associations was possibly because the professionals and workers who had been investigating him and 'getting him into trouble' were virtually all white and English. However, it is also possible that an unconscious contributory factor, as we have discovered after a numbers of years of therapy, was that there might have been some serious sexual abuse in his background by an Englishman.)

Although I did not, of course, in reality belong to either category he chose to place me firmly in the direction of the latter: an honorary Vietnamese (and therefore friend not foe). This distortion of external reality actually served to facilitate the assessment (and later therapeutic alliance when he commenced psychotherapy).

Similarities can be deceptive

Firstly – and I am stating this from experience – even in situations where there appears to be some similarity between the client and therapist, let us say, in terms of ethnicity we can discover that there are significant cultural or other differences. For example, I have worked, both at Respond and elsewhere, with Bangladeshi clients where because of profound regional differences in culture or language I have found it harder to understand and express myself to such a client than, for example, with a white, English person. Nevertheless the superficial similarity can still serve as a facilitator to a sort of a therapeutic alliance and a trust of sorts.

Adverse reactions to perceived similarities

On the other hand, the projective processes can sometimes operate to produce adverse effects. We came to learn from another organization of how a Somalian man had expressed great discomfort at the possibility of being referred to a Somalian therapist because of fears that the community would somehow find out (that he was having to seek therapeutic help). For this man it felt safer to work with someone who he perceived was distant from his community than to work with someone 'closer' and thus in his mind risk discovery and being stigmatized. Outside of Respond, I have worked with Bangladeshi clients where similar somewhat paranoid feelings have been experienced around confidentiality and also with some Muslim clients where fears existed of being judged by their fellow Muslim. If such a person has actually made it into the consulting room and has begun work then it has usually been possible to reassure them firstly through the therapeutic contract (including statements relating to confidentiality), and then through their discovery of the therapeutic process. However, my guess is that many potential clients do not even get to the first meeting stage because of such factors.

The nature of the referral process at Respond, where clients rarely refer themselves, means that the client has less choice of therapist than in a private situation. However, in this area of adverse reactions to perceived similarities (and more generally) this can ironically prove to be a blessing in disguise as the restriction in choice (and, we might say, freedom) serves to provide an opportunity for the client to face and hopefully work through the projective and paranoid processes.

The 'unhealthy' use of identifications: Khalid

Khalid, a middle-aged Bangladeshi man, used the perceived similarities in terms of country of origin and religion to attempt to create what felt to me like a somewhat unhealthy space of secrecy and exclusion, where the two of us would be united or allied against all the white workers and professionals. There was a feeling on my part that it was as if he was forcibly or somewhat seductively trying to draw me into his world. His use of language was quite telling in this. Despite knowing that I had some difficulty in understanding the dialect of Bengali he spoke and despite being able to speak fluent English himself he would regularly speak in that dialect, again with a tone of shared and exclusive intimacy. In this mode he was willing to disclose problematic aspects of his external life including his petty crimes and dangerous behaviour. However if I said anything which indicated that I did not in fact share his world or that I was not willing to collude in his secret life, he would feel hurt – I think in his mind I would be temporarily experienced as 'one of them' – and he would miss sessions or threaten to stop coming.

Mismatching: Simon

Simon, a white man in his twenties, was known to have expressed racist feelings to some of his workers. However, in view of times, availability, logistical and other considerations he was referred to me. After a couple of sessions it seemed that his attitudes got the better of the (seemingly positive) relationship that was developing between us and he terminated the therapy in a somewhat sudden, cold, cut-off way. I felt that perhaps it would have been too much of a betrayal to that hateful, racist side of him to allow the growth of positive feelings towards and a trusting relationship with someone whom he was supposed to dislike and mistrust even though there was genuine contact and moments of warmth in the sessions we had together.

After this experience we wondered about the wisdom of referring a client to someone who belonged to an ethnic group towards which the client had racist, hateful feelings. However, again the matter is complicated. For example, had Simon requested a white, English therapist on the grounds that he did not like (or, let us say more mildly, did not feel comfortable with) Blacks and Asians, could the Respond referral committee have possibly complied with his wishes and thus colluded with clear racist feelings? And yet we do not generally have problems with providing a female therapist for a female client requesting such, and similarly for a male client wanting to work with a man.

The above examples highlight how varied the ways that possible similarities and identifications – or in the final vignette, possible dissimilarities – may be perceived and employed by clients for various purposes and depending on the internal world they arrive with. In some of the cases the perceptions served an initially valuable purpose cementing the therapeutic alliance even if based on distortions. In other cases they may have been unhelpful to the therapeutic process. However, in all cases in the course of the therapy the identificatory distortions could not be sustained but were gradually replaced by elements of the 'real' therapeutic relationship akin to the discovery of the therapist as a new object (Baker, 1993).

A detailed clinical case: Hassan

When I first met Hassan, a young Iraqi man with mild intellectual disabilities, he was involved in a risk assessment by another therapist at Respond. Although the assessment sessions themselves had ended, I had been asked to see him in his home environment and to meet members of his family there in order to obtain information and formulate impressions in that context which might contribute to the assessment. In a private moment in our meeting he expressed his deep shame based on his religious beliefs relating to his predicament; his anxieties of what might happen as a result of his sexual offending behaviour; and his hope that by being Muslim and 'foreign' myself, I might be able to understand him better and perhaps help him in some way.

A few months later, Hassan was referred to Respond and then to me for psychotherapy. His referrers were interested in him working therapeutically on his inappropriate sexual feelings and activities but were also concerned that he would probably have to struggle with difficult emotions that might arise in relation to certain court proceedings. What became clear was that although he still felt an identification with me, there were now some opposing forces. Firstly, he associated me with Respond and with the risk assessment which he believed had been a significant factor in the restrictions that were being placed on his life. Secondly, having had the experience of being assessed it was extremely difficult for him to accept that he was now involved in a different process to that of assessment even though this was clarified and stated to him on a number of occasions. Thus began a long and painstaking process of establishing trust through his repeated discoveries that I was not actually responsible – even through association – for the constraints on his life nor was I here to assess him. (I adopted the practice of discussing with him any reports I was required to write and obtaining his permission for material I disclosed).

Hassan related to me experientially and emotionally in various ways. One such was that I would be a member of the set[3] of professionals who had (in his opinion) misjudged him and were now putting barriers between him and his family and restricting his life. This might lead to mistrust and anger (which, however, he was eventually able to recognize as arising from that dynamic). At other times I would be experienced as a fellow Muslim very much on his side and able

---

3   I should mention that although I am not using the terms in exactly the same ways, much of this description in relation to sets and membership of sets is stimulated by the concepts discussed by Ignacio Matte-Blanco in his books (Matte-Blanco, 1975, 1988) and in the description by Patrick Casement (Casement, 1985).

to share the pain of his predicament and conflicts. The sessions were, indeed, often painful in that for the first few months the threat of serious disruption to his family situation because of his misdemeanours hung over him. He almost always arrived in a highly anxious or angry state, and regularly used the sessions to relieve his distress.

Hassan often talked about religious matters in our sessions. Here my knowledge of Islam and my experience of Muslims proved to be useful because it enabled me to distinguish in his descriptions between what were generally held Islamic tenets or prevalent practices and what were more expressions of Hassan's own inner world and psychic conflicts. For example, in his darker moments he would believe that his intellectual disability and his related current difficulties were a form of punishment from God – a view that as far as I knew (and that at other times Hassan acknowledged) had no basis in Islam. With this knowledge it was easier for the two of us to recognize and access the feelings of shame, guilt and internalized parental hostility that were behind such religious constructs.

Looking back, and thinking about the sorts of issues discussed above in relation to equal access and matching considerations, I wonder if Hassan would have been able to stay in therapy at Respond as long as he did – nearly three years – had he not been referred to someone whom he saw as coming from a similar religious and cultural background. My belief is that he would not have been able to do so. His identifications with me as a fellow Muslim and 'foreigner' just about allowed him to hang on emotionally to the therapy until the negative forces lost their power, during which time a genuine trust in me and in the therapeutic process had built up.

Conclusions

As human beings, actual or perceived differences in others can make us feel anxious. We can respond to such anxieties in various ways. We may attempt to minimize such differences in our minds – a sort of pretending that we are all the same, possibly feeling safer or more comfortable in the process. Alternatively, we might go to the other extreme and mentally highlight or exaggerate differences, thereby distancing ourselves and treating the other almost as a different species. In working with our client groups at Respond we are faced with differences that are almost impossible to ignore but, perhaps surprisingly, despite the various manifestations of intellectual disability that enter sessions it is possible to lose awareness of the fact that we are working with clients who have intellectual disabilities. (I have regularly had this experience and I know of colleagues who have felt similarly.) I believe that this does not stem from some unhealthy denial or distortion of reality as described above but that it arises out of a contact in those moments at a level that somehow gets 'under' the disability. Perhaps this is partly because, as Sinason (1992) states, 'However crippled someone's external functional intelligence might be, there still can be intact a complex emotional structure and capacity' (p. 74).

An experience I have had at Respond – which I continue to experience but have learned to allow for – is that of meeting, for the first time, a client who has intellectual disabilities, and discovering that I find their speech almost unintelligible. The feelings that are then evoked are closer to a fleeting panic than mere anxiety. I think that the experience is along the lines of: 'How am I ever going to understand this person and what if I never do?' Of course, with time and perhaps with a heightened attunement or simply familiarity with that person's idiom it becomes possible to understand and also easy to forget previous feelings.

I believe – and I am aware that this is somewhat speculative, but again I am reassured to hear of similar experiences of colleagues at Respond – that the panicky feelings stem from a combination of a deep human need to understand other human beings, together with being in a situation where it is not readily possible literally or metaphorically to walk away – a defence that might be available in other contexts. The sort of relationship and encounter in psychotherapy involves contact and engagement at a profoundly human level where surface differences can be temporarily lost sight of.

I suppose what I am reaching towards in giving these examples is that, despite the massive manifest differences in disability, experience of sexual trauma, ethnicity and so on, the psychotherapeutic encounter is essentially a meeting of souls and in our best moments can be, and is, experienced as such.

References

Baker, R. (1993) The patient's discovery of the psychoanalyst as a new object. *International Journal of Psycho-Analysis 74*(6), 1223–1233.

Casement, P. (1985) *On Learning from the Patient*. London and New York: Tavistock.

Kareem, J. and Littlewood, R. (1992) *Intercultural Therapy: Themes, Interpretations and Practice*. Oxford, UK: Blackwell Scientific Publications.

Matte-Blanco, I. (1975) *The Unconscious as Infinite Sets*. London: Duckworth.

Matte-Blanco, I. (1988) *Thinking, Feeling, and Being*. London: Routledge.

Mohamed, C. and Smith, R. (1997) Race in the therapy relationship. In M. Lawrence and M. Maguire (eds), *Psychotherapy with Women*. London: Macmillan.

Respond (1997) *Equal access to equal quality*. EAP Proposal Document, Respond, London.

Sinason, V. (1992) *Mental Handicap and the Human Condition: New Approaches from the Tavistock*. London: Free Association Books.

Chapter 9

Therapy for life and death

A focus on the Respond Elders Project

Noelle Blackman

As I push Edith's wheelchair out of the waiting room along the corridor and into the therapy room she complains bitterly to me of the aches and pains in her ageing body. Specifically, she tells me about the bruises she suffers every day as she's lifted and moved, enduring the indignity of physical dependence. Edith delivers her litany of complaints each week as we move from one space into another to begin her weekly psychotherapy sessions. I understand her as railing against the pains of growing older and being less able to do things for herself.

Edith is in her late seventies and suffers from advanced arthritis in her hands and shoulders. Over the past few years she has also lost the ability to walk. Edith was referred to Respond when it came to light that she had been sexually abused over many years while in her twenties and thirties. However, what seems to preoccupy her more at present are the many losses that she is experiencing as she gets older. As we enter the therapy room she lifts her skirt to show me a large bruise on her leg: 'Jane did it when she lifted me onto the toilet', she says. I wonder whether she is reminding me of her earlier sexual abuse, and if the hurt she feels inside is evidenced by these external patches of pain. As well, I am anxious that she may have been roughly handled. Edith often shows me bruises and I regularly ask my case manager (see Chapter 11 for more explanation of this role) to raise my concerns with her referrers and ensure as far as we are able that proper lifting and handling procedures have been followed. Each time, we are assured that she is being carefully looked after and I can only conclude that her body is indeed becoming more frail. I recognize that part of my work with Edith is to be a witness to this process. She is angry but she is also in some way delighted to be able to show me what is happening.

During the sessions I see more evidence of this frustration as Edith lunges forward from her wheelchair to pick her bag up from the floor or grab a pen from the table. She often comes dangerously close to toppling out of her chair altogether. She sighs and moans with her exertions, but she does not ask for my help. I comment on her visible need to do things for herself, and she grunts and carries on busying herself with sorting out her bag.

Opposite the therapy room there is an office block and Edith has developed a fantasy flirtation with 'a man' that she 'sees' in a window there. As far as I can tell, the room is empty but Edith waves and smiles coyly. When this happens I think about Edith as a young woman and I wonder about her different experiences with men. I see her as flirtatious, and as enjoying their company. I wonder how she feels now she is an old woman; making sense of what the men think of her now? Despite her frailty, her feisty, lively character remains strong. I ask her what she would like to say to the man in the office window: 'I'd ask him to be my boyfriend', she says. 'And what do you think he would say?', I ask. Edith winks at me, knowingly. I find myself wondering again about her past experiences of abuse, but also of the apparent pleasure she derives from her flirting. I think about her early family life. What men were there and how did she feel about them, and they about her? There is scant information available about Edith's life and she is able to tell me very little. However, the therapy allows me to think and wonder, and to share my thoughts with her. In therapy, she is in the presence of a person who is interested about her whole life, about the young Edith, as well as the elderly Edith, and together to share this vision of her varied past.

Edith is lucky to have been referred to Respond. Psychotherapy is not widely available to people with intellectual disabilities (McGinnity and Banks, 2002) and there are misconceptions that older people generally are incapable of change and therefore not suitable candidates for psychotherapy (Van-Etten, 2006). Older people with intellectual disabilities may therefore face extra difficulties in accessing treatment, even though they are more likely to be facing significant and other major life changes.

In this chapter I will discuss some of the issues that affect people with intellectual disabilities as they grow older and, drawing on the work of the Respond Elders Project, I will explore a specific service response to the needs of this group, with a particular focus on its therapeutic practice. As well as psychotherapy and counselling for older people with intellectual disabilities, the Elders Project provides a free telephone helpline that can be accessed by older people with intellectual disabilities, their families and care workers and professionals. In addition, the project delivers more formal training and face-to-face consultancy. This approach, in which the wider context and network of an older person's life is addressed as well as their specific therapeutic needs, has been beneficial. Through the Elder's Project we are often asked to support older people and their carers at traumatic points in their lives. For example, professionals from either intellectual disability or palliative care services may contact the helpline when they are first involved in the care of someone with an intellectual disability who has been given a diagnosis of a terminal illness. At this point, there may be a sense of shock and panic about what they should be doing. Discussing the situation on the phone can make it easier to think of a way forward. It will be crucial at this point to decide when to begin to talk to the person about what is happening to them and support them to make informed choices where possible, and in accordance with their capacity to consent.

Current advances in medicine and improvements in diet and living conditions mean that people with intellectual disabilities, just like everyone else, are living longer. This brings new considerations for professionals and services working to support them. These present a number of challenges both to service providers and to our wider society. Although demographically forecast for over a decade, it is only very recently that the needs of an ageing population of people with intellectual disabilities have begun to be recognized (Hogg and Lambe, 1998; Mental Health Foundation, 1996). Because of the possibility of their lifelong dependence on carers, there is a risk that people with intellectual disabilities will be regarded as perpetual children even into old age. This may also be seen as defensive – a way of not recognizing their complicated adult needs for sexual and other relationships and for independence. However, the tendency to infantilize people with intellectual disabilities also contributes to a difficulty in responding appropriately and sensitively to their needs as they age. As referenced in other chapters, Hollins's concept of the 'Three Secrets' (Hollins and Sinason, 2000) identifies sexuality, dependency and death as core issues underlying the experience of intellectual disability. People with intellectual disabilities that have specific needs relating to their ageing and death challenge these secrets (or taboos) in the minds of those who must plan for and deliver their care. In addition, Todd (2002) discusses the 'social death' to which society has historically condemned people with intellectual disabilities, by exiling them to live in institutions. Todd notes how hard it is for staff today in intellectual disability community residential settings to consider supporting people through terminal illness.

To think about death and ending may seem incongruous with the focus that service provision has more recently placed on issues of empowerment. Staff may often have fought hard to support the person with an intellectual disability to live a full and active life. Recognizing the imminent end of that life may, for carers as for so many of us, be something they would prefer not to think about. However, many homes for people with intellectual disabilities are described as 'homes for life'. If this is to be a practical reality then services must also address how the homes will meet the needs of people with intellectual disabilities who are coming to the end of their lives.

Older people with intellectual disabilities are not a homogeneous group. While some may have spent many years of their lives in institutions and have had little or no contact with family members for many years, others will have lived sheltered and isolated lives in families. Such families may have chosen to ignore medical advice to surrender their disabled child to an institution and pretend that they had never been born, and subsequently soldiered on, suspicious and mistrustful of services. Because these families have avoided contact with services it is difficult to know exactly how many older people with intellectual disabilities there are living with family members. However, the Department of Health Paper 'Valuing People' (2001) estimates that at least 25 per cent of people living with family carers over the age of 70 are not in contact with services. These families are thought to be suspicious of help, some not even accessing the GP for their disabled adult child except in extreme emergencies. They are often accustomed to managing without any support, such as respite care, and are often wary of attempts by professionals to offer their services or advice. (Wandsworth Rathbone, 2002) Before improved life expectancy, families might have reasonably assumed that their disabled child would pre-decease them. As a result, they may not have made plans for their child's long-term future. It may also be the case that the prospect of life for their child without their care is simply too terrible to contemplate (for more exploration of this see Chapter 5). Services, at their best, may now work in alliance with families to ensure maximum independence for people with intellectual disabilities by, for example, supporting moves to more independent accommodation and residential care at age-appropriate times. However, for older families, this more enlightened thinking may have come too late. In addition, it may have been parental fears that their disabled children would be abused and neglected in residential care that have caused them to seek to provide care at home for as long as possible, and beyond the time at which it may in the best interests of their adult child. Sadly, reports such as the very recent Health Care Commission reports from Cornwall and Surrey (2006, 2007) may reinforce these fears. As stated in the GOLD report on research carried out by the Foundation for People with Intellectual Disabilities (2002), 'In order to plan for the future, families need to have the emotional space to deal with the uncertainty which the future will inevitably present' (Walker and Magrill, 2002, p. 57).

This 'emotional space' is something that the Respond Elders Project aims to provide, although we first have the task of ensuring that such families know of the existence of the project and, crucially, feel that it is a service that they can trust. One of the first steps that the Elders Project has taken towards this was to set up a partnership with another intellectual disability charity and two charities for older people. Together, we are in the process of producing a leaflet signposting people to the four charities. This will be distributed to GPs, district nurses, pharmacists and any other professionals who encounter older families in their daily work. It is hoped that this first step may encourage families to begin to talk to others, thereby taking the first steps towards creating a space to think and plan.

It is our experience that the dynamics between older parents, their adult son/daughter who has intellectual disabilities, and siblings can often be complex. The nature of managing for decades in often very difficult situations and in isolation can lead to intricate co-dependent relationships. In these families, attachments may have become deeply ambivalent or enmeshed (Bowlby, 1979). From very early, parents may have given their child the unconscious message that they will not survive unless they stay very close to the parents because others around them do not really care. This may leave the child with very confused feelings about extrafamilial relationships and they may become clingy and demanding. This can also create difficulties in sibling relationships, where brothers and sisters may become part of the overprotective pattern or, alternatively, feel excluded and resentful.

It is also the case that in some families, as parents become older and more frail, the caring roles become reversed and the disabled adult may become the carer for the elderly parents or siblings

(Walker *et al.*, 1996; Magrill *et al.*, 1997). This position of carers may not have been explicitly recognized or acknowledged by families or by services. Situations such as these can cause additional emotional complications for the person with intellectual disabilities when their relative becomes too frail to be cared for at home or, indeed, when they die (Blackman, 2003).

The GOLD research project (Foundation for People with Learning Disabilities Report, 2002) also highlighted that, within these older families, there was interdependence in many areas of family life, including physical care, domestic responsibilities such as cooking and cleaning, financial affairs and emotional support. The research states that 'both parties [are] providing each other with companionship and love which can make the prospect of "letting go" very difficult for some older carers' (p. 42).

As other chapters in this book (for example, Chapters 1, 5 and 10) have explored, notwithstanding contemporary changes in service provision and the current emphasis on inclusion and empowerment, there remain unconscious attitudes of hate and fear that may, in reality, lead to the exclusion and isolation of people with intellectual disabilities from mainstream society and lead to their complex emotional needs being neither recognized nor met. We also know that older people may be marginalized in a society that prizes youth, beauty and economic productivity. Thus, an older intellectually disabled person may face double discrimination, and feel doubly excluded from society.

We know that as people get older their health is likely to worsen and that, eventually, a high proportion of the older population will contract a terminal illness, such as respiratory disease or cancer. This likelihood increases with longevity. People with illnesses that have a long dying phase should, ideally, be offered palliative care. This is defined as 'The active total care of patients whose disease is not responsive to curative treatment. Control of pain, of other symptoms, and of psychological, social and spiritual problems is paramount. The goal of palliative care is achievement of the best quality of life for patients and their families' (WHO website, 2007). However, it is known that palliative care is not often accessed by older people in care settings (Addington-Hall and Higginson, 2001) or people with intellectual disabilities (Hogg *et al.*, 2001).

Case study: Stuart

I was asked to support Stuart, a man with intellectual disabilities in his late thirties, who was in the terminal phase of cancer. The staff team had not talked to Stuart about the fact that he was dying; although they felt that he might want to talk about it, they had felt unable to broach the subject themselves.

As a therapist, beginning work with a new client, I was struck by the strangeness and difficulty of my situation: I was to meet Stuart and straight away begin to talk about his death. I arrived at his house, anxious and unsure about what physical state he would be in. I was greeted at the door by a very thin but sociable and lively man. He had been told that I was coming to talk with him and very soon we were left on our own in the living room. I explained that the staff had told me that he was very poorly at the moment and that they thought that there might be some things that were worrying him and that if there were he could talk to me about them. Before long he was telling me that he thought that he would be going to heaven soon but that he was very worried about this. I asked what in particular was worrying him and he told me that he was worried that he might meet his Mum and Dad in heaven. After exploring this with him a little bit more, I discovered that his parents had been very strict and punitive with him when they were alive. They had now been dead for some time, and Stuart was worried that he was going to meet them once again in heaven. Together, we explored his concept of heaven, and it turned out not to be too different from earth. I explained that if it was such a large place there would be plenty of room for him to be there without having to be near his parents. This seemed to alleviate his anxiety and, in fact, not long after our meeting, Stuart died very peacefully. I had been very impressed by Stuart's awareness of his imminent death and his clarity in facing it, despite the fact that no-one involved in his care had dared to talk to him about it. I reflected on how hard it must have been for him to have been alone with his knowledge. Stuart, like many people with intellectual disabilities, had a fine emotional intelligence and had been attuned to the severity of his illness, although the details of it had not been formally disclosed.

Another important health issue for older people is dementia. Stuart-Hamilton (2006) states that 1 per cent of 60-year-olds will show symptoms of dementing and that this percentage doubles with every five years of life beyond the age of 60. Thus, the longer a person lives, the greater is the likelihood of their developing dementia. People with Down's syndrome are prone to early onset dementia, with symptoms presenting from age 50, and sometimes even younger. (Holland *et al.*, 1998). This is thought to be due to the presence of an extra 'X' chromosome, which is the cause of the syndrome. Historically, it has been extremely difficult within mainstream palliative care to access services for people with dementia, with or without intellectual disabilities. GPs and some professionals may still not be aware that Down's syndrome is linked to early onset dementia and diagnosis may be a more difficult process because the symptoms may be different from those in the general population (and so requiring specific training to identify) and may also be confused with the intellectual disability itself.

It is well documented that for people with intellectual disabilities many illnesses are diagnosed later than for the general population (Disability Rights Commision, 2006; Mencap, 2004, 2007; Tuffrey-Wijne and Davies, 2007) This means that by the time diagnosis is made, fewer treatment options are available to the patient with intellectual disabilities. The reasons for late diagnosis are various and complex. Intellectually disabled people may have poor access to screening services, suffer poor primary health care in the community due to gaps in the training of health and disability professionals and have greater difficulty than others in communicating their symptoms in ways that can be readily understood.

The Elders Project recently took a call from a member of staff who was supporting a woman with Down's syndrome who had recently become very anxious about walking, particularly using stairs or stepping off the pavement. The staff had thought that perhaps she was developing arthritis, but after a brief examination the GP could find nothing wrong. However, the staff, with their knowledge of the woman's character, continued to be concerned. A helpline adviser recommended that they request a test for Alzheimer's (an early sign of which is to be unsteady, and to experience difficulty in judging the transition from one place to another). The test was done, and Alzheimer's confirmed.

Underlying the fact that health care for people with intellectual disabilities is not equitable, there may, again, be unstated attitudes concerning assumptions about quality of life, the relative value of the lives of those who have intellectual disabilities, and the capacity to consent to treatment (Mencap, 2007). Wolfsenberger (1983) wrote of a 'deathmaking' culture surrounding those with intellectual disability and we may see this in force in the field of medical ethics and decision-making. Such assumptions may result in people with intellectual disabilities not getting the range of options regarding treatment that others do.

In accordance with 'ordinary life' principles of care, many people with intellectual disabilities are now living in small houses in which access may become difficult as mobility diminishes. In addition, staff may have been inadequately trained or prepared for meeting the needs of residents with intellectual disabilities as they get older. As a result, people may have to move at short notice and in a state of crisis, when an emergency occurs. In moving on, they may lose touch with people whom they care for and who care for them, and find themselves living somewhere where they are not known and neither is their life history. If a person with a intellectual disability lives in a generic older people's home they again may find that the staff there lack specific understanding of their condition and find themselves marginalized in what is already a marginalized service. Many older people with intellectual disabilities have no family to advocate for them and may need support in order to maintain relationships with any family or friends that they have. It is well known that close relationships are important for people's psychological well-being. As people age, and either their family members become too frail to continue to visit or they die, it is important that support services work hard to ensure that clients do not become confused and isolated. It is often difficult for people to remember their own history and they may have little access to prompts such as photos and mementoes. The intellectual disability may make it difficult to remember things or to carry a sense of timescale or order. It is therefore extremely important for services and professionals to encourage reminiscence and life story with people who are important to them. In addition to the challenges that people with intellectual disabilities may face in getting their health needs met as they get older and face their own mortality, it is also the case that they may struggle to have their emotional needs taken seriously. This is where psychotherapy has an important role to play.

Case study: Edward

Edward was in his late sixties when he was referred for psychotherapy. His behaviour had changed and he was becoming uncharacteristically angry with staff and residents. Previously a sociable man, he began to spend increasing amounts of time alone in his bedroom. Edward had moved out of his family home in his early forties, shortly after his father had died. He still maintained close contact with his mother and until shortly before the time he was referred, he would go home to stay with her every weekend. His mother was in her late eighties and was beginning to become very frail, having recently had to spend some time in hospital. Staff knew that it was unlikely that she would remain in the family home for much longer, and plans were under way for her to move into a service for older people. These changes in his mother's health meant that Edward saw far less of her and rarely went home any more. Edward had worked for 20 years as a cleaner in a small factory and the deterioration of his mother's health coincided with him being retired, against his wishes, from his job.

When I first met Edward I was struck by how well dressed, how formal and how polite he was. Following an assessment, he said he was keen to come back and see me again and we began to meet each week for 50-minute psychotherapy sessions.

On entering the therapy room each week, Edward would ask me questions about the age of pieces of furniture in the room: 'How old is that?' he would say, pointing to the small table. I asked how old he thought it was, and what that might mean. Edward always said that he thought the furniture was 'very old' and also that it was 'past it' and should be thrown away and replaced with a new piece. I asked him if he thought that his work had thought the same about him. 'In a way', he said. Although he clearly found it painful to think about, Edward also appeared to experience some relief in voicing his feelings, albeit through the analogy of worn-out and rejected furniture. I felt also that Edward was talking about his mother and her increasing age and frailty. She too was becoming more 'useless' to him as she became less able to care for him and take an interest in his life. We talked about this and his sadness at no longer being able to go to his family home and do things the way he had done them all his life. However, Edward was lucky that before his mother had become ill she had put together several photo albums of different periods of Edward's life. They were full of pictures of different family members at times of holidays, reunions and celebration. She had labelled them clearly and Edward and I were able to use them to reminisce with. Edward talked a lot about his father, who had died a long time before but for whom he had never really grieved. It became clear that Edward was very aware that his mother was approaching the end of her life although no one was really talking to him about it.

In sessions, Edward complained a lot about various aches and pains, particularly the arthritis in his hands. He would often blame these on other residents who he said were always 'playing up'. However, it gradually emerged that he was aware of his own ageing and impending mortality. He was noticing all too clearly that his body was not working as well as it used to. He expressed the fear that when his mother died there would be no-one to remember him when he died, and no-one to attend his funeral or to tend his grave. I encouraged him to talk about whom he was important to and in what ways he would be remembered and missed when he was no longer alive. He had a lot of nieces and nephews who were clearly fond of him and also friends from college, from the house he lived in and also his church. Edward's anxiety began to dissipate and his behaviour calmed down. I also engaged Edward's support staff in the therapy process indirectly. I supported them to recognize the importance of giving Edward the opportunity to talk about the things that he was facing at this time in his life. Up to this point, they had felt anxious about raising difficult issues with him in case they upset him. They had been unaware that he was thinking about these issues himself anyway but in a very lonely and unsupported way.

The bereavement needs of people with intellectual disabilities have, in our experience, often gone unacknowledged and unsupported. This is particularly the case when people move in crisis from the family home when a parent dies (Oswin, 1991; Blackman, 2003). This type of bereavement is particularly complicated as there are often multiple losses – of the family home, the role within the family, the local neighbourhood and the familiar routines and family ways. They may now suddenly find themselves in a situation where they are surrounded by people who have not known them before the death and know nothing about them or their life history. It is hard for any of us to have to make a new life and to tell our story to people whom we don't know at a time of significant emotional upheaval. For a person with an intellectual disability it will be harder still – perhaps impossible.

Edward was fortunate that his mother was still able to take an active part in his life after his father's death and that although he had to move out of the family home, he still visited it regularly. However, he had not, until receiving therapy, been able to grieve for his father, and I came to understand through my work with him that he had been afraid of upsetting his mother. He behaved in ways that accorded with her own pattern of grief, which was to bury her feelings of distress and loss. Edward was able to reveal his sadness only in the presence of a trusted therapist whom he did not feel he needed to 'protect' from the extent of his feelings of loss.

Case study: Mary

Mary, a woman with mild intellectual disabilities, was referred for psychotherapy while in her late thirties. While in his early twenties, her older brother had been killed in a tragic accident. He had not had an intellectual disability and was a graduate on the cusp of a promising career. Mary's family had been devastated by his death. The following year Mary's father had died suddenly, and Mary and her mother spent the next ten years locked in terrible grief together. The grief was complicated by Mary's belief, unspoken until she came to therapy, that it should have been her that had died as she was the one that was damaged, rather than her brother who had been poised to lead a 'successful' and 'useful' life. She felt acutely guilty and that she was a burden, who had nothing valuable to contribute to her family life or to society.

It had been additionally difficult for Mary to access emotional support for herself because her mother had refused any offers of bereavement support. This left Mary feeling guilty if she experienced things differently from her mother. Even coming to therapy represented a significant and potentially destabilizing challenge to their relationship. It was not until Mary's mother died that Mary was supported to grieve for her and also to express some of her anger about her mother's inability to deal with her own grief. Through therapy, Mary was able to move on in her journey to accept the pain of the multiple losses she had experienced and their effects on the course of her life and her sense of self.

This chapter has focused on the many emotional challenges that growing older may present to people with intellectual disabilities. There has been discussion about the different life experiences people may have had, such as growing up in institutions or within families and in a society hostile to their very existence. Many older people with intellectual disabilities will have experienced traumatic separations and losses and, on top of these, now face the normal challenges of ageing. As they experience current bereavements or face the end of their own lives, it is important that the emotional difficulties and unhappiness associated with these multiple losses be recognized. It may be that support services can be helped, through training and supervision, to respond to the particular needs of their elderly service users. In some cases psychotherapy is indicated, particularly if a person has become anxious or depressed as a result of unrecognized fears, or unmourned losses from the past.

The Elders Project has demonstrated that it is possible to provide a service that can respond to the complex and multilayered needs of older people with intellectual disabilities.

References

Addington-Hall, J. and Higginson, I. (2001) *Palliative Care for Non-Cancer Patients*. Oxford, UK: Oxford University Press.

Blackman, N. (2003) *Loss and Learning Disability*. London: Worth Publishing.

Bowlby, J. (1979) *The Making and Breaking of Affectional Bonds*. London: Tavistock.

Disability Rights Commission (2006) *Mind the Gap*. Stratford-upon-Avon, UK: DRC.

Foundation for People with Learning Disabilities Report (2002) *Today and Tomorrow: The Report of the Growing Older with Learning Disabilities Programme*. London: Mental Health Foundation.

Health Care Commission (2006) *Investigation into services for people with learning disabilities at Cornwall Partnership NHS Trust*. London: HCC.

Health Care Commission (2007) *Investigation into services for people with learning disabilities at Sutton & Merton Primary Care Trust*. London: HCC.

Hogg, J. and Lambe, L. (1998) *Older People with Learning Disabilities: A Review of the Literature on Residential Services and Family Caregiving*. London: Foundation for People with Learning Disabilities.

Hogg, J., Northfield, J. and Turnbull, J. (2001) *Cancer and people with learning disabilities: Part 1: The evidence from published studies; Part 2: Experiences from cancer services*. Kidderminster: British Institute of Learning Disabilities (report prepared for the Department of Health, England).

Holland, A. J., Hon, J., Huppert, F. A., Stevens, F. and Watson, P. (1998) Population based study of the prevalence and presentation of dementia in adults with Down's syndrome. *British Journal of Psychiatry 172*, 493–498.

Hollins, S. and Sinason, V. (2000) Psychotherapy, learning disabilities and trauma: New perspectives. *British Journal of Psychiatry 176*, 32–36.

Magrill, D., Handley, P., Gleeson, S., Charles, D. and Sharing Caring Project Steering Group (1997) *Crisis approaching: The situation facing Sheffield's elderly carers of people with learning disabilities*. Sheffield: Sharing Caring Project.

Magrill, D. (2005) *Supporting Older Families: Making a Real Difference*. London: Foundation for People with Learning Disabilities.

Mencap Report (2004) *Treat Me Right*. London: Mencap.

Mencap Report (2007) *Death by Indifference*. London: Mencap.

Mental Health Foundation (1996) *Building expectations: Opportunities and services for people with a Learning Disability*. London: MHF.

Oswin, M. (1991) *Am I Allowed To Cry? A Study of Bereavement Among People Who Have Learning Disabilities*. London: Souvenir.

McGinnity, M. and Banks, R. (2002) *Royal College of Psychiatrists' Working Group Report*. Poster presented at IASSID European Congress, Dublin, Ireland.

Sinason, V. (1992) *Mental Handicap and the Human Condition: New Approaches from the Tavistock*. London: Free Association Books.

Stuart-Hamilton, S. (2006) *The Psychology of Ageing: An Introduction* (4th ed.). London: Jessica Kingsley.

Todd, S. (2002) Death does not become us: The absence of death and dying in intellectual disability research. *Journal of Gerontology Social Work*, Nos 1 and 2, 225–239.

Tuffrey-Wijne, I. and Davies, J. (2007) This is my story: I've got cancer. 'The Veronica Project': An ethnographic study of the experience of people with learning disabilities who have cancer. *British Journal of Learning Disabilities 35*(1), 7–11.

Valuing People (2001) *A New Strategy for Learning Disability for the 21st Century*. London: Department of Health.

Van-Etten, D. (2006) Psychotherapy with older adults: Benefits and barriers. *Journal of Psychosocial Nursing and Mental Health Services 44*(11), 28–33.

Walker, C., Ryan, T. and Walker, A. (1996) *Fair Shares for All: Disparities in Service Provision for Different Groups of People with Learning Difficulties Living in the Community*. Brighton, UK and York, UK: Pavilion Publishing and Joseph Rowntree Foundation.

Walker, C. and Walker, A. (1998) *Uncertain Futures: People with Learning Difficulties and their Ageing Family Carers*. Brighton, UK and York, UK: Pavilion Publishing and Joseph Rowntree Foundation.

Wandsworth Rathbone (2002) Looking Forward Survey. In *'Today and Tomorrow' – The Report of the Growing Older with Learning Disabilities Programme*. London: Foundation for People with Learning Disabilities.

Wolfsensberger, W. (1983) *The Principle of Normalisation in Human Services*. Toronto, Canada: National Institute on Mental Retardation.

World Health Organisation (WHO) website – www.who.int.

Chapter 10

In one ear

The practice and process of telephone counselling

Debbee Arthur, Winnie McNeil and
Samantha Russell Small

Helplines are often viewed as points to access advice or information rather than sources of therapeutic input. However, the first official helpline call was made on 2 November 1953 to a young vicar, Edward Chad Varah. After he had officiated at the service of a 14-year-old girl who had taken her own life he was inspired by the coroner's comment that the tragedy might have been averted if the girl had had somebody to talk to, so he set up a telephone service from his church in London. He took 27 calls in the first week. Since those initial calls, the number of helplines and the variety of services offered by them has mushroomed, with the Telephone Helplines Association directory listing nearly 1,300 helplines throughout the UK. This is perhaps unsurprising given the advantages of accessibility, availability and anonymity that a helpline confers. The phone can also be less intrusive than face-to-face work and the caller has control, allowing them to disclose issues at a time and pace comfortable for them. This chapter will explore the work of a helpline that is specific and unique in that it was established to provide help in the particular area of sexual trauma and intellectual disability, with a brief to provide direct support to people with intellectual disabilities – a group that traditionally have found it difficult to access help for themselves.

The Respond Helpline was established in 1999 as a response to the significant number of calls the organization was receiving from people whose lives had been affected by abuse, whether the victim themselves, their families or carers and professionals. It was recognized that a helpline could support people on a national basis. The percentage of callers with intellectual disabilities has grown from under 10 per cent in the first year of its existence to over 50 per cent in 2006. A Freephone number was introduced as soon as possible in order that the helpline could offer this support without any charge to the caller. This is particularly important to people with intellectual disabilities, who often have limited incomes.

Much of the work of the helpline consists of providing an immediate response to a specific question. Information is given and callers may be signposted to other agencies. We also respond to enquiries via letters and e-mails and have recently introduced a text service. However, whatever our task, we are always drawing on the core skills of listening, clarifying, and responding in order to provide the central conditions of a counselling relationship. We may have to do this in a single conversation which lasts, typically, only 30 minutes. All our interventions are underpinned by our efforts to provide the unconditional positive regard, empathy and congruence which are associated most closely with a Rogerian, person-centred approach.

Unconditional positive regard, also known as acceptance, is allied to being non-judgemental but is essentially more active. This is particularly important to convey to people with intellectual disabilities, who have very often been stigmatized, bullied and deprived of knowledge, particularly in the areas of emotional stress identified as: the disability itself, loss, dependency needs, sexuality and the fear of being murdered (Hollins and Sinason, 2000). It is our experience that these are central issues in our work and are frequently a theme of helpline interventions.

Barrett-Lennard (1981) proposed the idea of an 'empathy cycle'. This involves the counsellor actively attending to, and being receptive of, what the client is expressing. The counsellor resonates internally with some aspect, or aspects, of the client's experience. Then, at a suitable point, and often tentatively to begin with, the counsellor communicates their awareness to the client. The client who can hear this has a sense that another person has at least partially grasped what they are going through, however painful, terrifying or mysterious it has been to them.

Another aspect of the empathy cycle is to clarify which aspects of the experiences and feelings are particularly troubling at this point. A client who is disclosing sexual abuse may be tormented by the content of their memories, and flooded with traumatic affects. Much later, they may have more conscious feelings such as anger at the failure of another family member to protect them, or guilt that they had experienced sexual pleasure during the abuse, or that they still feel love for their abuser.

The helpline counsellor knows that listening can in itself be healing, as reflected in the comment made by a client, 'Thank you for listening to me, everyone else thinks I'm a nuisance'. Like a practitioner working face to face, however, they have to be sensitive to the unconscious dynamics of therapeutic interventions. A call may be a 'cry for help' – over-dramatized by a client who craves attention and feels they have to make their story 'exciting' to retain the listener's interest. Or the counsellor may find themselves feeling that they are being asked to collude in perverse acts, for example when it becomes apparent that a caller is masturbating or self-harming while talking to the helpline. The telephone counsellor attempts to connect with the distress that may be hidden within the caller. Even the 'hoax caller', so unloved by helplines, can sometimes be reached. One young man called our helpline several times alleging that he was the victim of serious sexual abuse. Due to the extremely repetitive nature of his accounts, and an absence of the affect that we expect to hear in callers' accounts, we suspected that his calls were hoax calls. Eventually he was challenged by a counsellor who suggested that he was struggling with his sexuality and sexual fantasies and empathized with him that his feelings were overwhelming him. He agreed, and expressed relief that he was being understood. His calls then ceased.

One of the integral aspects of a helpline is that of caller anonymity, and this is particularly relevant to a caller who may be disclosing, possibly for the first time, abuse they have suffered – or indeed, abusive thoughts and feelings they may be experiencing themselves. However, anonymity also can bring its own dilemmas when as counsellors we feel that someone may be at risk. Our confidentiality policy directs us to explain to callers that any information they give us will be contained within the organization unless we feel there is a grave risk to an individual. However, as explained later in a case study, we may feel someone is at risk and yet are unable to act on that information as the caller has chosen to remain anonymous. The counsellor can then be left with a feeling of impotence and frustration at not being able to protect a vulnerable caller. Another aspect of contacting a helpline that resonates with our particular client group is the fact that it is the caller who has control of the process. The caller makes the choice to contact us: they can go at their own pace and are able to end the call whenever they wish. As a demographic group it is recognized that people with intellectual disabilities lack control over many aspects of their lives, and it is usually the services they receive that hold the power within the relationship. However, when contacting a helpline the caller is the one with the control and that in itself can be an empowering experience. It is not unusual for a caller to angrily end a call when they are struggling with containing difficult feelings and to blame the counsellor for making them feel that way, only to call back after they have reflected on the conversation and ask to continue the dialogue, and therefore to choose to maintain the relationship.

Longer-term telephone counselling

In addition to regular 'opening hours' during which a variety of unpredictable calls may be received, many of which will be 'one-off' contacts, the helpline also provides counselling, at prearranged times, to a number of regular callers. These are callers who have previously phoned the helpline over a number of weeks and have undergone an assessment by the helpline team. If it is felt that the caller would benefit from an opportunity for more input, and will be able to make use of the therapeutic space provided by consistent telephone support, then the caller is offered a regular slot. This is similar to face-to-face therapy in the sense that the therapist and client agree on a contract that is then adhered to. An arrangement is made for the client to call at the same time each week and the length of the call is stipulated (usually 40 minutes). As such, this ongoing work is subject to many of the same pressures and dynamics of face-to-face work. Clients may 'act out' and try to sabotage the therapeutic boundaries that are in place. The boundaries are of paramount importance and are central to all psychodynamic practice. However, as the following case studies show, with this client group, they also need to be flexible and, at times, revisited and redrawn. They have to be clearly agreed upon and, if necessary, reassessed.

Case study: Becky

Becky is a 24-year-old female, who has moderate intellectual disabilities. She lives independently but receives daily input from social services for both living and social skills. Becky's abuse started early. She was neglected at home, and recalls being allowed to have a bath only if her mother was 'being nice'. Her clothes were always dirty, her nappies were not changed for hours on end and Becky also remembers not having food on a regular basis. She was known to social services from the age of three, yet remained in her mother's care despite being chronically sexually abused by her brother and a family friend. When she was 12 years old, Becky's brother was released from prison. She says, while blaming herself for the further abuse, 'I knew what my brother did to me was wrong, but Mum knew and she didn't stop it'. This incestuous abuse eventually ended when Becky was admitted to hospital. She had been attacked internally with a knife. After this incident Becky was removed from her mother's care and put in a residential home. Due to her past experiences Becky found it difficult to adjust. She recalls running away on several occasions, she would often get into cars with strangers, where she would be assaulted again.

Before Becky called us she was receiving help from a therapist. However, Becky told us she could not engage with her, saying, 'She wants me to tell her everything. It's like going through it all over again.' During this time, to cope with her pain, Becky had been taking potentially lethal overdoses three or four times a week. Becky stopped seeing her therapist after an incident that she described thus: 'She pushed me too far – so I hit her'. Shortly afterwards Becky began to call the helpline.

From this story we knew we had to let Becky control what she told us and when. We also, initially, took her calls as and when she made them. Person-centred telephone contact allowed Becky to 'set the pace' of the help she received and for her, this was essential to the process as it allowed her to feel safe. This view has been confirmed by the fact that Becky chooses to write to her counsellor when she has particularly painful memories to share, rather than verbalize them on the phone. Again, she is the one choosing what material to share and how to communicate it.

At first, Becky's ability to contain the number of times she called the helpline spiralled out of control. Initially she stuck to our rule of 'one 30-minute call a day' but after a few weeks she started to call as many as 12 or 15 times a day. In addition, there were many silent calls that we also believed to be from her. We felt that Becky needed the holding and containment that contracted counselling could provide. Some callers are scared of this provision, as their previous experiences of broken attachments have often left them believing that no-one is able to maintain a relationship with them. However, Becky was able to grasp the positive aspects of building a trusting relationship and told us that she thought she could work well in these sessions. We agreed to two sessions a week for 40 minutes a session. We recognized that asking her to reduce this to just one session a week was unrealistic; Becky was not able to control her need to talk to us. Her ego was simply not strong enough to contain the unbearable thoughts and memories she held within herself.

For the first couple of weeks Becky was unable to stick to the contract. She would call a couple of times a day and we were careful to remind her of what we had agreed and to avoid getting drawn into a conversation with her. In her contracted sessions, which she never missed, we talked about the contract. She was adamant that she wanted to stick to it: 'You've worked me out, haven't you?' she said; 'You know that I'll try anything to push the boundaries, but you're good, you won't let me and that's what I need'.

In her abusive childhood Becky had not been able to develop firm boundaries between herself and others: the people she trusted and should have formed positive attachments to had always violated her boundaries, often in the form of sexual abuse. We had demonstrated a therapeutic robustness that, at an individual and an organizational level, could contain her chaotic inner world. Of course she retained control over the contracted sessions, and could choose if to call and when to end the contact. It was our observation that this simple power also helped Becky regain some control over her life. This was demonstrated in various ways, perhaps the most profound being the reduction in number of suicide attempts (she didn't take an overdose for many weeks). Also, Becky was able to enrol in college. This was something she had tried to do for many years, yet always sabotaged at the last minute.

Becky was able to stick to the contractual agreement for nearly two months and during this time she took only one overdose. Becky then had a setback when she attended a multidisciplinary meeting that intended to plan the next stage in her life with her full involvement. She left the meeting furious, stating, 'They're all arseholes, they don't care about me'.

In the following days she reported nightmares where she found herself naked in the middle of a boardroom. She felt stupid and wanted to hide, but she realized that there was no need as no-one looked at her; they either couldn't see her or chose not to. In this meeting she felt that the very people she trusted and believed cared about her had failed to acknowledge her independence and need to make her own decisions about her life and was left feeling suicidal, so she self-harmed by taking overdoses and cutting herself. During this period Becky renegotiated so that, during this time of crisis, she would speak to her counsellor three times a week. We felt this was in her best interests and that sticking rigidly to the pre-arranged boundaries would be detrimental to Becky. She seemed to respond well to this and stuck to the new contract for a further three months. In addition, she took no further overdoses.

In our experience, transference and countertransference are as significant in phone work as in face-to-face counselling. During the months that Becky used the phone counselling services the counsellor was able to discern changes in the transference. She first viewed her therapist as a magical figure that could make everything better. She would ask her counsellor to 'wave your magic wand and make it all go away' – not dissimilar to a young child who believes their parents can fix all their problems. As the relationship developed these feelings changed, and a significant point was when Becky told the counsellor she was stuck in a dark 'cave'. The initial reaction of the counsellor was to say, 'Perhaps I can help you out of the cave.' Becky replied that there was nothing anyone could do to help her out – she felt she was stuck in the cave; unreachable. Then the counsellor asked if she would like her to join her in the cave. Becky readily agreed. The transference appeared to shift to her feeling as though the counsellor was more sister than mother: a person to whom she could tell her deepest worries who wouldn't judge or tell her off; someone who could bear to be with her without needing to rescue her. Indeed, it can be argued from this example that the lack of visual cues and clues when working on the telephone can actually enhance the transference relationship (Rosenfield, 1997). We find transference (in its many forms) an essential tool in our work with clients. When Becky explained her nightmares of how invisible she felt, it was her counsellor who felt worthless and insignificant. Through being aware of these feelings the counsellor could then reflect this back to Becky. This can be explained as projective identification, when 'the therapist feels what the ego of the patient feels' (Symington, 1986, p. 260). The pain is thought to be too great for the patient's ego to bear, so it is projected into the therapist for them to hold. Our experience of telephone counselling is that this occurs as often and with as much impact as face-to-face therapy.

A few months later, Becky discovered that she was pregnant. This was the result of an inappropriate relationship with her carer and precipitated a significant crisis for Becky, who due to her suicide attempts was sectioned for her own safety. This crisis was mirrored by her counsellor who felt distraught that this had happened; all their joint hard work had so quickly been undone. The counsellor also felt guilty that she hadn't realized that the 'boyfriend' Becky had spoken of had actually been the same person she referred to as her carer. It remains the case that at times we need to think carefully about the narrative accounts offered by clients. They may not always reflect the lived reality, and, because of the nature of telephone work, we may lack the means to establish their veracity.

Throughout her time in hospital Becky continued to call at the correct time for each of her sessions. The countertransference shifted again. The counsellor felt very maternal towards Becky. This was not only a time that she needed protecting, but also one in which she needed to understand how to be a mother. For Becky this was especially painful and difficult as she had no effective role model. Becky was able to express powerful emotions as she talked to her counsellor about her early experiences with her mother. She felt angry towards her mother yet still yearned for affirmation from her. Becky talked also of her hopes that she would be able to care for her own baby. As Becky moved towards the birth of her baby, she moved into a new house, with additional support. She took no further overdoses and continued to call the helpline for her sessions.

Our work with Becky lasted for over 12 months. We are in the position of being able to offer support to our callers over long periods of time, if necessary. Thus the client may experience upheavals and crises, yet the helpline remains a consistent presence in their lives. They can access it as and when they feel they need to. In the context of lives that are characterized by frequent disruption and high turnover of carers, this can be valuable in itself and an attachment, or 'organizational transference', can form to the helpline as a whole.

Case study: Amy

Multiple traumas and losses are a characteristic of the histories of many people with intellectual difficulties. Like a number of helpline callers, Amy brings with her a very troubled past and many complex and challenging behaviours that we have to try to respond to over the phone, often with little or no contact with other members of her support network. Amy is a white working-class female in her early twenties who has mild intellectual disabilities. She has been calling the helpline for several years, and has had three different counsellors in that time. She did not show any obvious signs of protest or distress when she was first asked to speak to a different counsellor, which suggests that she hadn't established a particular attachment to the existing one. However, it was obvious that she relied quite heavily on her sessions and seemed to appreciate her counsellor's input. It seemed that this caller's transference relationship was indeed with the helpline as a whole, but it also indicated her history of disrupted attachment and how moving on from one person to the next was what she had come to expect in her life. Amy had been in temporary hostel accommodation, and prison, and had lost her flat in the community. Her parents are divorced but she remains in regular contact with both of them. Her relationships with her mother and her sister are full of conflict and ambivalence.

Like many of our clients, Amy has the template of both victim and perpetrator on her psyche. The helpline works with perpetrators as well as victims, believing along with our colleagues in Respond that we need to address both aspects and not split off one part of the work by working only with the 'good' victim and neglecting the 'bad' abuser. There is also recognition that many abusers have been victims themselves, especially as our callers are from a group that is particularly vulnerable to abuse of all kinds.

Amy was raped when she was 15 by three youths who were known to her. She had also been severely bullied within her home community. She was recently convicted of arson and was held in a medium secure unit for people who have a dual diagnosis of intellectual disability and mental illness. Amy had a serious drinking problem when in the community, but in a residential setting this was not an issue. She has never been in paid employment and feels she was a failure at school. Amy has had ongoing physical health problems and, in line with the findings of the Disability Rights Commission (2006), she has, like others, found it difficult to access the specialist medical help she requires.

A close relative of Amy's was murdered in horrific circumstances and much of our work with Amy has focused on her grief over this traumatic loss. Amy is alternately in denial of her grief and its impact on her and protesting about how this incident has affected her emotionally, saying that it is what is responsible for all her acting-out behaviours. Amy also projected her own feelings of vulnerability and need onto others, especially her mother and her cousins. She then concentrated on trying to look after them, instead of herself.

We were quite challenging with Amy – asking her to look at what led her to start fires. She found this very difficult and resisted accepting the serious consequences of this behaviour – how her life and those of others were put at risk and how it led to her imprisonment and the loss of her home. Such a refusal to face what she had done generated feelings of frustration, sadness and anger in the counsellor. It was helpful to see these as a communication of how Amy herself was feeling. Amy was also able to express anger about the fact that she had felt alternately overprotected and babied by her family because of her label of intellectual disability, and then had not been protected sufficiently by them from severe bullying.

The work with Amy could feel slow at times, and her inclination to deny the reality of her actions was hard for the counsellor to tolerate. However, it is our view that, through the telephone counselling, Amy experienced some containment and some emotional support with her overwhelming grief. She expressed her appreciation of the support she received from the helpline, particularly when we were able to act as advocates and encourage her social worker to put more support in place to help prevent the bullying that Amy was experiencing.

Case study: Ben

Helplessness as a feature of the work was also experienced in our work with Ben. Ben called the helpline at the behest of his father, who, along with his mother, was becoming increasingly distressed by his sexual behaviour. He had told us in his initial call that Ben was masturbating inappropriately, particularly in the presence of his mother and older sister. As far as his family was concerned, Ben's behaviour was incomprehensible. It left them feeling anxious, confused and vulnerable. In his call, Ben disclosed to the helpline that he had been abused by a family friend and another person. The details of the abuse were highly concerning, especially as his description of his perpetrators in masks led us to fear that he may have been ritually abused. Ben understood that we would need to pass this information on so he could be protected. We spoke to Ben's father, who seemed to us to be desperate for help. He gave us their contact details, which we passed on to social services. It then transpired that these details were incorrect. It appeared that, despite his initial wish that we should become involved, he was now rejecting any help we could offer. Over the next four weeks Ben continued to call us, but had to wait until his mother was out to do so. He also started to masturbate while on the phone to us, but responded compliantly when asked to stop. He refused to give us his address and we were left feeling helpless and hopeless. Ben has since stopped calling.

Vicarious traumatization

Another significant issue in our work on the helpline is that of vicarious traumatization. This is the process defined by Saakvitne *et al.*
(2000) as, 'The negative transformation in the self of the helper that
comes about as a result of empathic engagement with survivor's
trauma material and a sense of responsibility or commitment to
help'. At a specialist conference for disability therapists, Dr Nigel
Beail (2006) told of his work with a man with intellectual disabilities
who described a sexual attack in which the perpetrator defecated
into his mouth. Beail described feeling 'sick as though this was happening to him'. There are occasions on the helpline that the recount-
ing of traumas can have an immediate and direct effect on the
counsellor. An obvious example was when a young woman disclosed
being repeatedly raped by her father, grandfather and uncle from a
very young age. She described being gagged and not being able to
scream no matter how hard she tried. After the call the counsellor
felt her chest constrict and fill with emotion that she simply couldn't
verbalize. The counsellor felt the gagging that the caller described.
She had to go for a walk to shift this feeling.

As helpline counsellors the material our clients bring to us goes
directly into our ears via our headsets, and although there has been
no research about the effect this may have on the ear, we have
observed that all three of the team have experienced ear infections
since working on the Helpline – something none of us had suffered
from previously – and the ear that was affected was the one used to
listen to clients. We have wondered if the impact of hearing repeated
stories of trauma could cause a physical reaction in the listener's ear.

Unlike a therapist working face to face, the helpline counsellor is
not able to rely on the picking up of information or feelings through
body language or facial expression. In the context of telephone
counselling the counsellor must demonstrate sensitivity and patience
in order to detect the clues in, for example, the caller's tone of voice,
silences, or a moving away from the topic. The counsellor needs to
be alert constantly to which interventions the client can bear or is
defensively avoiding. Helpline counsellors also need to bring awareness to the impact their voices may have on the callers. One caller
who demanded that the counsellor sing her nursery rhymes seemed
to respond to the soothing tone and musicality of the counsellor's
voice as much as to the content. This caller also screamed at the
counsellor at times in a way that hurt the counsellor's ear. The tone

and the force of the communication can be as primitive as a baby's cries and in this case seemed to require the understanding of a mother of an infant as to the nature of the distress. Suzanne Maiello (1995) describes a girl of 10, with severe intellectual and emotional disabilities, who screamed songs at her therapist. Maiello says, 'When she violently screamed her songs, she seemed to split and project her rage into her voice which became a container for emotion that could not be verbalized' (p. 38).

The growth in the number of helplines over the past few years indicates that they offer a very particular type of service that resonates with people in need. However, it has been a significant challenge to ensure that our helpline is truly accessible to people with intellectual disabilities. Obviously, for people to use a helpline they have to know about it, so accessible publicity is essential. Making information accessible to people with intellectual disabilities is at the heart of the self-advocacy movement, which came to the UK from Canada in 1984. At this time, people with intellectual disabilities started to speak up for themselves about how they wanted to live their lives, and what was important to them, thereby challenging the imbalance of power within traditional services. Valuing People (2001) included a report from the service users' advisory group called 'Nothing About Us Without Us'. This phrase sums up the essence of service user involvement and means that organizations that provide services for people with intellectual disabilities need to consult with the people who have the experience of using services and are therefore, in many ways, the true experts.

The helpline consulted with a number of people with intellectual disabilities, soliciting their feedback on the publicity we were minded to distribute. From this initial user consultation we developed the Respond Action Group. The group meet on a monthly basis, are paid for their work, and contribute to Respond in a variety of ways: they advise on accessibility and undertake outreach visits to residential homes, self-advocacy groups, etc. in order to inform potential callers about the service. In addition, group representatives sit on consultative groups for bodies such as the Metropolitan Police and the Crown Prosecution Service as well as giving presentations and workshops at conferences.

In 2002 the helpline became a full member of the Telephone Helpline Association (THA), the professional body that regulates the industry, and in 2003 it was shortlisted for a THA award in the category 'Most innovative way of reaching the target audience'.

Accessible pages were added to the Respond website looking at subjects such as 'What is abuse?' and 'Bullying'. The action group are acutely aware of the sensitivity needed when discussing the issue of abuse and for the organization it is considered essential that the voice of people with intellectual disabilities is at the heart of Respond.

The onset of new technology has challenged Helpline counsellors to support people in ways other than on the telephone. E-mail is now often used by our callers, although it is more likely that the need of someone contacting us by e-mail is that of supportive advocacy. As described in the following case study, transference relationships can exist in this format.

Case study: Ellen

We received a desperate e-mail from a mother, Ellen, describing serious abuse of her son, Mark, who has intellectual disabilities, by two professional sports coaches. A young man who had formerly been outgoing and excelled at his sport had become withdrawn, depressed and distrustful. He had his nose broken by the male coach. Money was taken from him and he was indecently assaulted and verbally abused. The sport's governing body had eventually expelled the pair, but as the Protection of Vulnerable Adults (POVA) regulations did not at that time extend to sports coaches, Mark's mother was appalled to discover that there was nothing to stop this couple setting up another club in another town.

From her e-mails it seemed that Ellen had formed a highly idealized transference relationship with the counsellor who supported her. To quote from one e-mail, 'Your messages always seem to arrive when I am at my lowest ebb'. However, it would seem that she had no desire to extend and change this relationship to the more immediate form of telephone support, because despite it being offered, she declined it. It would seem for Ellen that the prospect of communicating verbally with this idealized figure might have shattered that illusion. She seemed to prefer to maintain her image of her counsellor as 'saviour'. Perhaps also, e-mails afforded her greater distance than telephone contact. Even more than the phone caller, the e-mailer retains anonymity and control over the contact.

This chapter has described some of the complexities of providing a telephone counselling service. The need for good-quality support and supervision is paramount and no less important than it is for face-to-face work. However, unlike face-to-face work with vulnerable clients at Respond, the telephone counsellor has no context in which to place the client. We do not have access to reports or assessments; we can only work with what the client chooses to tell us, some of which may of course be fantasy. Telephone counsellors participate in team supervision sessions and the helpline as a service is seen as integral to the work of the organization. However, in addition we receive monthly supervision from an external supervisor who, crucially, has experience of telephone work himself and therefore not only can work with the client's material but also can understand the intensity with which a telephone counsellor can experience the vicarious trauma and can contain that for the team. Supervision offers a space to explore the particular pressures that telephone work can place on an individual, and the team as a whole. A helpline team also needs to find ways of offering support to the counsellors on a day-to-day basis, as, especially during busy periods that can never be predicted, a counsellor may have little or no time to debrief following a particularly intense or difficult call.

The Respond Helpline offers multiple services: emotional support, regular counselling sessions, information, advocacy and outreach work and this places demands on the workers to be present, adaptive, thoughtful and well informed at all times. In turn, those workers need the support and mindfulness of the organization they work for. With those qualities in place a helpline can offer an extremely valuable service to its callers, who may find that speaking on the telephone about their experiences is their first step towards a greater understanding of their own lives. For people with an intellectual disability who are so often socially isolated and lack intimate friendships or relationships, being able to pick up the phone and be listened to, believed and acknowledged may be even more than that: it may be a lifeline.

References

Barrett-Lennard, G. T. (1981) *The semi-autonomous phases of empathy*. Paper presented at the meeting of the American Psychological Association, Los Angeles, USA.

Beail, N. (2006) *Vicarious traumatisation*. Talk at the annual conference for the Institute of Psychotherapy and Disability, York, UK.

Disability Rights Commission (2006) *Mind the Gap*. Stratford-upon-Avon, UK: DRC.

Hollins, S. and Sinason, V. (2000). Psychotherapy, learning disabilities and trauma: New perspectives. *British Journal of Psychiatry 176*, 32–36.

Maiello, S. (1995) The sound-object: A hypothesis about prenatal auditory experience and memory. *Journal of Child Psychotherapy 21*, 23–41.

Rosenfield, M. (1997) *Counselling by Telephone*. London: Sage Publications

Saakvitne, K. W., Gamble, S. G., Pearlman, L. A. and Lev, B. (2000). *Risking Connection: A Training Curriculum for Working with Survivors of Childhood Abuse*. Lutherville, MD: Sidran Foundation and Press. Quote from www.tsicaap.com/research.htm.

Valuing People (2001) *A New Strategy for Learning Disability for the 21st Century*. London: Department of Health.

Chapter 11

Outside in

The effects of trauma on organizations

Tamsin Cottis and David O'Driscoll

As we have seen earlier, notably in Chapter 3, the therapeutic relationship between a therapist and a client with intellectual disabilities is not a simple dyad. Working as part of the client's network of support is a recognized feature of therapy with people with intellectual disabilities (see Sheppard, 2003) and should be acknowledged in this book too. However, working alongside other carers is not the only thing that expands and alters the therapy dyad. Sobsey's (1994) ecological model (see Introduction) recognizes that individual relationships exist in an environmental and cultural context whereby each affects and is affected by, the other. Similarly, therapeutic work with traumatized, intellectually disabled people will be affected, dynamically, by the personal, social and cultural experience that the client with intellectual disabilities brings into the therapy room. These elements will also refract and resound in the organization that is providing the therapy service. In this analysis we are helped by an understanding of fractal processes, i.e. the way in which, as Hopper (2003) explains, in many realms of the universe, parts seem to manifest the same fundamental structures as their wholes. That is to say, the therapist works hard to provide a high-quality therapy experience, and the therapy service itself exists as part of a wider environment. In this wider context, therapy may, for example, be regarded as a waste of time and money because the client with intellectual disabilities is never going to 'get better'. The negative view that whatever the emotional benefits, the cognitive deficits will remain, and so the therapy is pointless, may leak into the therapy process. In addition, the staff on whom we rely to bring the clients to therapy, and to support them sympathetically, may be poorly paid and relatively unsupported in their ancillary roles. As identified in Chapter 1, work with people with intellectual disabilities may not carry high status in a society that does not value disabled citizens or view them as having a meaningful contribution to make. All these issues come with the client into the therapy room, along with their personal experiences of trauma and abuse.

The following case study demonstrates the effect of ecological processes and also highlights how elements of the client's traumatic experiences may be witnessed in the events and behaviour of those individuals and organizations involved in their care.

Case study: Susie

Susie had been sexually abused by John, the deputy manager of her day centre, over a period of two years. Aged 35, she had moderate intellectual disabilities. Susie had two older sisters, both of whom were married with children. Before attending the Day Centre she attended a special school. Susie left the family home three years prior to referral, following the death of her mother, to live in a semi-independent supported flat.

Susie talked in therapy of the way in which John groomed her for the abuse, taking her first on special trips, giving her special jobs to do in the centre and spending time alone with her. The relationship gradually became sexual, with sex taking place in the Art Room at the centre, and then later at Susie's flat. She described how he persuaded her to keep their contact secret because he did not want his wife to find out about it. Susie talked in therapy of how he made her feel special and attractive, and although he penetrated her with objects, and had anal sex, which she found shocking and shameful, she was thrilled by his attention. She believed herself to be in a reciprocal relationship with him, and that the only obstacle to their being an ordinary couple was his marriage.

However, following disclosure from another service user, it became known that John was sexually abusing at least four other female centre users. Susie was appalled to find that she was not, after all, 'special' and, in distress, told her key worker what John and she had been doing together. In therapy, when recalling her shock at this discovery, Susie became enraged, attacking a male disclosure doll, stamping on it and tearing out its hair.

We can see how Susie's experiences – of sexual degradation, loss, betrayal and shame – are coloured by her position as a woman with intellectual disabilities. It was partly this that made the attentions of a non-disabled man so exciting and pleasurable and heightened her susceptibility to John's attentions.

There are links here with a therapy matrix that cannot be concerned only with the 'here and now' of a conventionally understood psychoanalytic relationship – i.e. one in which the therapist is working only with the transference, and everyday details are seen primarily as matters to be interpreted rather than significant in their own right. In working with people with intellectual disabilities it is especially the case that their lived experiences, culturally and historically, cannot be divorced from current experiences as presented in the therapy session.

Susie's staff were horrified at what had happened and they too felt betrayed by John, whom they had regarded as a trusted and respected colleague. Susie's keyworker in particular felt the vicarious pain of her abuse, along with guilt that she had not realized that it was taking place. The manager of the centre, a personal friend of John, at first refused to believe the allegations that centre users made. In the absence of action from him, Susie's keyworker felt compelled to take her concerns to the next management tier (as her organizational guidelines said she should). As a result of her actions, both members of staff eventually lost their jobs, leaving the centre traumatized and leaderless. Susie's keyworker then found herself to be the target of staff distress and, as the whistleblower, found herself scapegoated and very much 'on the outside'. She turned to Respond for telephone support.

In circumstances such as these, it is not surprising that teams can implode, and it is common in the aftermath of such cases for damaging and sometimes irreparable splits to occur in a staff team. Chapter 6 has considered the idea of 'acting out', i.e. the way in which painful past experiences manifest in offending behaviour, often in highly complex ways. Organizations working with people who have intellectual disabilities will not be immune from their own staff sometimes behaving like this. It could also be argued that unsupported exposure to a client's traumatic experiences will exert a stress of its own and acting-out behaviour may be more likely. In such circumstances, colleagues of an abusive staff member will be affected by the shame, fear, guilt and anxiety that are characteristic of abuse and, like Susie's team, have to deal with feelings that they had somehow colluded with the abuser, or had been in denial as to his actions.

An organizational interface with sexual trauma will inevitably affect the internal dynamics of the organization. We know that sexually abused patients may have enduring difficulties with authority and parental figures; that for them men are usually experienced as abusers or potential abusers and women as people who may have failed to protect them. In the clinical session there are many expressions of these difficulties, but, ecologically, they can travel from the therapy room into the organizational structure. It may be, for example, that a staff team projects the suspicion of authority, brought in by client material, into its own governing body. Splitting is common in families where there is incest, where issues of blame and responsibility become perverted. It is also a feature of many organizations that work with trauma. There may be multiple splitting between staff and management, men and women, therapeutic and administrative staff. Gender issues may be more than usually pronounced.

There may also be structural issues that serve to heighten vulnerability to organizational trauma. In many organizations in this field, for example, funding is not secure and the organization's existence can feel precarious because of this. In addition, responsibility for the sound financial and legal status of a voluntary sector organization rests with a Board of Trustees. Staff, especially in organizations where there are high levels of trauma in the nature of the business, may have a greater than usual need for strong leadership, containment and holding. Trustees look to the director to keep things in order and rely on him/her to help them fulfil their role effectively. For this to work, there need to be robust management procedures allied with high levels of trust and communication between staff and trustees. In any organization these take time to develop and will not endure without careful and thoughtful management attention. Financially and managerially, fears of annihilation may be pervasive.

There are also particular features that arise from working with intellectual disability and connect with organizationally held fears of death and dying. Hollins and Esterhuyzen (1997) have written extensively on the obstacles – societal and intrapsychic – that are placed in the way of people with intellectual disabilities who have lost someone they love. It is important also to consider, as we have seen in Chapter 5, the loss that may be experienced by a parent when they learn their child has a disability. Mourning, grief, despair, envy and hate may need to be split off or encapsulated. Organizations and, indeed, individuals, working with people with intellectual disabilities may find themselves on the receiving end of projections and projective identifications that then become subsumed into the cultural and interpersonal fabric of the workplace.

We know from our experience that an inauthentic cohesion can develop in families, in which family members become tightly bound together around the disabled child – caught in a feeling of being 'on the outside' of society, which mirrors the social exclusion experienced as a consequence of disability. Similarly, working professionally in the intellectual disability field can be affirming and rewarding, though sometimes these rewards can seem fleeting and difficult for workers to internalize. As with families, there is also a risk that the rewards can be exaggerated and inauthentic cohesion will flourish – cohesion as a defence against the awful truth of the disability. Dartington *et al.* (1981) have written of the tendency in disability support services to deny the impact they can have on clients, or to only see what they want to see.

Bion (1961) has written of the two tendencies in the life of a group. The first he termed 'work-group mentality'; this is where the group is working together towards an agreed task. There is a sense of reality inside the group. The second is where the group's behaviour is directed to meeting the unconscious needs of the group members. In this way the group reduces anxiety and internal conflicts. Bion termed this latter activity 'basic assumption mentality'. He distinguished three basic assumptions: dependency (baD) fight–flight (baF) and pairing (baP). They are detected by the feeling and tone in the atmosphere of the group. In the (baD) group, members are 'hanging on' to the words of the group leader as if all knowledge is within him. In (baF) there is the idea that there is an enemy to be found either inside or outside the group. Finally, in the (baP) group, members believe that two members, a pair, either within the group or outside will bring some salvation.

Hopper (2003) has identified a fourth basic assumption, denoted as I:A/M.

I = incohesion and arises as a result of trauma. A = aggregation – a tendency to split into separate, self-protecting, 'crustacean-type' units, working in isolation. M = massification – a group that clings together, amoeboid-style, admitting no dissent or difference. As Elizabeth Lloyd (2006) says, in describing her work with a Respond-based group of intellectually disabled women who had all been sexually abused, 'As a group of traumatised individuals it is possible to think of the women in the group in terms of Hopper's fourth basic assumption lurching between aggregation and massification in their attempts to ward off re-enactment of trauma . . . A process of reparation – a literal repairing of torn psychic skin – was taking place in the group.'

Obholzer (1994), writing about his work as a consultant to a school for physically disabled children, describes how, when he first began his work there, the head never called staff meetings. He understood this to be a defensive move on the part of the staff as it protected them from having to face the intense difficulties, notably a feeling of helplessness, that they all faced in relation to the support of profoundly disabled children, many of whom had life-limiting conditions. It also increased the incidence of splitting: between different staff groups; between the school and parents; and between the staff and outside professionals.

Our experience at Respond has been that the creation of a space in which the whole team (including non-clinical staff) meets monthly with an external facilitator has gradually allowed the team to process some of the effects of the work and also to feel able to claim a sense of healthy difference. It is our view that a climate in which difference can be celebrated is also a climate in which each individual person with intellectual disabilities can be understood, valued and appreciated. This 'talking and thinking' space has become a forum for close observation of, and reflection on, the group dynamic processes and contains some elements of the dyadic therapeutic space. It is a model of team support that operates in addition to clinical supervision and to individual line management. It is something we advocate, and at times help to provide, for our partner organizations that have an interface with intellectual disability and trauma.

Intellectual disability services may be caught up in a conflict between a conscious desire to create an environment where service users have freedom of choice as autonomous beings, and the – usually unconscious – need of the staff group to defend itself against the anxiety and sense of helplessness evoked by the presence of disability. Sinason (1992, p. 12) has described some of the difficulties and tensions in working with people with intellectual disabilities: 'Where something is seriously wrong that cannot be repaired, we often seem to be reminded of our mental and physical frailty and mortality. This leads to some of the most inspired preventative or reparative work on the one hand or to blaming, scapegoating, disowning on the other.'

If we are to work productively with the most damaged and vulnerable members of society we have to recognize the powerful impact of that damage and vulnerability, but strive not to over-identify with it. It is our experience that a regular space for the team to explore and reflect on the potentially toxic effects of exposure to trauma is a crucial factor in ameliorating the traumatic effects of the work on personnel and helping to maintain a diverse and healthily functioning, thoughtful team.

We also recognize the need to work thoughtfully with the workers close to the client, and with the wider community of those working with people who have intellectual disabilities. Sheppard (2003), drawing on Rustin's (1998) work with children's therapy, has identified three ways in which a therapy organization can foster good contact with referrers and supporters of clients. These are: to support staff to allow individual therapy to take place; to consult with staff groups to help them think about their roles; and to provide training for staff.

Since its inception, Respond has provided a wide range of short- and long-term training to many professional groups from all sectors that provide teaching and training opportunities for staff to address issues of loss, shame and mourning. In response to the need to support staff to allow individual therapy to take place, a case manager is allocated to each client referred to Respond. The case manager is never the therapist and is the first point of contact for referrers. It is their job to nurture the relationship with external agencies. We recognize that therapy may come under attack and thus have procedures in place to help ameliorate this: when a client is referred for therapy, the spotlight is on their difficulties, on the painful experiences they may have had and on the consequence of these. As such, it is an acknowledgement that all is not well and that bad things have happened. This can be profoundly significant for the patient, but also for others who care for him/her. For example, Audrey in Chapter 7, with her sorrowful incantation at the loss of her daughter, could no longer be characterized simply as a difficult older lady with a tendency to repeat herself in an apparently meaningless way. She became instead a mother who had lost a child. Her social worker was obviously able to face this painful situation, and referred her to Respond. However, her other carers were thereby compelled to go on the same journey. How might they respond?

In her study of nursing, Menzies Lyth (1958) wanted to find out why nurses were leaving hospitals in such significant numbers. In talking to the nurses she found that they experienced a plethora of uncomfortable emotions due to the intimacy of the role. She proposed that the structure and culture of an organization should support its members in processing unsettling feelings such as anxiety, guilt, hatred or uncertainty. Menzies Lyth termed these feelings 'socially structured defence mechanisms'. Similarly, residential care systems should also support staff with the sometimes difficult emotional consequences of their working relationships. There have been a number of research studies claiming that residents interpret relationships with staff as friendships, and feel that the staff are the most important people in their lives (Mattison and Pistrang, 2000). While this relationship can, on the surface, seem to be rewarding for staff, it can also be stressful, bringing up a variety of conflicting feelings ranging from love to hate. Menzies Lyth found that nurses often found change difficult because they had established ways of working that helped them defend themselves against feelings of anxiety. Therefore, to try to change ways of working generated more anxiety and often resistance. Furthermore, a response to their anxiety was for nurses to stop thinking about what might really be happening and instead to split off their uncomfortable feelings, blaming them on the management. A dynamic of 'them' (the uncaring management) and 'us' (the put-upon nurses) emerged. It is our experience that such dynamics are common in many services, particularly at times of stress. In services for people with intellectual disabilities they may mirror the 'inside/outside' experience of families and may also link to parental 'introjects' carried by the staff, who transfer unresolved feelings regarding their own parents on to the management.

Audrey's referral could have been experienced as a challenge to her team's previously held views of her. It also meant they had to acknowledge a profoundly sad story. It would be unsurprising if they resisted this, and defended against the vicarious pain of Audrey's experience by minimizing it or denying it. In addition, there may have been more conscious resistances: because the loss was a long time in the past, they may have felt it would be more trouble than it was worth to dig it all up again. The client was difficult to work with and the therapy could have been experienced as a reward for her difficult behaviour. Audrey's therapist had the tools of her professional training to draw on. She was part of a team of colleagues attuned to, and prepared to face, the sorrow in the work with Audrey, and which was supported by skilled supervisors in doing so. The escorts, who were responsible for a difficult and stressful journey by public transport each week to bring Audrey to her session, had no such cushion of support.

To make things easier for all, Respond provides written information for the escort who brings the client to the service. It contains practical advice such as what to do when they first arrive and who to talk to if they have a query about the therapy. We always ask that the escort stays in the building for the duration of the session as, for most clients, this adds an important containing layer to the therapy process. While the escorts wait, on comfortable sofas, they are provided with free tea and coffee. In this way we recognize the importance and value to the client of a good escort. We are also acknowledging the difficulty and significance of the escort's role in ensuring that the client arrives for therapy in good time, and experiencing minimal additional stress. At times, it may be helpful to provide more direct consultation for staff teams, as in the following.

Case study: Miss A

Miss A was referred for psychotherapy for her depression and self-harming. During the course of her treatment, Miss A disclosed how she was sexually abused in a private nursing home by the home manager over a number of years. As a consequence she could behave very negatively towards the residential staff, whom she experienced as intrusive and infantilizing. Miss A was full of complaints to the therapist of how the staff would 'move stuff around my kitchen' or 'hang around my flat'. This proved to be very difficult for the staff, who found that even basic support work with her was problematic and that they were often met with a sullen and negative response from Miss A. Miss A would also go on 'midnight rambles' to other residents' bedrooms. This was upsetting to all parties, and staff started to develop policies in response to this behaviour. For example, a rule was introduced that residents had to stay in their flats after 10.30 pm.

In our work with the staff, the case manager from Respond explored how Miss A's intensely hostile feelings were in part due to her past experiences. Emphasis was placed on the ways in which this past trauma continued to serve as an emotional template for her present-day interactions with carers. Past experience of abuse also affected her behaviour – night times had been upsetting and Miss A had never been able to process this trauma. As a result, she continued to experience disturbance at night, and communicated this to others by wandering. We also gave the staff a space to discuss some of their negative feelings about supporting her.

Obviously, a meeting such as this will find its way into the therapy. The therapist, and often the client, knows that such a meeting has taken place. The therapist may find out information that the client would not have told her directly. The distancing effect of a third person, who understands the significance of the countertransference, can help the therapist to process the effects of external realities on the therapy. It is a complex and difficult process, and clearly one that the therapist in private practice with non-disabled clients is unlikely to experience. Supervision is a vital arena for exploring and understanding the consequences of such 'professional intrusion' into the therapy dyad.

As therapy for Miss A and support for the team progressed, Miss A's negative feelings towards staff did not disappear entirely. It seemed, though, that one consequence of her exploring her past experiences in therapy was that the projection of those feelings onto staff lessened in intensity. Concurrently, the staff team began to feel more positive towards Miss A and most moved away from a position of irritation and resentment at her negative behaviour.

Those supporting people with intellectual disabilities may struggle with their unconscious negative feelings towards their clients. In the paper 'Hate in the Counter-transference' (1947), Winnicott lists a number of reasons why a mother hates a baby and explains why the mother needs to contain her feelings. Intellectual disability workers may experience similar feelings in their caring quasi-parental roles. We may have difficulty in acknowledging our more negative emotions as we worry that these can only be viewed as unprofessional or uncaring.

Wolfensberger (1983, p. 25) wrote that, 'normalization incorporates the explicit assumption that consciousness is preferable to unconsciousness and that negative feelings and dynamics should and usually have to be made conscious in order to be adaptively addressed'. This idea seems often to have become lost in our contemporary efforts to make normalization a reality for people with intellectual disabilities in all aspects of their lives. Cardona (2000) has written on the use of denial as an organizational defence: '[It] disables people from thinking, and therefore from bringing about any change. Facing reality, on the other hand, can restore some confidence in their reality to influence their destiny if the external threat cannot be overcome' (p. 142).

It was important that Miss A's team had the opportunity to mourn the way they used to work and to acknowledge their anxieties about the future. It is the purpose of our contact with staff teams that understanding and empathy for the position of their clients who have intellectual disabilities should be promoted, in tandem with our respectful recognition of the pressures and difficulties (often invisible to the outside world, and thus unacknowledged) that staff face in their professional roles.

In conclusion, we can see that Sobsey's (1994) ecological model of abuse has relevance in considering work with organizations, and the impact of working with trauma on individuals and teams. In earlier chapters in this book, we have seen the extreme and complex emotional cocktail that clients with intellectual disabilities who have been sexually abused bring with them into the therapy room. The therapist is daily encountering their multiple (and often unmourned) losses, the deeply ingrained sense of shame, and active symptoms of unresolved trauma, much of it unavailable to the conscious mind of the patient. Our work also involves us working across generations, with the parents and siblings of our clients, and may encompass work with their children. It is our experience that this work can be very hard to bear. The impact of the work on all those engaged in it can be powerful and primitive and, if unrealized and unprocessed, potentially damaging to client, therapist and staff teams alike.

References

Bion, W. R (1961) *Experiences in Groups and Other Papers*. London: Tavistock.

Cardona, F. (2000) *Ending and regeneration: Reflection on the emotional experience of ending a consultancy assignment*. Unpublished paper presented at the ISPSO Conference, London, UK.

Dartington, T., Miller, E. and Gwynne, G. (1981) *A Life Together: The Distribution of Attitudes around the Disabled*. London and New York: Tavistock.

Hollins, S. and Esterhuyzen, A. (1997) Bereavement and grief in adults with learning disabilities. *British Journal of Psychiatry 170*, 497–501.

Hopper, E. (2003) *Traumatic Experience in the Unconscious Life of Groups: The Fourth Basic Assumption: Incohesion: Aggregation/Massification or (ba) I:A/M*. London: Jessica Kingsley.

Lloyd, E. (2006) *Can the centre hold? The development, survival and growth of a charitable organisation providing therapeutic support to people with learning disabilities who have experienced trauma, and training and advice for their carers*. Paper presented at Group Analytic Society Conference, London, UK.

Mattison, V. and Pistrang, N. (2000) *Saying Goodbye: When Keyworker Relationships End*. London: Free Association Books.

Menzies Lyth, I. (1988) *Containing Anxiety in Institutions*. London: Free Association Books.

Obholzer, A. (1994) Fragmentation and integration in a school for physically handicapped children. In A. Obholzer and V. Zagier Roberts (eds), *The Unconscious at Work: Individual and Organisation Stress in the Human Services*. London: Routledge.

Rustin, M. (1998) Dialogues with patients. *Journal of Child Psychotherapy* 24(2), 233–252.

Sheppard, N. (2003) Working with care staff and organisations. In S. Hodges (ed.), *Counselling Adults with Learning Disabilities*. London: Palgrave.

Sinason, V. (1992) *Mental Handicap and the Human Condition: New Approaches from the Tavistock*. London: Free Association Books

Sobsey, D. (1994) *Violence and Abuse in the Lives of People with Disabilities: The End of Silent Acceptance?* Baltimore: Paul H. Brookes Publishing Co.

UK Home Office (2006) *Achieving Best Evidence in Criminal Proceedings: Guidance for Vulnerable or Intimidated Witnesses, including Children*. London: Home Office Publications

Winnicott, D. W. (1947) Hate in the counter-transference. In *D. W. Winnicott Collected Papers: Through Paediatrics to Psychoanalysis*.

Wolfsensberger, W. (1983) Social Role Valorization: A proposed new term for the principle of normalization. *Mental Retardation 21*, 234–239

Chapter 12

Life support or intensive care?

Endings and outcomes in psychotherapy for people with intellectual disabilities

Tamsin Cottis

Any exploration of the questions, 'Has therapy helped this person with intellectual disabilities?' and 'How can we tell?' has to engage with a number of related issues. Firstly, what is known about the efficacy of psychotherapy with this client group in general? What research is there and what does it tell us? What are the challenges to conducting research with this client group? Also, what does our particular experience at Respond tell us about how it helps? How can our clients, who in the main receive long-term, psychoanalytic psychotherapeutic treatment, be seen to have benefited from that treatment? How do we, as an organization, respond to the pressure to demonstrate its effectiveness to our stakeholders?

There is also the important question of what the place of psychotherapy for people with intellectual disabilities in the broader service context should be. Can it be considered a psychotherapy specialism? If so, what steps are being taken to establish it as such? How should therapists doing this work be trained and in what settings should they offer treatment? In addition to thinking about individual cases, it is important to consider the ways in which, in service terms, psychotherapy should be made available to people with intellectual disabilities. For example, Respond is a medium-sized voluntary organisation with a clinic base in Central London. Long-term plans are for regional expansion but such growth is necessarily slow – especially as funding remains a persistent challenge to the development and indeed survival of an organization such as this. The previously cited report from the Royal College of Psychiatrists (2004) identifies a number of service models for the provision of psychotherapy to people with intellectual disabilities, including: the voluntary sector; a community intellectual disability team; provision within a specialist psychotherapy institution; and another from within a hospital intellectual disability psychiatry service.

The present picture is of a geographically *ad hoc* service provision and the report recommends that ways be found to make treatment more uniformly available. It would seem that, as the report says, 'No single professional group or statutory or voluntary/independent agency can plan or deliver these services in isolation' (p. 57).

The report also highlights the training needs of the work and recommends developments in both specialist and mainstream therapy trainings. Progress within the Institute of Psychotherapy and Disability may lead to the opportunity to train as a disability psychotherapist, though again it is important to consider the relative benefits of a separate and specialist training, as weighed against the risk of the further marginalization of this potentially isolating and overlooked field of psychotherapy. It is to be hoped that debate on this issue will continue to be vigorous and thoughtful.

The first thing to say about research into the efficacy of psychotherapy for people with intellectual disabilities is that most of it is case-based and qualitative and very little of it refers to the psychodynamic and psychoanalytic psychotherapy that is the focus of this book. However, Nigel Beail's research (Beail and Warden, 1996) studied the effect of long-term treatment on both the symptoms and self-esteem of those referred for long-term treatment. He found that in his small sample group symptoms decreased and self-esteem increased. A later study (Beail, 1998) also found that aggressive behaviour in men with learning disabilities in the sample group diminished following psychotherapeutic group treatment. Beail *et al.* (2005) explain that research that involves randomized control trials is not always feasible in this field and that it may not be possible or preferable to find matched controls. They cite Salkovskis' (1995) 'hourglass model' of research to argue that there is a place for naturalistic studies. Using a naturalistic exploratory practice-based study of the effectiveness of individual psychodynamic psychotherapy provided in routine clinical practice, Beail *et al.* concluded that people with intellectual disabilities can benefit from such therapy. Additionally, the research itself has generalizability to clinical practice and provides some suggestions regarding length of treatment and participant characteristics.

Bichard *et al.* (1996) conducted research that included the use of a control group. They used the Draw a Person (DAP) test and found that in seven out of eight participants the drawings became more sophisticated or detailed, suggesting a more integrated sense of self on the part of those who had received psychotherapy. The control group did not show the same improvement. Bichard *et al.* also solicited feedback from carers, most of whom felt that patient's symptoms had improved or disappeared.

These studies in themselves highlight some of the major difficulties in conducting quantitative research. The first is that sample groups are likely to be small. It is not suggested in this book that every person with an intellectual disability needs psychotherapy; rather that, just as for the general population, there may be some people with intellectual disabilities (according to the government White Paper *Valuing People* (Department of Health, 2001), 1.2 million people in the UK have 'mild to moderate learning disabilities' and 210,000 have 'severe or profound learning disabilities') for whom it is the treatment of choice. This means that while therapy that is undertaken will be specialized and intensive and very likely long-term, it is the case that, in any geographical location, there will be a limited number of potential referrals. Establishing a control group may be practically and ethically difficult. Attempts continue to obtain funding for a large-scale, multi-setting research project – begun in 2000 and led by Professor Sheila Hollins at St George's Hospital – but have so far proved unsuccessful.

It is pertinent to suggest that if treatment were more readily available perhaps there would be more referrals. This question was addressed in the report of the Royal College of Psychiatrists (2004). The report surveyed 424 responses from psychiatrists on the mailing list of the Faculty of Psychiatry of Learning Disabilities of the Royal College of Psychiatrists, and psychologists on the mailing list of the Section for Learning Disability of the British Psychological Society. In response to the question, 'What do you believe to be the demand for psychotherapy for people with intellectual disabilities?', the majority of respondents said 'moderate' and 83 per cent of responses indicated a moderate or high demand. The report (pp. 28–29) says:

> The particular vulnerability of this client group to sexual abuse, loss, psychiatric disorder, consequences of institutional care . . . was elaborated in many responses. Reference was also made to the particular problems of people with mild learning disabilities and personality disorders; an area where clients often fall between service eligibility criteria.

The Bichard *et al.* (1996) research also highlights a significant issue in researching the efficacy of therapy: that carers will have an influence and view on how much it has helped the patient with intellectual disabilities. Chapters 9 and 10 have drawn attention to the ways in which, notwithstanding concerted attempts to redress this, many people with intellectual disabilities still do not have the opportunity to make choices and operate as autonomous individuals. It is highly likely that the patient's carers will have initiated the referral for psychotherapy. As Hodges (2003, p. 45) has pointed out and as our experience at Respond confirms, very few patients with intellectual disabilities self-refer. Referrers, whether family members or paid carers, may have a strong practical, emotional and financial investment in the success or failure of treatment. It may have been their growing sense of concern that precipitated the referral. For example, to take a sample of 10 cases from Respond (six men and four women, all of whom ended their therapy in 2006 or 2007), all but one of the men were referred primarily because of their offending behaviour. All the women were victims of sexual abuse and two of those also presented violent and aggressive behaviour. All the referrers would have obvious 'symptom' benchmarks by which to assess the value of therapy. Although therapy is not offered as 'a cure' for offending and challenging behaviour, it is the case that such behaviour may be a communication of some pain or distress (see Chapter 6) and all concerned would be looking to see distress alleviated and symptoms diminish – of offending behaviours but also of self-harm and depression. People with intellectual disabilities are surrounded by others who will have a view on their progress. It is likely that the views of these people will form part of any evaluation of treatment. As we have seen in Chapters 3 and 11, it is also likely that their opinions of the value of the therapy will find their way, through the transference, into the treatment.

Another relevant, but hard to assess, factor is that by making the referral, the carers themselves extend the network of support around a troubled individual. Sometimes this sense of containment, or access to a professional and supportive voice can reduce anxiety around a client, and thence symptoms may also diminish because the carer no longer feels so alone and may therefore be less anxious in their dealing with the client. The client's own fears of annihilation can, in our experience, be experienced in the transference, by the professional worker in any setting.

Ecologically, research may also be influenced by an existential question raised throughout this book. Are they worth it? That is to say, is the happiness of people with intellectual disabilities, or their emotional stability, or their capacity to make the most of their life opportunities for love and work, important to us as a society? As shown in Chapter 1, the 'episodes of interest' in psychotherapy for people with intellectual disabilities that have occurred over the past 80 years or so have taken root only in the past 10–15 years. It is almost as if we still need to fight continually the urge to ask, 'Is it worth it?' It is a toxic question, which can get into the work itself and also, I would argue, act like lead boots on the feet of potential researchers. Along with Nigel Beail (1998; Beail and Warden, 1996; Beail et al., 2005), the question is addressed by innovative and pioneering practitioners such as Alvarez (1992) and Sinason (1992), who do not evade the question but respond to it with life-affirming and hopeful vigour, passion, insight and enthusiasm. Additionally, The Royal College Of Psychiatrists Report (2004, p. 17) has a pragmatic and robust response to this which, it is to be hoped, will underpin learning disability psychotherapy services in the future:

> The evidence base for treatment choice in psychological therapies and counselling has been elaborated on by the Department of Health in its publication 'Guidelines for Treatment Choice in Psychological Therapies and Counselling' [2001]. People with learning disabilities experience similar disorder to the general population, and there is a known vulnerability to mental illness and psychological problems. Although treatment choices for these conditions were not specifically considered for people with learning disabilities, no evidence was presented that psychological therapies do not work for this client group.

From this starting point we can say that people with intellectual disabilities are entitled to psychotherapeutic treatment and have been shown to benefit from it.

Notwithstanding this central tenet, we at Respond have had to address the ways in which our patients come in and out of their treatment. This has been an evolving issue at Respond and the ecological processes described in earlier chapters can once again be seen to be in operation.

To take a small sample of 10 cases:

- three finished at the mutual agreement of client, referrer and therapist, after treatments of between two and seven years
- two ended because the patients' symptoms worsened and they were hospitalized (after treatments of one and three years)
- one client moved away, and it is not known whether treatment was continued elsewhere
- two patients chose to stop attending after treatments of one year each, although the referrer and the therapist would have liked them to have continued in treatment
- one patient was withdrawn from treatment because his mother no longer wished him to attend, after ten months of erratically attended weekly sessions.
- one patient had to stop attending because funding was withdrawn against the recommendation of the therapist and the expressed wishes of the patient, after six years of treatment.

Case 1: A patient is hospitalized

When Sheila was referred for psychotherapy, she had recently moved to a large group home, after many years living in a secure unit. Her childhood had been traumatic and characterized by a sexually abusive father and a mother, herself with intellectual disabilities, who was unable to protect her. She had also been abused by her brothers and pimped by them to men in the local community. Her level of intellectual disability was moderate but emotionally she was profoundly impaired, lacking empathy, insight and an apparent capacity for thought that might lead to an understanding of her violent and irrational behaviour. It is worth noting at this point that many patients referred to Respond seem to have become disabled more by their traumatic life experience than by any congenital impairment.

Sheila would say, without affect, 'I attacked the staff because I was thinking about the past. About what my dad did', and be furious at the sanctions that had followed each attack – utterly unable to empathize with the hurt and pain she caused, or apparently to control her violent anger. Although she was never physically violent towards me in two years of therapy, I was aware that many parts of her thinking remained unavailable to me. I was reminded of the neuroscience research that is now showing the permanent and terrible damage that can be exacted on the infant brain, especially to the right hemisphere, which is subjected to extreme neglect and trauma (Schore, 2001). The ways in which this research appears to mirror and complement attachment theory is both fascinating and encouraging. Sheila had experienced gross deprivation and abuse in her infancy and I saw in her how 'the massively stressed child, with only primitive abilities to cope with overwhelming arousal induced by relational trauma and at the limit of her fragile regulatory capacities, experiences intense affect dysregulation, projects a distressing communication, and then instantly dissociates' (Schore, 2001, p. 65).

We knew, on taking the referral, that a talking therapy that was relational and took a view of the significance of the early traumas she had endured might not be effective for Sheila. The risk that she would become too dangerous to be contained was ever-present. However, she seemed to experience some benefits from the treatment, and was able to accept some therapeutic interventions from me. I was, however, conscious of the fact that at times my interpretations might be 'too close and too hot' (Blake, 2001, p. 81). She would, for example, shout at me, 'Don't say that! Why are you getting on at me?', if I tried to make a link between her frustration and loneliness and her angry outbursts. I recognized that I had an opportunity to be a 'thinking audience' for her. Transference interpretations were more difficult for her. She found it difficult to see me 'as if' I was someone else and felt very easily 'got at', experiencing my attempts to explore her violent and abusive behaviour as persecutory. However, I began to see a pattern to her violent outbursts, and to encourage Sheila herself to examine the state of mind that precipitated an attack. After 18 months she responded to my question, 'How were you feeling before you hit C?', with a burst of emotion, 'But I wanted to phone my friend. She wouldn't let me!' At last, she had accessed affect in her motives – not the deadened, 'I was thinking about the past. What my Dad did', response. Sheila's violence continued outside the sessions, however, and the staff remained very obviously sceptical about our approach in ways that could feel both undermining and dispiriting. Outside therapy, Sheila was encouraged to control her behaviour through punishment and reward. In therapy we did not engage with these techniques but instead began to play. Although very tentative to start with, Sheila gradually turned towards the dolls' house in the room and we would make up stories about people in the house. Sometimes these stories told me about her abusive past – for example, 'The baby is in bed with the daddy; they're having sex. He's three. He's old enough to have sex', but more than that, her affect and the mood in the room were transformed when we journeyed into her imagination. We both relaxed, time flew by and there was laughter from both of us. As Blake (2001) describes with his patient, David, I too found that play enabled the interpretations to become hearable.

This sense of life and movement in the sessions was in stark contrast to the effects on me of her silencing rage or indeed of her conscious narrative: as she listed what she had eaten that day, what she would buy from the shops and which staff would be on duty when, the sessions would feel deadening. I sometimes used to wonder how I would make it to the end of the 50 minutes. She would fix her gaze on me, adhesively, and was able to say that she hardly dared to blink in case I disappeared while her eyes were closed.

It was exceptionally difficult for Sheila to internalize my presence as a 'good object'. At each break she would say, 'This is the last one', as if unable to hold in her mind the many previous times we had broken up and reunited. The past damage to Sheila's emotional world had been severe and profound. Consequently, I was thrilled to see her even slightly lose herself in play, and also to experience a relaxing of the throttling stuckness of her mind when she talked about the here and now. I felt what I was doing was working to bring her mind to life; that I was, in Alvarez's (1992) term, engaged in a process of therapeutic reclamation, and functioning as 'an alerter, an arouser and an enlivener' (p. 60). However, it was also clear to me that 'recovery' was unlikely to occur for Sheila. I recognized that changes would be small. We might perhaps hope for longer gaps between explosions in the home. I hoped that, in time, she might begin to be able to feel something more towards people than a desperate, adhesive attachment or a sadistic sexual anger. However, one day, following the departure of a male member of staff with whom she was infatuated, Sheila's attack on a staff member was so vicious that they felt they could no longer care for her in safety and she was returned to a secure setting. The ending of her therapy was abrupt and brutal. We had no chance to say goodbye. I could only imagine the trauma she had been through, and recognized that weekly treatment for three years was not enough in itself to prevent the agonizing and brain-damaging legacy of the past from overwhelming her self-control.

Case 2: A patient is withdrawn

Andrew, aged 19, and with moderate intellectual disabilities, was referred to Respond after his mother had found him in bed with her 25-year-old stepson. Andrew himself was unable to talk about what had happened. In the wake of this traumatic discovery, the relationship with Andrew's stepfather broke down and his mother was highly distressed and traumatized. She was vigorously pursuing a prosecution of Andrew's stepbrother, although the police had told her that Andrew would not make a reliable witness and with no other evidence regarding actual abuse, or on issues of consent, were reluctant to take further action.

After the event, Andrew became very distressed and disturbed. He began to wet his bed and became very clingy towards his mother. Alone and estranged from her husband, his mother neared a breakdown herself, converting that desperate energy into her pursuit of justice. She at first latched very positively on to Respond. She found herself taken seriously and supported. She applied her considerable skill and energy to successfully acquiring funding for therapy for Andrew.

Although we cautioned against it, Andrew's mother had, I think, held out hope that in sessions, Andrew would 'open up' and say more about what had occurred with his stepbrother and that this would help with an eventual prosecution. In fact he talked little about that, other than to indicate he had liked his stepbrother and found him sexy. His upset was that he was 'gone now' and he 'missed him'. It seems possible that whatever had happened between them was consensual – in stark divergence from his mother's view of events.

Andrew also used the sessions to explore, through drawings, his feelings of sadness and frustration that his siblings were involved in sexual relationships and marriages and had children, while he was still living at home, 'like I'm still a little kid'. Despite our vigorous efforts to be clear, in a conscious way, with his mother about what therapy for Andrew might be, the reality was found to be threatening and too different from what she had wanted it to be. She found it difficult to experience Andrew establishing a therapeutic relationship that was separate from, and independent of, her. Her goal for therapy was that questions about the abuse would be answered, and they weren't. She withdrew Andrew from his therapy despite our attempts to preserve the treatment space for him. Andrew himself seemed powerless to resist his mother, although he had worked well in therapy, and seemed pleased to be there and able to make use of the thoughtfulness and interest of his therapist. It was a frustrating outcome – and the treatment ended peremptorily and prematurely.

Case 3: A mutually agreed ending

Mandy was first referred following a brutal sexual attack in her home by a member of her extended adoptive family. Aged 23, with moderate intellectual disabilities and with elective mutism that had endured since her early teens, Mandy presented at assessment as totally silent and extraordinarily impassive. Her attacker had been seen fleeing from the scene of the crime and was quickly arrested. Mandy was able, through a specialized interview in which she used simple signs (Makaton) and symbols (PCS) and indicated 'yes' or 'no' answers, to give a relatively thorough account of her attack. The perpetrator received a lengthy prison sentence. Although initially distressed, within days of regaining consciousness after the attack Mandy was her calm, silent and impassive self. However, all around her there was distress, guilt, and eventually a family breakdown that led to Mandy having to leave the adoptive family, against her wishes. She moved first to a group home, then to a shared flat and eventually into her own flat. Mandy's therapy lasted for seven years.

The referrer, acting in the months immediately following the attack and before the family broke down, felt that post-traumatic counselling would help Mandy. In fact, Mandy remained outwardly calm about the attack itself until year five of treatment, when her attacker was to be released from prison. At this point she became angry and upset and was able to communicate through pictures and gestures that she wished him to be made to live well away from her and she feared he would seek her out. She also used the symbols and question-and-answer communication that had become our shared language to revisit her feelings about the original attack.

Mandy found the enforced move from her family very upsetting at first, and indicated her sense of injustice, anger and rejection. As her therapist, I began to realize that therapy might have a part to play in enabling Mandy to become less passive and more assertive in her communications. We compiled a 'picture vocabulary' and each session would start with the pile of pictures on the table between us. Mandy would go through them and find the ones that reflected what was on her mind at that time. In this way she was the 'initiator' of

our conscious communication – a role she rarely, if ever, played elsewhere. She was accustomed to waiting for others to approach her,
and thus to set the content and pace of any interaction. In the
absence of her words, I became acutely interested in all the other
communications available to her and absorbed in what Racker (1968,
p. 42; quoted by Edwards, 2001) calls the 'analytic microscopy', i.e.
'our growing capacity to understand and recognise the unconscious
processes underlying the patient's every phrase and mental movements, each silence, each change of rhythm'. In addition to her
silence, Mandy's face was very inexpressive. She would smile, but
only slightly. She rarely frowned and only once cried in the session.
When she did so, although she was terribly upset following an
immensely stressful journey to the session, she remained silent. In
those first five years, therapy that might initially have been seen as
one thing, actually became another. It gave Mandy the experience of
an 'other', working as an attuned mother would, to understand the
meaning of her communication, whatever it was, in order to make
contact with her. I realized that breaks made reaching her more
difficult although she would not acknowledge any feeling in relation
to the absence of sessions for the first three years. In the countertransference I felt superfluous and insignificant at these times.

I began to realize that it was the way in which Mandy related to
people that had the most profound impact on her life, and it was not
clear how much she maintained a sense of control through her
refusal to talk, and how much her silence was in fact beyond her
conscious control. Mandy could express contempt effectively – a
dismissive turn of the mouth and movement of the hand. Her sense
of humour was also available to us in the sessions. By the time the
therapy ended, Mandy was an assertive person, very much more able
to make her wishes felt. Midway through the treatment she initiated
a complaint about a member of staff who she felt had treated her
with disrespect. The complaint was taken seriously and the staff
member sacked. I saw a new confidence but, alongside, a sense of
truimphalism in Mandy at this time. A few months later, a similar
process was initiated by her, this time apparently without foundation. In therapy, I wondered about the revenge she was enacting on
her failed carers of the past, and how she was enjoying her new sense
of power. Mandy was also contemptuous and rejecting of her adoptive mother when it was decided she could no longer live with her. I
saw in this the extent of her anger, and her capacity to express some
of the rejection she had experienced in her own life. I also saw and

felt this anger in her refusal to make eye contact with me in the session after a break, or her switching off from me when she felt that I could not offer unmediated support in the second staff dismissal action.

However, I felt that Mandy experienced my lively interest in her as helpful and in some way an effort to 'imitate the natural processes that characterize any mother with her own infant' (Winnicott, 1965, p. 19; quoted in Edwards, 2001). Using toy animals, as well as the picture symbols, which we adapted and personalized to enhance our communication, we spent many sessions exploring Mandy's feelings about the birth mother who had been unable to care for her, and for her siblings, who had been adopted and were also lost to her. These lost siblings remained a theme, and source of sadness right to the end of the therapy.

With work as long-term as this, which starts with a traumatic event but takes us back to the earliest years of an exceptionally difficult life that has resulted in the most complex responses affecting body and mind, it was difficult to know when the work would ever end. Valerie Sinason (2005) has talked of psychotherapy as a 'life support'. To continue a medical analogy, we may, especially in a case like Mandy's that begins following a specific incident of trauma, feel that we are providing intensive care through therapy. The therapy, which aimed to focus so intensively on her internal world, to give her an experience of being deeply thought about, which incorporated humour, empathy, understanding, and the courage to face the negative as well as the positive transference, was quite rightly a long-term process. Alvarez (1992) writes about her 30-year treatment of Robbie, an autistic boy (then man).

For Mandy, the deprivation and lack of her early life was enormous. She had never experienced being the focal point of another's joyful and loving gaze. Therapy, in a way, can offer this positive experience for the first time. However, the damage done by the deprivation makes the 'taking in' of the love and attentive thought very difficult, and the work is time-consuming. It may also be the case that the cognitive deficit, as well as the emotional experiences, makes it more difficult for the 'helpful other' to be internalized as a good object. All those who have been engaged in helping a person who has intellectual disabilities to acquire new skills will know how long it can take for them to master an apparently simple task and how many times the new skill may need to be practised before it is truly learned.

Throughout her therapy, Mandy remained silent – rediscovering her voice had never been a stated aim, but it was a continued point of reference for us as she struggled to understand why it had disappeared. She was able to identify fear as a significant reason to stay silent – a fear of her own voice and the power it might have, and also a deeply held fear of being laughed at, the shame and humiliation of having a voice that wasn't 'right'. She had found, conversely, that her silence could be a draw, and she could derive a sense of power from denying this contact to others as contact had been denied to her – by her birth mother, herself disabled and overwhelmed by the demands of six children, and later, by her adoptive mother who was unable to offer her a home following the invidious traumatic aftermath of the attack. The transference and countertransference were crucial elements of the treatment. For example, I could draw on the way that Mandy's withdrawal from contact with me made me feel. We could jointly feel the pleasure that came from a growing and rewarding mutual capacity to understand one another.

Mandy herself brought the sessions to an end. In the early years of treatment, there had been very little communication between us and her network. Relations were cordial enough but her silence and isolation seem to be mirrored in the quiet and minimal contact that existed between us and her other carers. The treatment fees were paid, but we had no contact with carers on a day-to-day level. Mandy's escorts were generally kind and reliable, but also very quiet. However, after two years of treatment, this began to change. Mandy's social worker would phone at intervals saying, 'Mandy wants you to know that . . .'. I would raise this in the sessions and Mandy would tell me more and we would explore it together. Sometimes she would indicate that she wanted me to raise a subject with her keyworker or social worker. Before ending, Mandy initially told her social worker that she didn't want to carry on coming and that she was ready to finish her treatment. With Mandy's consent, the social worker passed this information on to me. We explored why – she was ready for a change, she said; she wanted to move on; she had talked enough about the past; she was no longer fearful of her attacker. I felt so many different things at this point, including a great deal of sadness and loss – almost as if one of my own children was leaving home. I could see, however, that Mandy was moving on in a highly appropriate way but one that also marked an ending of the therapeutic relationship between us. I suggested we work towards an ending some sessions ahead. Mandy said she wished for only four more sessions. I would have liked more but she forced the pace. We talked about where her emotional support might come from when therapy ended and what she wished for herself in the future. Her years of therapy had been marked by a growing independence, and she was poised now to move into her own flat. With Mandy's consent we convened a meeting of people whom she wanted to know about the therapy and what might happen next. It was very much a thoughtful 'handover', with the therapist and case manager protectively wanting to make sure that her carers would really know Mandy and know what was in her past. Mandy herself had been clear that she wanted to focus now on the future. It was sad, and the ending still felt, to me, a little premature, but I felt confident that Mandy had controlled the process. It could not, I think, have been a 'better ending'. However, in being initiated clearly by the patient and in such as way that we had the opportunity to prepare for it thoughtfully, it was unusual.

These three cases provide a snapshot of some endings. There has, as yet, been no systematic quantitative research into how and why treatment might end for patients who have intellectual disabilities. The cases reveal, however, some of the pressures and external expectations that may impact on the treatment. In Mandy's treatment we can see that, with long-term funding, a supportive network and a growing assertion and autonomy on the part of the patient, therapy can end in a thoughtful, planned and mutually satisfying way. In Sheila's therapy, although the ending was unsatisfactory and Sheila herself could be seen to have 'got worse', or at least to have failed to 'get better' she nevertheless, in her psychotherapy, had the opportunity to experience something akin to a maternal function, of bringing the mind to life through 'the perception and expression of non-verbal emotional expressions embedded in facial and prosodic stimuli and unconscious levels' (Schore, 2001, p. 59).

There are difficult questions about how long therapy should last. I feel that this is an important area for practitioners in the field of intellectual disability and one that has wider fractal links. In our current society there is a prevailing culture of promoting 'independence'; that is, of minimizing an individual's dependence on state provision in whatever form. This may, of course be primarily a consequence of capitalist, growth-driven economies, which, as we have seen, can be hostile and unforgiving environments for those who may never be economically productive. Thus, NHS patients are moved out of hospital as soon as possible, with pressure on families to provide after-care. In schools, current emphasis tends to be on 'learning' rather than 'teaching'. In statutory social services, many personnel have a significant 'gate-keeping role' – to assess who should (and should not) receive services. It is our experience that much emphasis can be placed on the 'throughput' of clients through social services care, with pressure on social workers to close a case. The elderly are increasingly obliged to pay for their own care and not to look to the state for financial support in alleviating the increasing dependence of old age.

Debate as to the guiding philosophy and the consequences of this spirit of 'anti-dependence' is beyond the scope of this book, but, as we have seen, many people with intellectual disabilities have a life-long need for more than usual practical, emotional and financial support. It may be that for the therapeutic reparation and reclamation of which Alvarez writes, even a seven-year treatment could be seen as terribly short, when weighed against the brain-damaging consequences of early infant deprivation. We should not be afraid to make this point to funders, to referrers, to researchers, to patients and to our therapist colleagues.

References

Alvarez, A. (1992) *Live Company: Psychoanalytic Psychotherapy with Autistic, Borderline, Deprived and Abused Children*. London: Routledge.

Beail, N. (1998) Psychoanalytic psychotherapy with men with intellectual disabilities: A preliminary outcome study. *British Journal of Medical Psychology 71*, 1–11.

Beail, N. and Warden, S. (1996) Evaluation of a psychodynamic psychotherapy service for adults with intellectual disabilities: Rationale, design and preliminary outcome data. *Journal of Applied Research in Intellectual Disabilities 9*(3), 223–228.

Beail, N., Warden, S., Morsley, K. and Newman, D. W. (2005) Naturalistic evaluation of the effectiveness of psychodynamic psychotherapy for people with intellectual disabilities. *Journal of Applied Research in Intellectual Disabilities 18*, 245–251.

Bichard, S. H, Sinason, V. and Usiskin, J. (1996) Measuring change in mentally retarded clients in long term psychoanalytic psychotherapy – 1 The Draw-a-Person test. *NADD Newsletter 134*(5), 6–11.

Blake, P. (2001) 'Think outside, not inside': Making an interpretation hearable. In J. Edwards (ed.), *Being Alive: Building on the Work of Anne Alvarez*. London: Routledge.

Department of Health (2001) *Valuing People: A New Strategy for Learning Disability for the 21st Century*. London: The Stationery Office.

Edwards, J. (2001) First love unfolding: Developmental and psychoanalytic perspectives on first relationships and their significance in clinical work. In J. Edwards (ed.), *Being Alive: Building on the Work of Anne Alvarez*. London: Routledge.

Hodges, S. (2002) *Counselling Adults with Learning Disabilities*. London: Palgrave.

Picture Communication Symbols Book (various years) Solana Beach, CA: Mayer Johnson.

Racker, H. (1968) *Transference and Counter-transference*. London: Karnac.

Royal College of Psychiatrists Council (2004) *Psychotherapy and learning disability*. Report CR116, London: Royal College of Psychiatrists.

Salkovskis, P. M. (1995) Demonstrating specific effects in cognitive and behavioural therapy. In M. Aveline and D. A. Shapiro (eds), *Research Foundations for Psychotherapy Practice* (pp. 191–228). Chichester, UK: Wiley.

Schore, A. (2001) Neurobiology, developmental psychology, and psychoanalysis: Convergent findings on the subject of projective identification. In J. Edwards (ed.), *Being Alive: Building on the Work of Anne Alvarez*. London: Routledge.

Sinason, V. (1992) *Mental Handicap and the Human Condition: New Approaches from the Tavistock*. London. Free Association Books.

Sinason, V. (2005) Talk at CARI Conference, Dublin, Ireland.

Winnicott, D. W. (1965) *The Relationship of a Mother to Her Baby at the Beginning*. London: Tavistock.

Glossary

Attachment theory is a descriptive and explanatory framework for understanding the relationships between human beings. Most of attachment theory as we know it today is derived from the work of John Bowlby and stresses the attitudes and behaviours of young children towards their adult caregivers. However, a wide variety of social behaviours, occurring at all ages, is subsumed under the term 'attachment'. These can include care-seeking by children or others, peer relationships of all ages, romantic and sexual attraction, and responses to the care needs of infants or sick or elderly adults. Attachment behaviours are accompanied by emotional experiences that motivate the behaviour, as well as by cognitive and memory functions. Types of attachment include secure attachment, avoidant attachment, ambivalent attachment and disorganized attachment.

Autistic spectrum disorder (ASD) (sometimes referred to as **autism spectrum**) is classified in the APA's *Diagnostic and Statistical Manual of Mental Disorders* (Fourth Edition; DSM-IV-TR) and the International Statistical Classification of Diseases and Related Health Problems (ICD-10) as five pervasive developmental disorders (PDDs) characterized by widespread abnormalities of social interactions and communication, as well as severely restricted interests and highly repetitive behaviour.

Autism is one of the five autism spectrum disorders. Of the other four ASDs, **Asperger's syndrome** is closest to autism in signs and likely causes. Unlike autism, Asperger's has no significant delay in language development.

Clinical psychologists study and apply psychology for the purpose of understanding, preventing and relieving psychologically based distress or dysfunction and to promote subjective well-being and personal development.

Cognitive behavioural therapy (CBT) is a psychotherapy based on modifying everyday thoughts and behaviours, with the aim of positively influencing emotions. The general approach developed out of behaviour modification and cognitive therapy, and has become widely used to treat psychopathology, including mood disorders and anxiety disorders. The particular therapeutic techniques vary according to the particular kind of client or issue, but commonly include keeping a diary of significant events and associated feelings, thoughts and behaviours; questioning and testing assumptions or habits of thoughts that might be unhelpful and unrealistic; gradually facing activities that may have been avoided; and trying out new ways of behaving and reacting.

Countertransference is defined as a therapist's feelings toward a client. A therapist's attunement to their own countertransference is as critical as their understanding of the transference. Not only does this help the therapist regulate his/her own emotions in the therapeutic relationship, but it also gives the therapist valuable insight into what the client is attempting to elicit in them. Once it has been identified, the therapist can ask the client what their feelings are toward the therapist and examine the feelings the client has and how they relate to unconscious motivations, desires, or fears.

Down's syndrome or **Trisomy 21** is a genetic disorder caused by the presence of all or part of an extra (21st) chromosome. It is named after John Langdon Down, the British doctor who described it in 1866. The disorder was identified as a chromosome 21 trisomy by Jérôme Lejeune in 1959. The syndrome is usually identified at birth and its incidence is estimated at 1 per 800 to 1,000 births.

Financial abuse can take many forms, from denying the victim all access to funds, to making them solely responsible for all finances while handling money irresponsibly. Money becomes a tool by which the abuser can further control the victim, either ensuring financial dependence on them or shifting the responsibility of keeping a roof over the family's head onto the victim.

Forensic psychotherapy is the psychodynamic treatment of offenders and victims.

Makaton is a form of communication that uses sign and gesture based on BSL. It can be used alongside speech to support communication skills.

Object relations theory is the idea that the ego-self exists only in relation to other objects, which may be external or internal. The internal objects are internalized versions of external people, primarily formed from early interactions with the parents.

Person-centred therapy, also known as client-centred therapy, was developed by the humanist psychologist Carl Rogers in the 1940s and 1950s. He referred to it as counselling rather than psychotherapy. The basic element of Rogers's new way of therapy was to have a more personal relationship with the patient, to help the patient reach a state of realization whereby they can help themselves.

Physical abuse is abuse involving contact intended to cause pain, injury or other physical suffering or harm.

Post-traumatic stress disorder (PTSD) is a severe and ongoing emotional reaction that results from exposure to extreme stress and/ or trauma. Clinically, such events involve actual or threatened death, serious physical injury, or a threat to physical and/or psychological integrity, to a degree that usual psychological defences are incapable of coping with the impact. The presence of a PTSD response is influenced by the intensity of the experience, its duration, and the person involved.

Psyche is the Ancient Greek concept of the self, encompassing the modern ideas of soul, self and mind.

A psychiatrist is a doctor who specializes in mental health and is certified in treating mental illness. As part of their evaluation of the patient, psychiatrists are one of only a few mental health professionals who may prescribe psychiatric medication, conduct physical examinations, order and interpret laboratory tests and electroencephalograms, and order brain-imaging studies.

Psychoanalysis is part of the family of psychological theories and methods based on the work of Sigmund Freud. As a technique of psychotherapy, psychoanalysis seeks to discover connections among the unconscious components of patients' mental processes. The analyst's goal is to help liberate the patient from unexamined or unconscious barriers of transference and resistance, that is, past patterns of relating that are no longer serviceable or that inhibit freedom. The patient will usually see the therapist more than twice a week for at least a year; it can often last for several years.

Psychoanalytic psychotherapy draws on theories and practices of analytical psychology and psychoanalysis. It is a therapeutic process that helps patients understand and resolve their problems by increasing awareness of their inner world and its influence over relationships, both past and present. It differs from most other therapies in aiming for deep-seated change in personality and emotional development. The relationship with the therapist is a crucial element in the therapy. The therapist offers a confidential and private setting that facilitates a process where unconscious patterns of the patient's inner world become reflected in the patient's relationship with the therapist (the transference). This process helps patients gradually to identify these patterns and, in becoming conscious of them, to develop the capacity to understand and change them.

Psychodynamic psychotherapy has a primary focus on revealing the unconscious content of a client's psyche in an effort to alleviate psychic tension. In this way, it is similar to psychoanalysis and psychoanalytic psychotherapy. However, psychodynamic therapy tends to be briefer and less intensive than psychoanalysis. It relies on the interpersonal relationship between client and therapist. In terms of approach, this form of therapy also tends to be more eclectic than others, taking techniques from a variety of sources rather than relying on a single system of intervention.

Psychological abuse or **emotional abuse** refers to the humiliation or intimidation of another person by an individual or group. Psychological abuse can take the form of physical intimidation, controlling through scare tactics and oppression. It is often associated with situations of power imbalance, such as abusive relationships and child abuse. Any situation in which the repeated and extreme impact of a situation affects a person's emotional and rational thinking, in such a way as to impact their later lives adversely, could be termed psychological abuse at some level.

Psychological trauma is an emotional or psychological injury, usually resulting from an extremely stressful or life-threatening situation.

A psychologist is a scientist and/or clinician who studies psychology, the systematic investigation of the human mind, including behaviour and cognition. Psychologists are usually categorized in a number of different fields, the most well recognized being clinical psychologists, who provide mental health care, and research psychologists, who conduct substantive and applied research.

Secondary handicaps. In 1981, while studying patients with learning disabilities, Neville Symington found that his patients' levels of ability and impairment varied considerably. He speculated that not all of the handicap was organic. Valerie Sinason later developed his ideas and described a number of defence mechanisms frequently employed by intellectually disabled individuals to protect them from the 'awfulness of realizing they are different' (Sinason, 1992; see References in Introduction). These mechanisms are defences against meaning and constitute 'secondary handicaps' that complicate the original handicap. Skills and intelligence present are attacked and denied.

Sexual abuse is the threatened or actual sexual exploitation of another.

Splitting is a coping mechanism whereby an individual, unable to integrate certain particularly difficult feelings or experiences into the overall ego structure, compartmentalizes his or her reaction to those feelings or experiences. This is also often referred to as ego disintegration or, in extreme cases, dissociation.

Systemic therapy, or family therapy, is a professional attempt to study, understand and cure disorders of the interactional whole of a family and its individual members as family members. The aim is that the interactional patterns that prevent individual growth will change.

Transference is an unconscious redirection of feelings for one person to another. It is a reproduction of emotions relating to repressed experiences, especially of childhood, and the substitution of another person for the original object of the repressed feelings.

The unconscious is the term used to describe all the contents that are not present in the field of consciousness. These drives and feelings can cause us to act in ways that can be counterproductive in terms of how we want to act.

Valuing People, produced in 2001, was the first White Paper concerned with intellectual disability for 30 years. It stressed the need for care in the community wherever possible. It set out the principles of working with people with intellectual disabilities, e.g. respect, inclusion, choice and user empowerment. All services are meant to involve people with intellectual disabilities in their planning and to incorporate the above principles in their practice.

Index